MIDNIGHT TALKS AND MORNING GOALS

An unapologetic hostel tales of dreamers and doers

ASIF N K JANI

INDIA · SINGAPORE · MALAYSIA

ISBN
Paperback 979-8-89610-666-1
Hardcase 979-8-89673-463-5

This book is a tribute
to my daughter Manha Khan,
my father Qaisar N. K. Jani,
my mother Seemin Khan, and
my three sisters: Bushra, Ayesha, and Sana.

I express my genuine gratitude towards my family for being my unwavering support during my writing journey. It would be unjust not to acknowledge my two friends, Amim Ahmad and Farha Fatma John, who stood by me throughout my writing journey. They were always there for me, day and night, serving as my source of relief from stress. Even at odd hours like 3 AM, they never hesitated to listen to me.

I am deeply grateful to all of you.

CONTENTS

CHAPTER 1

FROM BHAGALPUR TO CSHM: BUILDING A NEW CIRCLE OF FRIENDS

Bhagalpur, once known as the Silk City of India, holds a special place in my heart. Although I was not born in Bhagalpur, I was raised there in an affluent Muslim family. Growing up with a dozen cousins in a joint family, we never felt the need for friends as we had each other. Our ancestral house, resembling a haveli, had over 50 rooms and was always bustling with activity. We were fortunate to have a dozen helpers who took care of our home, including our dear Najia Bua, who looked after me when I was young. I was enrolled in St. Joseph School, but I must admit, I was a difficult child to handle, and going to school was something I dreaded. However, my parents were wise enough to understand my excuses. Cricket was my passion, and after school, I would have to study Arabic, as it was mandatory for all Muslim children. I would pray that my Moulvi Sahab would not show up for the Arabic lessons. After studying, it was time for me and my cousins to play cricket on the large field in our campus until sunset. The summer vacations were my favourite time, as it meant endless hours of playing and having fun with my cousins. Bhagalpur will always hold a special place in my heart as it provided me with a comfortable and memorable childhood.

Growing up in an aristocratic family certainly had its advantages and disadvantages. As a child, I was fortunate enough to enjoy the care and attention of my family, with everything I wanted being provided for me. I have fond memories of playing in the mango orchard near our house and indulging in sweet mangoes with my cousins during the season. However, as I entered my teenage years, these privileges began to feel suffocating. The strict security measures in place due to ongoing gang wars in Bhagalpur meant that I was not allowed to leave our campus without an escort. This started to weigh down on me, and I knew that I needed to leave Bhagalpur once I finished my 10th board exams for my future studies. It was during this time that I met Mehboob Alam, the nephew of a family friend who was studying at Hindu College. He left a deep impact on me, and I still admire and respect him greatly. His success, having completed an MBA from XLRI Jamshedpur and now serving as the South Asia director at FMCG company, inspired me to break free from the constraints of my aristocratic upbringing. I eventually dropped out of St. Joseph's School and graduated from a different school, determined to carve out my path in life.

After giving my 10th board exams, it was time for me to leave my city and move to another place for my further studies. Like every other teenager, I spent a lot of time researching which school to join after 10th. Having been to Delhi a couple of times on vacation, I was adamant about getting into any school in Delhi. My relatives in Delhi had sent me a few application forms, and I applied to 6-7 schools, anxiously waiting for the results. I was not worried about my scores, but rather about getting admission, as I did not want to continue my studies in Bhagalpur. My dad's business partner and family friend, Prince Bhai, suggested that I move to Delhi for better opportunities. He even booked three tickets for me, my dad, and himself to visit Delhi. I finally got my results, and while they were not exceptionally high, I was sure to get admission to an average school in Delhi. We reached Delhi and stayed at a hotel in Paharganj while visiting different schools. Unfortunately, most of them refused me admission in the science stream. Our last option was CSHM Public School in Mehrauli, a boarding school with a beautiful campus. I instantly fell in love with the school as soon as we entered the campus. After an aptitude test and interview, I was asked to wait at the reception area while my dad met with the principal. After a long wait, my dad came out and told me that I had been admitted, and we needed to complete some formalities. I filled out the form and was asked to send a demand draft from Bhagalpur. We were overjoyed and went back to our hotel to rest as we were mentally and physically exhausted. That evening, my dad treated me to a famous restaurant in Old Delhi, Karim's. We enjoyed our meal, and the next day, we took a train back to Bhagalpur at 8 PM. It was a bittersweet feeling to leave my hometown, but I was excited for the new chapter of my life in Delhi.

We embarked on an exciting journey from New Delhi station to Bhagalpur on the Magadh Express, which departed promptly at 8 PM. Despite my excitement, I couldn't sleep properly on the train, eagerly awaiting our arrival. The next day, as we reached Bhagalpur around sunset, we were greeted with warm welcomes and a lavish dinner. However, my stay in Bhagalpur was short-lived, as within 10 days, I had to leave for boarding school. In those few days, we indulged in some shopping, and I purchased a holdall bag for my bedding, along with new clothes and shoes. As my departure day drew closer, my mother spent the last 2-3 days making snacks and sweets for me to take to my hostel. While I was happy and excited for this new chapter in my life, I couldn't help but feel anxious about leaving behind the comfort of my family for the first time. Sleepless nights followed as I woke up early on the day of my departure. It was a bittersweet moment as my family bid me farewell with sad expressions, and I too felt a tinge of sadness in leaving them behind.

As the day arrived for me to leave home and start my journey to the hostel, I couldn't help but feel an overwhelming sense of sadness. My dad, Prince Bhai, and I boarded the Magadh Express in the afternoon, and as the train started moving, tears began to stream down my face. I already started missing my home and family so much, but I tried to hold back my emotions since I was with my dad. Prince Bhai, on the other hand, was his usual lively self, especially when it came to food. We had brought dinner with us, but I wasn't in the mood to eat. However, I still had a small portion because it was the last meal my mother had cooked for me before going to the hostel. The thought of not having home-cooked meals for the next 8-9 months until winter break made me feel even more down. While I went to bed, Prince Bhai continued to eat from almost every vendor who came to our bogie. As we reached Delhi early in the morning, we headed to Hotel Marco Polo, where my dad used to stay whenever he visited Delhi. After freshening up and having breakfast, we were ready to go. The housekeeping staff helped us with our luggage before we started our journey to the hostel in a taxi. I must admit, as we left the comfort of the hotel and headed towards the unfamiliar territory of the hostel, I was scared. This was my first time away from home in a hostel, and I didn't know what to expect.

After a long and tiring journey of 30 km from Paharganj, we finally reached CSHM public school. It took us approximately 1 hour to reach our destination. As soon as we arrived, my heart started beating faster with excitement. The grand Qutub Minar was visible from a distance, indicating we were about to reach our destination. However, before we could enter the premises, the security at the gate stopped our car and asked for our documents, which we promptly showed. After parking our car, we headed to the admin office to complete the registration process. Once all the formalities were fulfilled, I was allotted room no. 7 in the hostel's east block. Accompanied by my dad, we went to meet the hostel warden, A N Singh sir, who then showed me my room. To my surprise, I found out that I would be sharing my room with three other students. Despite being a little nervous about living with strangers, I was excited to start this new chapter of my life at CSHM public school.

My dad and I were invited by A N Singh sir to have lunch at the hostel mess. I couldn't believe my eyes when I saw the size of the mess, where more than 500 students could eat at a time. The school had two huge messes, and after lunch, we went to collect my books and uniform. We walked back to the hostel, and I was helped by Prince Bhai and Dad to make my bed in my room. The moment for them to bid me goodbye arrived, and I walked with them to the parking area. Dad and Prince Bhai hugged me tightly, and as they left, I felt a wave of sadness wash over me. I stood there, gazing at the car until it disappeared from sight. The security guard closed the gate, and suddenly, I was all alone. This marked the beginning of my journey towards a new life, where I would have to learn to handle everything on my own.

As the clock struck three in the afternoon, I saw students leaving their classes and heading back to their hostel. Feeling homesick, I went straight to my room. The silence of the room made me even more emotional, and I started crying. Suddenly, I heard footsteps, and there stood my roommates, Mir and Faisal, both seniors from the Biology department. They introduced themselves, and then came my first friend on campus, Piyush from Gaya. He was very soft-spoken and made sure I felt okay. He instructed me on how it was my first day and seniors might rag me, which made me even more nervous. He asked me to change into comfortable clothes and started revising some chapters. He said we would go for snacks and tea at 4:30 PM but warned me not to look up, or else we might get caught for ragging. On our way to the mess, I saw Vikash bhai, a senior from my previous school, St. Joseph's. His familiar face brought some comfort in this new place. He recognized me and immediately greeted me with a warm smile. He told me to relax and assured me that if anyone asked me anything, I could just mention his name as a reference. This made me feel at ease, and we went to grab some snacks and tea. As we sat down to chat, Piyush told me about his experience on the campus over the past week. It was full of activity for him, but for me, it was different. I felt out of place, and all I wanted to do was return to my room. Piyush mentioned that he had been picked on by some seniors twice, but we both laughed it off and compared ourselves to ducks trying to find their way in a new environment. We eventually made our way back to my room where two seniors were studying. They were not very social and spent most of their time buried in books. One of them even went to the washroom every hour to smoke. I realized that they were not going to be much help when it came to adjusting to campus life. As the clock struck 7 PM, we headed to the mess for dinner, ready to take on whatever challenges the campus had in store for us.

As we entered the mess, Piyush led me to a table where his classmates were seated and eating. He introduced me to them, and I realized that I had not met a single boy from my section until now. After finishing our meal, we went back to the hostel and saw Piyush picking up books. He instructed me to take my subject book as 8-9 was prep time, where students sit in the classroom with one teacher present. He also mentioned that if I had any questions, I could go and talk to my teacher. Piyush then showed me my classroom, and as I entered, I sat next to the tallest boy in the class. He introduced himself as Ranjit Singh Bahadur, and we began talking. It was then that I realized he would become my best friend during my stay in the hostel.

Ranjit is a unique individual who possesses an indescribable charm. His tall, dusky frame and curly hair combined with his sparkling eyes exude a sense of liveliness and mischievousness. During his stay at the hostel, he quickly befriended every boy, and even during our first encounter in prep, he was more interested in chatting with his co-benchers than studying. Despite this, he noticed that I was feeling homesick and scared and made it his mission to make me feel comfortable with his words. After prep, he invited me to the canteen for tea, reassuring me that we could handle any senior students who might be there. Instead of taking me to the main canteen, he led me to the canteen for MBA students, where he was well-known by many of them. It was astonishing how he had managed to make so many friends in such a short time. The best part of going to this canteen was that we didn't have to worry about payment as it was often taken care of by the MBA students. Ranjit's friendly and outgoing nature made my time in the hostel much more enjoyable and eased my initial fears of being away from home.

After coming back from our half-hour break, Ranjit and I went to my room. He sat there for a few minutes before informing me that he had been allocated a room in the South Block. He mentioned that he would come and join us for breakfast in the morning. At 5 am, I heard an announcement over the speaker, reminding everyone to get up and go for a morning jog and some basic stretching exercises. I quickly put on my sports shoes and joined Piyush as we made our way to the ground. However, I couldn't help but look around for Ranjit, whom I had met earlier. Unfortunately, he wasn't there. After our jog, we returned to the hostel and went to the shower area, which was a long corridor with shower panels on both sides. As this was my first time seeing so many boys in their underwear and taking showers, I felt quite shy. There was laughter and splashing as the boys playfully interacted with each other. Piyush and I ended up taking a shower together before returning to our room to change into our school uniforms. As I didn't have a mirror, I borrowed one from Faisal bhai to comb my hair before heading to the mess for breakfast with my new friends.

Today was my first day at school to attend classes, and fortunately, Ranjit came to my room as promised. We walked to the academic block together, which was an impressive oval-shaped building with a large ground in the middle. As we reached the block, we could hear the school anthem being sung and saw the PT sir inspecting the students' uniforms. Unfortunately, I was late on my first day of class. After the assembly, which lasted for about 15 minutes, we were dismissed to go to our respective classes. Ranjit and I headed towards the PCB block, where our class was located. Being my first day at school, I was feeling a little nervous, but knowing that I had Ranjit by my side made me feel more at ease. We sat on the last bench, and I couldn't help but notice the group of boys who seemed to be the popular "last benchers." Next to Ranjit sat a boy who was around 5'4" and he spoke in fluent English. I assumed he was from the ICSE board due to his confident demeanour. He introduced himself as Debashish Mondal and told us that his parents were doctors at Asansol. In that moment, I realized that these last benchers would become my friends and make my school experience even more memorable. I believe that the reason why

Debashish was sent to stay at St. Paul School in Darjeeling was because his parents were busy with their professional commitments. As soon as we met, we both realized that we had similar interests and could easily become friends. However, before we could talk more, our chemistry teacher, Thakur sir, entered the classroom. While everyone stood up to greet him, the backbenchers remained seated as always. Thakur sir had a unique style of entering, where he would hold books close to his chest with one hand and use the other hand to signal students to sit down. It took about 5 minutes for him to take attendance as there were around eighty students in the class. He was one of the best teachers at CSHM, and I still hold a lot of respect for him. The class duration was 45 minutes, but it felt like time flew by in a matter of seconds before the bell rang, indicating the end of the session. As we were leaving, Thakur sir reminded us to come and meet him during prep time if we had any questions.

As the bell rang, announcing the end of our previous class, we all breathed a sigh of relief knowing that we had a five-minute break before our next class. Most of the students hurriedly gathered their belongings and rushed outside for some water or to use the restroom. However, a few of us stayed seated in class, engaged in animated conversations. Our next class was Biology, and we were all excited to learn from our teacher, who entered the classroom with a broad smile on her face. As I reflect on this particular moment, I realize how much effort our teacher put into trying to build a bond with us students. Unfortunately, back then, her efforts seemed to go in vain as most of us did not take her seriously. After taking attendance, she began teaching the lesson for the day. For us, this period was like a mini-vacation as we could do anything we wanted without being reprimanded. The backbenchers were busy cracking jokes and chatting away while our teacher patiently finished her session. However, just before leaving, she reminded us to be prepared for a question-and-answer session the following day to show that she meant business. She often did this as she was aware that students didn't take her seriously. Looking back on that moment now, I realize how much our teacher cared for our education and wanted us to succeed.

There was a 20-minute break before the next class, and since it was fruit break, my classmates and I headed to the central ground to stand in line for some fruits. I distinctly remember waiting in line for about five minutes to get two bananas. After that, my friends Ranjit, Debashish, and I decided to sneak out of the building and go to the canteen in the MBA block. After satisfying our cravings, we returned to our class. It was our physics class, and as soon as we settled down, our teacher entered the room. I can't recall his name, but he was a serious-looking man with glasses and a stern expression on his face. He often interacted with students during class and would ask questions related to the previous lecture. Today was no different as he started the session by posing questions to the class. As expected, he picked students from the backbenches first, much to their surprise and amusement. Since I was also sitting there, he suddenly turned to me and asked me a question. I had no idea what he was talking about, so I politely told him that it was my first day at school. He then asked me to sit down and told me to get notes from Anmol, a bright student from Bihar with a 100% scholarship. However, since I had not interacted with anyone yet, I had no idea who Anmol was. Anmol then stood up and said he would sit with me during prep time in the evening. He offered to give me his notebook after class so that I could copy it and revise during prep. It became clear to me that I needed to focus more on studying physics to avoid feeling embarrassed in class. As the class ended, I felt more at ease as those 45 minutes had been suffocating with the pressure of not knowing anything.

It was lunchtime, and we had a one-hour break before our next class. As we headed to our designated room to keep our bags, my friends Ranjit and Debashish came near my room. They started shouting my name, urging me to hurry up. Being on the first floor, I took some time to come down. They wanted to sit with their other friends at the same table in the mess, which was about 200 meters away from our hostel. As we reached the mess, I noticed a section reserved for girls at the entrance. I couldn't help but avoid looking at it. However, while crossing, I caught a glimpse of a girl and was certain that I knew her. She also seemed to recognize me and looked at me with similar feelings. Ranjit pushed me to hurry up, but I couldn't help turning back to take another look. The food served at the mess was a balanced diet, though not so tasty. It included chapati, dal, rice, salad, green vegetables, and raita. I was impressed by the fact that no other school provided such a nutritious diet. Vegetarians were served paneer while non-vegetarians had meat twice a week. During the registration process, I had chosen the vegetarian option, as being Muslim, we only ate halal food. Whenever we had no clue about the meat being halal, we turned into vegetarians. As we ate, I couldn't help turning back many times to see the girl from earlier. Next to her sat a beautiful girl. Ranjit and Debashish saw this, and they teased me for being a Romeo in our group. Little did they know, I was actually looking at the mysterious girl who seemed familiar to me. After finishing our lunch, it was our norm to keep the used plates in the designated area. I had eaten a lot as I was extremely hungry and had not eaten my last two meals properly due to being homesick and nervous.

While returning from lunch, I heard someone calling my name from behind. I turned around to see Amit Singh, a childhood friend from St. Joseph's school, with a broad smile on his face. He hugged me and exclaimed, **"Arey sala, tum bhi agayae yaha. Ab maza aayega"**

(Hey, you're here too! Now it's going to be fun. I couldn't believe how happy I was to see someone from my town in this new place. Amit told me that he was studying at India International School, which was a wing of CSHM, and they had their own hostel and mess. As we were catching up, I saw my friends Ranjit and Debashish waiting for me near the telephone booth. After giving Amit my room number, he said he would meet me after class. As I walked towards the academic block, I saw Zainab Aapa, my cousin, who was doing her MBA there. She came up to me and offered her help if I needed anything. She even promised to bring home-cooked food for me. Since it was only my second day in the hostel, I hadn't yet started craving home-cooked food. As I entered the class, Ranjit signalled me to sit next to him. It was an English class, and our teacher, Ravi sir, entered the room. He was a thin bachelor in his late 40s, standing at only 5'2. He later became one of my favourite teachers in school due to his polite demeanour and never scolding any students. He also made an effort to befriend almost every student in the class. This was the first lecture of the day that I actually paid attention to, despite his leniency.

There was a sense of relief knowing that I only had one class to attend that day. To my dismay, it was my least favourite subject, Hindi. As expected, a boring-looking ma'am entered the class, and I couldn't help but wonder why all Hindi teachers seemed to be the same. My apologies to all Hindi teachers for thinking this way. Ever since I was a child, I was never fond of Hindi as a subject. However, the best part of the lecture was when our teacher stood at the front of the class and started speaking like a parrot. It was quite entertaining, and my classmates and I were left to do whatever we wanted. The first few rows paid attention to the lecture while the last two benches were busy chatting away, much to the indifference of our teacher. My friends

Ranjit, Debashish, Abhishek, and I decided to play book cricket during the class. It was a new game for me, but I thoroughly enjoyed playing it. Our class seemed to go by in a blur, and even after it ended, we continued playing as there was no winner in sight. It was a fun period, and we didn't even realize when our class started and ended.

After a long and tiring first day at school, I decided to retreat to my room for some rest and a nap. As I entered my room, I found my roommate Piyush waiting for me. He had a worried expression on his face, probably because it was my first day and he wanted to make sure I was doing okay. But at the same time, there was a glimmer of happiness in his eyes as I mentioned that I had made a few friends. I could sense a hint of sadness in his eyes too, as he himself didn't have any friends and perhaps wanted me to be his best buddy, being his roommate. As I changed into comfortable clothes and settled into my bed, in just 15-20 minutes, I heard a knock on our door. Piyush kindly went to open the door, and to my surprise, it was Amit Singh with his two friends Vinod and Arvind, all from Bhagalpur. It was like a mini-Bhagalpur reunion in our hostel room. While we were all chatting and catching up, I noticed Piyush getting disturbed as he was trying to study. So, we decided to go outside and sit on a bench near our block. The four of us mostly talked about our hometown, Bhagalpur, and shared some funny memories. Around 4 PM, Piyush came up to me and suggested that we go to the mess for some snacks and tea. Even though I wasn't particularly interested, I went along just to keep Piyush happy. As expected, the tea served at the mess was quite pathetic, which explained why only a few students went there. The majority of students who visited the mess for tea were studious and nerdy types. After returning to the hostel, I copied notes from the book given by Anmol.

After dinner, it was prep time. Prep time was for self-study in the presence of subject teachers. As I got used to the routine, I must admit, unlike yesterday, I was not nervous. Even the teachers would talk amongst themselves unless some students had questions. My friends and I would take the farthest seats in the corner of the room, away from the teachers, and we would talk in low volumes. However, during one of my breaks, when I went outside to drink water, I saw a mysterious and beautiful girl standing near the water filter. I couldn't help but feel a little nervous as I quickly checked my appearance, making sure my Lee t-shirt from London, gifted by my cousin, was presentable. As I went near, our eyes met, and she asked if I was from Bhagalpur. Surprised, I answered yes and asked how she knew me. She introduced herself as Shalini Verma and told me that our families knew each other and she had been to my house a couple of times. When she mentioned her mother's name, I immediately recognized her. She went on to say that she was from Mount Carmel School, one of the finest girls' missionary schools in Bhagalpur. Shalini then introduced me to her beautiful friend Rachika Arora, and I nervously said "Hi" to her. Little did I know that this chance encounter would lead to a great friendship.

As I chatted with them for a few minutes, little did I know that the news of my conversation had spread like wildfire among our classmates. Apparently, someone had seen me talking to them and had informed Ranjit about it. In no time, both Ranjit and Debashish came to check on me under the pretence of getting water from the filter. I could tell from their cunning smiles that they were up to something. Shalini and Rachika, who were with me, also sensed something was amiss and bid their goodbyes, saying we would meet at the girls' canteen, which was open until midnight. It seemed like Shalini was feeling homesick and wanted someone to talk to, and we instantly hit it off as we had many things in common. Meanwhile, Ranjit and Debashish were making fun of me for talking to girls, but I kept my cool and pretended like nothing happened. They even teased me for making an effort on only my second day at the school. However, when I mentioned that our families knew each other, they couldn't help but burst into laughter and playfully say, "Our Romeo is very fast." After returning to class, we continued chatting and playing games until our prep time was over at 9 PM. As we walked out of the class, I saw Shalini and Rachika heading towards the girls' hostel. I purposely slowed down so that we wouldn't meet and give my friends more material to make fun of me.

I went to my room to keep my books and ditched my friends to go to the girls' canteen to meet Shalini and Rachika. But as luck would have it, my friends Ranjit, Debashish, and Ashish showed up and ruined my secret plans. They called out for me to come down to the canteen for tea, but I was exhausted and just wanted to sleep. However, they were determined and came up to my room on the first floor, carrying me on their shoulders and declaring me a hopeless romantic. I knew I couldn't escape their enthusiasm, so I reluctantly agreed to go with them but asked them to put me down. I had hoped to sneak away from my friends and meet the girls instead, but my irritation grew when they headed towards the MBA canteen. However, all of that was forgotten when we tasted the Nepali Maggie noodles and hot tea. I was instantly in love with the delicious food and enjoyed the company of my friends. We returned to the hostel at 10:30 PM, and I changed my clothes in darkness so as not to disturb my roommate Piyush. As I settled into bed, I realized that Piyush would have a tough time with my abnormal schedule. But that didn't stop me from planning to wake up at 5 am for an early morning jog and exercise session.

CHAPTER 2

SNEAKING OUT OF CAMPUS: MY FIRST PRIYA CINEMA ADVENTURE

As we got accustomed to our daily routine, life at the hostel became monotonous and boring. We had been living in a strict and disciplined environment for over a month now, with the only exception being a few small mischiefs like pretending to be sick to skip lectures. After completing our preps, we were sitting in the canteen when we overheard some seniors talking about their adventures outside the campus at Connaught Place. The idea of escaping the strict rules of the hostel intrigued us, and we decided to explore the area and find a way to sneak out. We went to the dhobi ghat and managed to climb over the 6-foot wall surrounding the school with some bricks. However, we soon realized that we were surrounded by barking village dogs and got scared, so we returned to the safety of the school. On our way back, we met some seniors who were smoking, and they warned us that we went in the wrong direction and that the area was not safe. They promised to show us the right way the next day. As we roamed around the hostel campus, we saw students chatting and playing sports like basketball and table tennis on the central lawn. But as I reached my block, I saw my roommate Faisal smoking near the washroom. When I asked him if it was safe to smoke here, he nonchalantly replied that no one checks after 11 PM unless there is an inspection. He even advised me to break some rules and make memories while living in the hostel. As I went to bed that night, I couldn't help but think about how everyone else seemed to be enjoying their time while we were stuck following rules and regulations at school.

I woke up at five in the morning to the sound of a loud announcement on the speaker and a knock on my door. It was A N Singh, sir, our hostel warden, reminding us to get ready for the day. I quickly 5r4got up and, along with my roommate Piyush, went to the ground for our morning exercise routine. As we were doing our exercises, I noticed that Ranjit was not there again. It was becoming a regular occurrence, and I couldn't help but wonder how he was managing to bunk exercise every day. After finishing our exercise, we returned to our hostel rooms and grabbed my soap case and towel and headed to the shower. It was now a routine for me to see other guys from my hostel taking showers in underwear—some with a chubby build, some thin, and some with different skin tones. Initially, I would carry my clothes with me to the shower, but now it had become so normal for me to walk down to my room in just a towel. The only thing that made me slightly self-conscious was when I had to walk past the girls' hostel wall, as their rooms on the first and second floors had windows that opened towards our side. However, in just a month's time, I had become so shameless that even this did not bother me anymore. I changed into my school uniform and headed to the mess for breakfast, feeling completely comfortable in my own skin.

It was a different day for me, as the only thing on my mind was to go out and see the world. I had been in Delhi for over a month now, but I hadn't explored anything yet. The conversations of my seniors echoed in my mind, reminding me of how much there is to see and experience in life outside of the hostel where I spend most of my days. Even my friends Ranjit, Debashish, and Abhishek seemed to share the same feeling. I couldn't even eat my breakfast properly, as I was too preoccupied with the thought of breaking out of our monotonous routine. During our fruit break, I confided in my friends about my desire to take a break and explore the city. To my surprise, they expressed the same sentiment. But since we only had a 15-minute break, we didn't get to talk much. As we headed to the mess for lunch, I saw two familiar faces—Shalini and Rachika. It had been a month since I had met them, and it was a pleasant surprise to see them again. Shalini exclaimed with joy, "Finally, you got some time to meet your friend from Bhagalpur!" Rachika, who had been listening to our conversation, had a smile on her face. I couldn't help but notice that it was the most beautiful smile I had ever seen. It radiated a sense of warmth and happiness that was contagious. We made plans to have lunch at the MBA canteen on Saturday if I was in the hostel, as I had plans to go out of the campus. However, in my attempt to impress Rachika, I accidentally disclosed my secret plan to sneak outside the campus. I quickly made up an excuse that my local guardian would be coming to take permission. As I returned to my seat, my friends teased me about keeping me away from girls as I may get distracted. Despite their jokes, deep down, I knew that it was time for a change and to break out of our comfort zones.

After our lectures were over, my friends and I decided to go explore the spot from where we could potentially go outside of our school campus. As we made our way towards the spot, we saw a few seniors effortlessly jumping over the walls. This sight gave us the assurance that this was indeed the spot that would lead us to freedom. It was conveniently located behind the shower area. We were both happy and scared at the same time, as we knew we were breaking the rules and could possibly get into trouble. However, for the seniors, this was a normal occurrence, and they seemed to have no fear of getting caught. It was thrilling for us to be part of this rebellious act and be among the first ones from our batch to go outside of our school premises. This spot became a symbol of adventure and freedom for us, and it will always hold a special place in our memories.

Ever since I stopped going to the mess for snacks and tea, my friends and I have preferred to go to the main canteen on campus. It has become the most happening place for us, not only for tea but also to make new friends outside of our group. While on my way to the mess for dinner, I bumped into an old friend, Amit Singh. He asked me where I had been as we hadn't met in days. To be honest, the homesickness and excitement of meeting students from Bhagalpur have faded away. I have known Amit since childhood, so it was always a pleasure to meet him. After meeting Ranjit, Debashish, and Ashish, I realized that friendship knows no boundaries. It is free from factors like region, religion, colour, or gender. As we walked towards the mess together, Amit and I caught up on old times. I promised him that we would catch up properly after our prep time. As I reached my table where my friends were having their meal, Debashish jokingly said, "Sala, kitna Bhagalpur Bhagalpur karte tumlog."

Going to prep was something I always dreaded. We were constantly asked to study and do our homework, which we rarely ever did. Instead, our time at prep was spent talking and making plans. My friends Debashish, Ranjit, and I always took our favourite corner seat. We were currently making plans for the upcoming Saturday, as it was a half-day and sneaking out would be easier. We wanted to skip our morning class and leave after breakfast, making sure to return before sunset. On weekends, there would often be inspections and attendance taken during prep, as even the school administration was aware that students would go out. The only way they could catch us was through attendance since there were thousands of students in the hostel, and keeping track of everyone was a difficult task. We assured each other that we would come up with a solid plan to avoid being caught. During our conversation, I heard about Priya Cinema for the first time, and we decided that we would go to Vasant Vihar to watch the Jim Carrey movie, Ace Ventura. This would be my second time watching a movie in a theatre and my first English movie. I couldn't wait for Saturday to come so we could put our plan into action.

We were all eagerly anticipating our trip to Vasant Vihar for a movie at Priya Cinema. However, our excitement was dampened by the fact that we had no idea how to reach there. None of us was familiar with the area, and we didn't know which bus to take. We considered asking a senior for help. After our prep session, we headed to the canteen for some tea and coincidentally met a helpful senior who guided us on the safest route to take. They also advised us to return before sunset, as the lane from the main road to the hostel was a 3 km stretch that we would have to walk. This was already part of our plan, so we were relieved. As we were enjoying our tea, I casually mentioned that I needed to meet my friend Amit Singh in his hostel near Principal Ma'am's office in the administrative block. My friends initially thought I was going to meet Shalini and Rachika in the girls' canteen. I asked them to come with me, and they decided to join me, and we walked over to Amit's hostel together.

As we entered Amit's room, I noticed him sitting at a table, completely engrossed in studying physics. Even though we were on the same campus, we attended different schools with the same teachers. It surprised me to see him studying post-prep, while I hardly ever studied during prep. He informed me that they had a physics test the next day, and it suddenly hit me that we might also have a test coming up as we shared the same teacher. Physics was always one of my toughest subjects, and the thought of the test made me anxious. We returned to our hostel, and I immediately went to my room, grabbed my physics book and notebook. It was no surprise to find out that I had a lot of catching up to do as I hadn't paid much attention in class. Piyush, my roommate, walked in and was surprised to see me studying. He asked if I had a test the next day, and I replied saying it was not until next week, but we could have a test on any day of that week. He advised me to study regularly instead of piling up chapters, as it was just the beginning of the session and things would only get more difficult in the next 7-8 months. There were also other subjects that I had not studied yet, and it was important to stay on top of things. I promised myself to study at least during prep from now on. I stayed up till midnight, trying to grasp the concepts of physics, and went to sleep with determination to do better in my studies.

Waking up the next morning was difficult for me as I had only slept for a few hours. I was tempted to skip my morning exercise and sleep for a few more minutes, but my plans were disrupted by A N Singh, sir, who came to my room and scolded me for sleeping after the bell and announcement. I tried to make an excuse, saying that I was not feeling well, but sir checked my pulse and declared me perfectly fine. Reluctantly, I got up and changed my clothes to head to the field for exercise. Upon my return, I still wanted to sleep, but there was no way to skip class. The only option was to miss my shower and sleep for a few more minutes. I requested my friend Piyush to bring some water so I could wash my face and hair and look presentable.

He kindly obliged, showing how much of a gem of a person he was. After freshening up, I changed into my school uniform and headed to the mess for breakfast, something I never missed during my hostel life. Later, along with my friends, I went to the academic block for our second lecture, which turned out to be a big surprise. Our physics test was scheduled for Saturday, and Ranjit, Debashish, and I were shocked and saddened by the news. We couldn't afford to miss the test as it would reflect in our final year's results. During our biology class, we discussed how we would have to cancel our plans for the movie this week. However, Ashish's optimistic attitude reassured us that we could plan everything perfectly now. While my friends were worried about the test, I was secretly happy as it meant I could keep my promise of going to lunch at the canteen with Shalini and Rachika.

After returning to my room, I took out my physics book and saw that I had to study two chapters for an upcoming test. However, both of these chapters were like French to me, and I knew I needed help to understand them. I spent an hour studying, but the concepts were still haunting my mind. I didn't want to ask my subject teacher for fear of being judged and receiving strict criticism in class. It was then that I realized the importance of having studious friends. Anmol was the first name that came to my mind, and with just one day left, I made sure to ask for his help. The next morning during breakfast, I saw Anmol eating with his friends, and I mustered up the courage to approach him. He assured me that he would sit with me after school to help me understand the chapters. I also found out that Ranjit, Debashish, and Abhishek were also worried about the test. Fortunately, they were in the same block as most of the good students. Anmol invited me to his room in the South Block, and we started studying. I was honest with him and admitted that I hadn't studied anything yet. He was surprised but said that with one day left, it would be difficult to understand both chapters completely. He suggested that we focus on just one chapter, as he believed that questions would be asked equally from both chapters. He also assured me that he would make sure I passed the test. Anmol had even locked his room from the inside so that we wouldn't be disturbed while studying.

None of my friends knew that I was studying in South Block with Anmol, as they were all busy with their own activities. At 7 PM, Anmol suggested that we take a break and go for dinner. We went to the mess and joined a table where a group of studious students were sitting, most of them wearing thick glasses. As I was about to sit down, I noticed Ranjit and Debashish entering the mess. For the first time, I felt selfish and ignored them completely. Unlike us, who used to discuss trivial things like who is dating whom and who is the most beautiful girl in school, these nerds were having a heated discussion about physics. Ranjit came to my table and whispered sarcastically in my ear, "Abey Topper, hum log ko Bhi Kuch Physics Padha Dae." (Hey, Topper, teach us some physics too). I laughed it off, knowing that I would go back to my friends after the test was over. Anmol overheard this and reassured me not to worry about passing as long as I studied regularly. This put me at ease, as my only concern at that moment was to get passing marks. After dinner, I went to the prep room and sat next to Anmol. He gave me 5-6 questions with solved answers that might come in the exam. He also explained that if I had trouble understanding any concept, I should just memorize it. It struck me that Amit Singh had appeared in today's test. I immediately went to his hostel to ask for the question paper, knowing that the same questions would most likely be asked in our test since the teacher was the same. To my dismay, the question paper was difficult, at least for me. Determined to pass, I went to my friends Ranjit and Debashish's room at midnight and showed them the paper so that they could also study and pass. They were overjoyed and even hugged me, calling me a master of cheating. After a few minutes, I went back to my room feeling exhausted from studying for hours. The next morning, I showed the question paper to my friend Anmol and asked him to solve it for me as I didn't have enough time to understand it. After lunch, he gave me the solved paper, and I went back to my room after class, locking the door from inside to study. I had instructed my roommate Piyush to tell anyone who came looking for me that I was not in the room. Despite all the effort and hard work, I was still anxious about the test the next day.

As usual during tea time, my friend Piyush was ready to head to the mess for some snacks and tea. He asked me if I wanted to join him, but I had a lot of work to cover and declined. Piyush took his thermos and left for the mess. About 15 minutes later, he returned with snacks and a full thermos of tea. He poured me a glass and told me to drink it for a refreshing feeling. I was grateful and thanked Allah for sharing a room with Piyush. At 7 PM, my friends called out to me for dinner, and after locking my room, I joined them. On the way, I saw two girls, Shalini and Rachika, near the mess. However, I was not in the mood to socialize and chat with them today. While we were eating, I asked my friends Ranjit and Debashish how their preparations were going for the test. They laughed and said, "Don't be a nerd; we are just aiming for passing marks." Deep down, I also just wanted to pass the test. While washing my hands after dinner, I saw Shalini and Rachika again standing behind me. I greeted them with a simple "Hi," and they responded with an overly dramatic "Helloooo." I explained that I was in a hurry to study for the test tomorrow. They smiled, and Shalini exclaimed, "When did you become so serious about studying? You guys are always out having fun." I smiled and promised to catch up with them at the canteen for lunch tomorrow. They replied in unison, almost forgetting that we had planned to have lunch at the canteen on Saturday.

I returned to my room with the determination to memorize all the answers for the test. I stayed up late into the night, going over each question and its corresponding answer until I felt confident in my preparation. However, due to exhaustion, I ended up falling asleep and only woke up at 5 AM when my friend Piyush asked me about my progress. I assured him that I just needed to revise it one more time before the test. Piyush then came up with a plan to ensure that I had enough time to study. He promised to lock the door from outside so that our teacher, AN Singh sir, wouldn't disturb me. With this assurance, I started revising once again. Piyush later returned and unlocked the door for me. We quickly took a shower and rushed to have breakfast before heading to class for the important test. Thanks to Piyush's help, I was able to revise properly and felt ready to ace the test.

During the first lecture of Chemistry, I found myself constantly revising my Physics answers. Suddenly, the school bell rang, and our physics teacher walked in with question papers in his hand. He rearranged our seating arrangement, and I was asked, along with the other backbenchers, to sit in the front rows. I ended up sitting on the second row next to Heeba Wani, a girl from Kashmir who had previously lived in Saudi Arabia before joining our school. Heeba was known for her dedication towards her studies and had a bad impression of me. As I glanced at the question paper, I realized it was the same one that my friend Amit Singh had given me earlier. I felt relieved and started writing my answers, but soon realized that I had forgotten some important equations. Desperate for help, I turned to Heeba, but she rudely refused. With half-solved equations, I submitted my answer sheet. After the test, I could see the disappointment in my friends' eyes as they had also struggled to write well. However, I still held on to the hope that our teacher might be lenient while marking, and I might pass the test. As it was a Saturday, there were no classes after lunch. I headed back to the hostel and took a shower before joining my friends Shalini and Rachika for lunch. Dressed in my favourite light blue jeans and white shirt with sneakers, I took out some emergency money from my bag and headed to the canteen for lunch.

When I reached the canteen, I saw Pulkit bhai, a batchmate of my cousin Zainab Aapa, from MBA college. He recognized me and asked me to join him at his table. I politely declined, mentioning that I was with my friends. But he insisted, saying that my friends were welcome to join us when they arrived. As soon as Shalini and Rachika came, Pulkit bhai excused himself, saying he had some work to catch up on. He went to the canteen manager and said something. As a vegetarian, I had been eating the same food for months, so when I saw butter chicken on the menu, I couldn't resist trying it with some paratha. My friends also agreed, and we enjoyed our meal with some cold Thumbs Up, which Shalini had ordered. It was a perfect meal for us. This was the first time I had a conversation with Rachika, as I usually only spoke to Shalini when we met. Rachika would just exchange a quick "Hi" and "Hello." In our conversation, we learned that they were not quite comfortable with hostel life yet and hadn't made many friends. Rachika mentioned how much fun it was to have meals outside of the mess in the canteen with good friends. It was a memorable experience that brought us closer together.I felt a rush of happiness as I saw Rachika, the crush of many students from our batch, talking to me. It was a rare opportunity, as even the seniors were attracted to her. However, my joy was short-lived as I noticed my friends approaching the canteen where we were sitting. I was afraid that they would make fun of me if they saw me with Rachika and Shalini. Luckily, they headed towards the lawn tennis court behind the canteen, where our friend Debashish used to play. I headed to the counter and asked for the bill. To my surprise, the staff told me that it had already been paid for. Confused, I asked how that was possible. The staff informed me that Pulkit bhai had paid for our meal. I was relieved as I had saved my emergency money. I wanted to thank him, but he was nowhere to be found. When the girls suggested sitting for some more time, I had to decline as I didn't want to risk getting caught by my friends. As I headed towards the tennis court, I met Debashish and Ranjit and they asked why I was so well-dressed and why I hadn't joined them for lunch. To avoid their teasing, I lied and said that I wasn't feeling well. Abhishek jokingly said that I dress up nicely even when I'm sick. Ranjit then pointed out that my friends Shalini and Rachika were approaching us from behind, causing my heart to beat erratically.

Rachika turned to us with a big smile and said, "Thanks for lunch, Asif. We should definitely make this a regular thing and meet up more often." She then surprised me by saying that she would be treating for the next lunch outing. I was overjoyed at the thought of spending more time with them over delicious food. However, my friends couldn't resist teasing me about my little "lie.". Debashish jokingly said, "Sala date pe gaya tha aur bol raha tha, 'I was not feeling well." I had to defend myself by explaining that I had actually met them while going to the mess and they had invited me to join them for lunch. Ranjit chimed in, "You never dress up so nicely; why would she say thank you if they didn't pay?" We all burst into laughter, and my friends reminded me to not take things too seriously. It was a light-hearted moment that brought us all closer together, and I couldn't wait for our next lunch outing together.

That evening, my friends and I were mentally relieved from the stress of our exams. We decided to randomly roam around campus until it was time for dinner. As I entered the mess, I saw Heeba, a classmate of mine, eating in the girls' section. I felt an instant urge to scold her for not helping me during the test. I was annoyed just by seeing her face. However, as I passed by her table, she looked at me with fear in her eyes. Instead of confronting her, I gave her a smile and asked about her test. She replied, saying that it went well as the question paper was easy. Deep down, I was furious to know that she could have helped me too but chose not to. I had never interacted with any girls in our batch before, so the other girls sitting there were surprised and even a little stunned by my presence. Most of them disliked me and my friends because we were carefree and rebellious, and they were scared of us being backbenchers. I went to sit with my friends at our table, who also thought that I went there to confront Heeba.

That evening at prep, my friends and I were chatting and trying to come up with a plan to sneak out to the MBA canteen. We finally managed to escape and made our way to the canteen, where we sat and talked for a while. But soon it was time to head back to our rooms before the entrance door was closed. As I entered the room, my friend Piyush was anxious to know how my test went earlier that day. I told him the truth, how I had completely screwed it up. He nodded sympathetically and then suggested that I start studying during prep so that I don't face similar problems in the future. For the first time, he smiled at me and said, "You just studied for two days." His words made sense, but I couldn't help feeling a little bothered by them. As I lay in bed that night, his advice continued to weigh on my mind, but eventually, exhaustion took over and I drifted off to sleep.

Sundays were always highly anticipated by every student on campus, and this particular Sunday was no different. It was a day of rest and relaxation, with no early morning exercises to worry about. Piyush, like every other Sunday, went to the mess for breakfast at his usual time. He surprised me by bringing my breakfast as well and placing it on my study table. That table was usually just a place to dump my books and notes, but today it became a makeshift dining table. I woke up around 8:30 AM, and after getting ready, I ate my breakfast. I wanted to catch up with my friends in South Block, but they were all still asleep. Disappointed, I went back to my room and decided to take a nap. I woke up around 1:30 PM and headed for a shower. Piyush and I then went to the mess for lunch, and he seemed delighted that I was spending time with him. Sundays were truly the best days to unwind and spend quality time with a friend like Piyush.

Since Piyush was a commerce student and our interests were completely different, we didn't have much to talk about. However, he asked me about my plans after the 12th board exam. I wasn't sure what I wanted to do, so it was tricky for me to answer his question. I told him that I would be preparing for the medical entrance exam, and if I didn't clear it, my parents had already planned for me to study medicine in Russia. Piyush was impressed and said that my life was sorted. He shared that he wanted to become a chartered accountant and that the exam was very difficult. He felt the pressure from his parents' high expectations, and it made me feel bad for my own parents, who simply wanted me to pass the 12th boards. I went back to my room and thought about being more serious in my studies. But when I went to the prep room, I got distracted by my friends, and we were discussing health. Debashish, who was health-conscious, suggested we start playing sports and doing some push-ups in our rooms. We even planned to go play in the field the next day. As we went back to our rooms to sleep, I realized that I only went to my room when I had to sleep.

On Tuesday when our physics teacher entered the class, we noticed him holding an answer sheet in his hand. Instantly, my heart sank as I wasn't expecting this so soon. After taking attendance, he started distributing the answer sheets. It was a shocking moment when I heard my name being called out first, with only thirteen marks out of fifty. As I made my way from the last row to the front to collect my answer sheet, I felt humiliated and couldn't even look up. I could hear whispers from the girls' section, and I knew they were all happy about my low score. I wanted to confront them in anger, but I couldn't gather the courage. To my dismay, my friends Ranjit, Debashish, and Abhishek had also failed. The entire day, we all felt terrible and didn't talk much during prep time. Personally, I wanted to use my time for both fun and studies, but after seeing my result, I knew I needed to focus more on my studies. After prep, I went to my room and informed Piyush about my result. He comforted me and advised me to start studying, as it was just the beginning of the session.

On Thursday afternoon, after school, I headed to the badminton court to play. It was during this time that I had started playing badminton, and it quickly became the only sport I excelled at. My friends came along and watched my game, cheering me on. After the game, we decided to take a walk in the nearby field. As we walked, Ranjit asked me about our plans for the upcoming Saturday outing. We had all been feeling down for the past couple of days and wanted to take our minds off it. That Friday night, I even prepared my outfit—a pair of jeans and a Pepe t-shirt, which was considered expensive at the time. Seeing my preparations, Piyush asked if I had any plans for tomorrow. I didn't respond and went to the mess hall for dinner. During our prep time, we finalized our plans in detail. We made sure to meet A N Singh, sir, in our school uniform before heading to breakfast the next morning. After taking a shower and changing into my school uniform, I waited for my friends to come near my room. We then went to sir's chamber, which was in my block, to greet him. However, the sir scolded Ranjit for missing morning exercise. After breakfast, I waited for Piyush to leave for his lecture before changing into my fancy clothes and heading to the shower area to meet my friends. As we stood on the wall near the area, we were all scared to death. Ranjit encouraged us to jump and not be nervous as we didn't have the option to return to school.

As we excitedly jumped and started walking towards the left, heading towards the main road, we were pleasantly surprised to see a canteen in the distance. As we got closer, we noticed many seniors sitting there, smoking and enjoying their tea, Maggie, and bread omelette. We recognized a few familiar faces, and they asked us where we were headed. We informed them about our plan for a movie outing, and they were kind enough to give us directions on which bus to take and how to reach our destination, Vasant Vihar. They also warned us to return before dark as the road was not safe. With determination, we continued on and walked 3 km to reach the bus stop on the main road. Fortunately, we ran into the group of seniors again who were also waiting for the bus to Qutub Minar. We happily boarded the bus with them and later changed buses to reach Vasant Vihar. In just 45 minutes, we finally arrived at our destination and were grateful for the help and advice from our fellow seniors.

After getting off the bus, my friends and I found ourselves lost and unsure of where the theatre was located. We approached a tea shop guy for directions, and he kindly guided us to the cinema hall. As we reached our destination, we were amazed by the bustling atmosphere on Saturday. My friend Abhishek went to purchase tickets while the rest of us stood there, taking in the electrifying energy. It felt like all the beautiful girls of Delhi had gathered there at that moment. Personally, I have never seen so many beautiful girls together in one place. It was a mesmerizing sight, and I couldn't help but feel overwhelmed by their beauty. However, controlling my emotions in that moment was difficult. The temptation to fall in love with each and every one of them was strong, and if given the chance, I could have easily fallen in love 100 times in a day. Their radiant smiles, graceful movements, and captivating personalities were enough to make my heart skip a beat. But I knew that it was not realistic, and I had to remind myself to stay grounded and not get carried away by my emotions. We were witnessing something beyond our wildest dreams. Everyone was dressed in their most fashionable outfits, making us feel slightly out of place. To pass the time before our movie, we indulged in people-watching and bought cold drinks for a cool effect. Trust me, everyone looked so cool except for the four of us. During the movie break, we decided to buy some snacks but were taken aback by the high prices of popcorn. We settled for just two packs and shared them among ourselves. After the movie ended, we spent some time outside the theatre, soaking in the lively atmosphere. It was such a different life compared to our routine in the hostel. We made a pact to visit this place at least once a month, as we couldn't afford to go twice a month. That day was truly a memorable one, filled with new experiences and a promise for more fun times ahead.

After a long and tiring day, we finally took our bus for the return trip. As hunger struck us, we decided to grab a quick bite before catching the second bus. As we reached near the Qutub Minar, we came across a roadside Dhaba, which fortunately was serving halal chicken. We ordered chicken and butter roti and enjoyed our meal. It was already getting dark, and we realized we were running late. We got down from the bus, and two uncles on a scooter offered us a lift. They asked if we were from the hostel, and upon our confirmation, they dropped us near an illegal canteen. It turned out that they were from the same village and were happy to help us out. As we came near the canteen, we saw some of our seniors and felt relieved. We then made our way through a wall and reached the central lawn of our hostel. Everything seemed normal, and we saw AN Singh sir standing outside his office. We greeted him, and he seemed pleased to see us back safely. After exchanging pleasantries, we went to our room to change our clothes. I couldn't help but feel happy as it had been the best day in the hostel so far.

CHAPTER 3

SHIFTING TO NORTH BLOCK

Life at the hostel had been going smoothly until recently. However, living in the east block had become quite difficult and even painful. The warden of the hostel had his office in the same building, and he would always start his surprise visits or inspections from our block. To make matters worse, our vice principal, Bhardwaj sir, also had his office just below my room. My friends Ranjit, Debashish, and some others were asked to shift to the North Block, and I too wanted to move there so I could be with them. I wrote an application and submitted it to the warden and principal's office, but unfortunately, both of them refused. Principal ma'am stated that it was the responsibility of the warden to handle hostel arrangements, and there was no solid ground to shift me to the North Block. However, I didn't give up and continued requesting him whenever I saw sir in a good mood. Finally, one day he agreed and allotted me room number 12 on the first floor of the North Block. It was in an ideal location as I could see anyone coming towards my room. During the lunch break, I went to check out my new room and saw that it was a 4-room accommodation with only two students living there. My new roommates were Tarun Kataria and Sachin Khandelwal, both commerce students. We had seen each other around but had never talked before. They welcomed me warmly and offered to help me shift after school was over. With the help of my friends, we managed to carry my luggage to the North Block, and Tarun and Sachin helped me arrange my bed and clothes in the almirah.

Life in North Block was a whole new experience for me, and it was vastly different and interesting compared to my previous block in the east. The people there had a different energy and vibe, and I quickly made new friends. Two of my closest friends in that block were Tarun and Sachin. Tarun, who hailed from Malviya Nagar in Delhi, was full of life and had a typical Punjabi charm. He always knew how to make me laugh and never failed to brighten up my day. On the other hand, Sachin was from Bihar and was extremely serious about his studies. Being in the same commerce course, they often hung out together and had common friends. It was always amusing to be with them, and I often found myself spending time with them after classes were over. Overall, my life in North Block was filled with new experiences and friendships.

Sachin and I were excited to start our first year at our new school. We had joined few months back and were still getting to know our way around. But there was one student who seemed to know everyone and everything about our school—Tarun. He had been a student at our school for many years, and his experience showed. He was well-liked by his classmates and was even aware of hostel life, which was new to us. Many students would often visit our room just to talk to him. Our next-door neighbours were also students who had completed their 10th grade from the same school. I had only exchanged simple hellos with them, but one day, when we were sitting in our room, we heard a knock on our door. It was Manish and Satyakam, our next-door neighbours, coming to meet Tarun. He introduced me to them, and

I was happy to meet them, especially Manish, who happened to be from my native place, Bhagalpur. It was an instant connection between us, and we hit it off immediately. From that day on, we became good friends and spent most of our time together. Thanks to Tarun, Sachin and I quickly found a sense of belonging in new block with our new friends by our side.

My circle of friends was growing, but that did not mean that I had no time for Ranjit and Debashish. We continued our daily routine of eating all three meals together and hanging out in the canteen after lectures or prep time. Since we were now in the same block, I would either go to their room or they would come to mine. Mostly, they would visit me, as my room had an open terrace in front of it where we had made a sitting arrangement. A new canteen on the ground floor was started recently, and we would often buy tea from there and go sit on the terrace to enjoy it. Life was truly wonderful at the moment. I had appeared in a few more tests and managed to pass in chemistry while also scoring well in biology due to my strong memorization skills. Despite making new friends, I am grateful that I still had time for my old friends, Ranjit and Debashish, who have always been there for me through thick and thin.

I used to take walks with my friends Tarun and Sachin on our school campus. During one of these walks, Tarun introduced me to his friend Ashish Rawat. I was surprised to know that Ashish's cousin was a national shooter who had represented India in numerous tournaments. We exchanged pleasantries, and I found out that we had two things in common: we were both badminton players, and we both wanted to join the Horse-Riding Club. However, since my other friends were not interested, I didn't join earlier. But after meeting Ashish, we decided to practice badminton together and also go horse riding every alternate day. I was full of excitement and enthusiasm to try out horse riding and couldn't wait to get started.

The following day, I was bursting with excitement and energy as I was finally going to join the riding club. It was hard for me to focus during lectures, as all I could think about was my upcoming adventure. My friends Ranjit, Debashish, and Abhishek had no clue about my excitement, and during lunch, they asked me about the reason for my lost demeanour. I shared with them my plan to join the riding club, but they didn't seem too interested. However, they promised to visit the riding ground to cheer me on. I knew deep down that they were secretly hoping for me to fall so they could have a good laugh at my expense, as we were always looking for opportunities to prank each other. After the lectures, my friend Ashish and I headed towards the riding area and were asked to fill out some formalities. We were introduced to our riding instructor, who preferred being addressed as "Ustad Ji" instead of sir. His unconventional title only added to my excitement, and I couldn't wait to get on the horse and start my journey as a rider.

During our first day of horse-riding class, we couldn't help but notice that the majority of students were small kids. Our instructor, Ustad Ji, noticed our concern and informed us that another girl from our batch would be joining us and she would be arriving at 4 PM, as our class timings were from 4 PM to 5 PM. As we entered the stable, we saw around twenty magnificent horses. Ustad Ji told us to choose a horse as we would be riding the same one every day. He also explained that horses are very sensitive animals and it would take about a week for both the horse and us to get accustomed to each other. He assured us that the horse would eventually get used to our riding style and it would be easier for us to control it. This made me realize the importance of building a strong bond with our horse in order to become skilled riders.

Mamita, a girl from Manipur studying humanities, entered the riding area around 4 PM. It was my third month in the hostel, and I had never seen her before. As we were about to select our horses, I wanted to take the white one, but it was already taken by Ashish. Mamita had chosen the black one. I asked Ustad Ji, our instructor, which horse was the fastest, and he replied with a smile that it depends on the rider. He suggested that I take "Chocolate," a chocolate-coloured horse who was known to be the fastest but difficult to control. Ustad Ji instructed us to open the rope and walk with our horses to the riding area, a long stretch of sand. All three of us were scared as the horses made strange sounds and kicked. Ustad Ji warned us to never stand behind the horses in the beginning and taught us how to put on a saddle and sit on the horse. With our hearts beating fast, we hopped on our horses and started riding. Ustad Ji and his assistant held onto the ropes for the first few minutes until we got comfortable. That day, we just sat on the horses as they walked slowly. By the end of the session, we had gotten used to riding and had to take our horses back to their stable and tie them up. Ashish and I talked during the ride, but we didn't speak to Mamita that day. As we dismounted, we were relieved and happy with our first riding experience.

After returning to the hostel and not finding my friends there, I knew they must be at the canteen. I went there, still feeling upset, and asked them angrily why they didn't come to see me. They apologized and said they had forgotten about it. Apparently, they had come to my room but assumed I was with Tarun and Sachin. Feeling guilty, they offered to buy me tea and insisted I didn't have to pay for it. On our way back to the hostel, they mentioned something about an adventure during or after prep. When I asked for more details, they refused to disclose any information and just told me to be prepared. They also warned me not to be a "Phattu" (coward) and assured me that all four of us would be together. While heading towards the mess, I saw my childhood friends Amit and his friend Arvind going in the same direction. I shouted their names at the top of my voice, and they responded with equal excitement. It was always a pleasant feeling to meet Amit, as we had known each other since we were kids. However, due to different school schedules and strict rules at the campus, it was difficult for us to meet often. After meeting them, I headed over to my mess and took a seat beside my friends. Even during meals, I couldn't help but wonder what kind of adventure my friends were planning for us.

As I was entering the prep room, I saw our English teacher, Ravi sir. He was assigned to monitor the class, and I immediately knew that we were in for an adventure during prep. Ravi sir was always my favourite and the coolest teacher in school. He had a unique way of teaching that made learning fun and engaging for us. Despite his attempts to be strict, I could see that he couldn't hold it for long as he often ended up laughing with us during class. I admired Ravi sir for his friendly and approachable nature, which made him stand out from other teachers. I always looked forward to his class, as it was guaranteed to be full of interesting discussions and activities. Seeing him in the prep room only added to my excitement, and I couldn't wait to see what adventure my friends had planned for us that day. I saw my friends Debashish and Ranjit giving me a mischievous smile. I knew what that meant; they were thinking of sneaking into the prep session. We had to wait for 15-20 minutes before we could leave one by one, as that was our strategy to avoid getting caught. Whenever we had to bunk prep, we would have to ask a batchmate for help to keep our books and collect them later. I requested my friend Manish, but he had his own plans in the canteen. He suggested giving my book to Jyot, who was his roommate and also my neighbour. I handed over my book and went to ask permission from our sir to use the washroom. I had to wait for my friends near the water filter, and within a minute, they all came out one by one. As I started walking towards the MBA canteen, my friends informed me that we were not going there. They started walking towards the North Block, and I started wondering why. But instead of taking a turn towards our room, they headed towards the shower area. It was then that I realized that we were going out of campus. I stopped them and asked about their plan. They revealed that they wanted to explore a notorious canteen outside of our campus, even though it was already 8:30 PM.

Hearing this, I immediately felt a wave of nervousness wash over me. This was our second time sneaking out of campus and the first time doing it in the dark. My heart was racing as we jumped over the wall and made our way towards the canteen. As we approached, I couldn't help but notice the presence of many seniors and a few of our batchmates. The fear of getting caught intensified, but at the same time, I couldn't help but feel a rush of excitement. It was a risky move, but I trusted my friends and knew that this night would be one to remember. With apprehension and thrill mixed together, we continued towards our destination, ready for whatever the night had in store for us.

As we entered the open space in the vegetable farm, we noticed that it was a popular hangout spot for students from our school. The owner of the canteen, fondly known as Tau (Uncle), had set up a seating arrangement in one corner with more than 100 plastic chairs. He had also placed a few charpais (cots) for the comfort of his customers.

It was evident that he knew the importance of providing a comfortable environment for his customers. We saw Vikash bhai, a senior from our school and from Bhagalpur, sitting on one of the charpais. He was quite overweight, and I couldn't help but wonder how he managed to jump from the wall, which was a common feat among the students. The atmosphere was lively and bustling, with students chatting and enjoying their snacks. It was clear that this open space in the vegetable farm had become a beloved spot for students to unwind and socialize.

As we settled into our chairs at the canteen, Tau's son appeared to take our order. Curious about the food options, we asked him what they were serving. To our surprise, their menu was quite limited, with only tea, bread omelette, and Maggie available. We noticed that they were also selling cigarettes, which seemed to be a popular item among smokers. We decided to order tea, and the young man asked us which brand of cigarette we wanted as well. When we told him that we didn't smoke, he chuckled and joked that we could have just gone to the school canteen for tea. Clearly, he was too busy with his work to pay attention to our reactions. Waiting for our tea, we noticed the flood of bright lights that illuminated the entire area. We were curious as to why there was such an excessive use of light. As our tea was served, we couldn't help but ask the canteen owner about the reason behind the bright lights. He chuckled and told us that we were new to the canteen and would eventually understand the need for such lighting. Some seniors sitting close by overheard our conversation and warned us not to pry too much into the matter. They then whispered to us that a few days ago, Tau was attacked with swords and had just returned from the hospital. Since then, to prevent any further attacks, they had been using floodlights as a precautionary measure. It was a harsh reality check for us, as we realized that even in our supposedly safe environment, there were incidents of violence that needed to be dealt with in such extreme ways.

It was our first visit to this place, and while everyone around us seemed full of life, we couldn't help but feel a sense of fear and uncertainty. Despite this, there was also a feeling of freedom in being in a new place. As we sat and ordered a second round of tea, I noticed my friend Manish and his friends approaching us. He greeted us with a smile and said, **"Sutta Marne aaya hai."** We politely declined, telling him that none of us smoke. Manish then joked, **"Yahan aana shuru hogaya to jaldi hei cigarette peena bhi shuru hojayega."** (Once you start coming here, you will soon start smoking too.). We laughed it off and didn't take his words seriously. We stayed at the tea stall until midnight and returned to our hostel quite late, feeling content and happy. Despite our initial fears, we had managed to have a memorable and carefree evening.

The next day, I went to the badminton court in the academic block to play with my friend Ashish. I always dreaded going to the academic block, but today I was happy and surprised to find that no one was playing there. It seemed that most students preferred other sports like cricket, football, lawn tennis, or basketball. Ashish and I did warm-up exercises and started playing a 3-game set. It was great fun playing with him, but during our second match, we were both exhausted and gasping for breath. Despite this, we continued with our third match, taking only a short break in between. It was clear that we needed to play regularly to improve our stamina. Our warden, Mr. A N Singh, also came to the court after seeing the lights on. He too was fond of playing but had no one to play with. He was overjoyed to see us and asked us to come every day to practice. We humbly informed him that we could only come on alternate days as we also go for horse riding.

He seemed a little disappointed but encouraged us by saying that if we practiced regularly, he would send us for an interschool competition scheduled in two months. Excited by this opportunity, Ashish and I made a pact to come every alternate day and on weekends for practice. We also realized that we needed better rackets, and Ashish assured me that he would ask his parents to bring them as they visited him every Sunday.

While I was on my way to dinner, I noticed Mamita walking towards our direction. As she came closer, she recognized me and greeted me with a simple "Hi." I replied with the same greeting, but we didn't have much time to talk as she seemed to be in a hurry and my friends were waiting for me outside the mess. Unfortunately, the food today didn't meet our expectations, and I found myself disliking the food at the mess. Although it was supposed to be nutritionally balanced, it lacked in taste. Feeling disappointed with the meal, I went over to Piyush's table and asked for some ghee and achaar. I knew he always had some with him. Pleased to see me after a long time, he happily shared some with me. However, as I walked away, I couldn't help but feel selfish for only meeting him after so many days for help. After dinner, we decided to voice our concerns about the food to the mess in charge. However, he seemed uninterested and kept telling us that even the chairman sir eats the same food, and if there was an issue, he would have informed them. Despite his dismissive attitude, he did offer us some dessert and suggested we enter through the back gate. Feeling slightly appeased, we left the mess and went to prep for self-study.

During my time in prep, I stepped out to drink water when I ran into Mamita again. I asked her where she was rushing off to during dinner time, and she replied that she doesn't eat at the mess and prefers the food at the canteen. She explained that she didn't like the food in the mess and usually depended on the school canteen for her meals. It was the first time she had been away from her family, and she mentioned that the food habits in Delhi were quite different from those in Manipur, her hometown. Mamita's father, who was a member of parliament, would often visit her in Delhi and bring home-cooked food for her. It became clear to me that Mamita came from a wealthy and powerful family. I had initially assumed that she was either introverted or arrogant because she didn't have any friends, but as we talked, it was evident that she was neither. Before we parted ways, Mamita asked me if I would be coming for horse riding the next day, to which I replied with an enthusiastic yes, as it sounded like a fun and exciting activity.

The next day, we arrived at the horse-riding club around 3:45 PM, and to our surprise, Mamita was already there. She informed us that we would have to wait for about 10-20 minutes before our session would begin. As we waited, I couldn't help but notice that the three of us were from different streams—I was from science, Ashish from commerce, and Mamita from humanities. This resulted in us not having much to talk about and having different friend circles. Ustad Ji then called us and instructed us to put the saddle on our horses and bring them to the riding ground. Today, we were left to do this on our own, but we helped each other out and successfully brought the horses to the riding area. Unlike yesterday, we were less scared and more confident as we sat on the horses and started riding. We even learned how to make the horses move out and turn, much to our delight. However, our session came to an end, and despite wanting more time, we had to give way for others who were waiting for their turn. After the ride was over, I noticed Ashish leaving in a hurry without informing us. Mamita and I walked back slowly towards the girls' hostel, where she invited me to join her for dinner since she knew I didn't like the food at the mess. I wanted to accept her invitation as I was also tired of the hostel food, but this was the time I usually spent with my friends Ranjit and Debashish at the mess. I declined her offer but promised to meet her after prep time. She said after prep time she does not go out of the hostel. She said goodbye and asked me to come on time for our next riding session. I understood why Mamita had no friends, but I hoped that our bond would grow stronger in the upcoming riding sessions.

My life was filled with excitement and joy, except for the constant struggle with my studies. I was having the time of my life and didn't even miss my family, as I would talk to them on the phone once a week. I had six subjects, and while I excelled in all of them, Physics was the one subject that gave me a hard time. I tried my best to focus on it, but I just couldn't grasp the basic concepts. Despite regular tests being conducted, I would always pass in every subject except Physics. It seemed like no matter how much effort I put I would fail every physics test. To make matters worse, my physics teacher would constantly put me on the spot during lectures, leaving me feeling embarrassed and defeated. Despite these struggles, I never stopped going to Tau's canteen with my friends. Tau had grown fond of me, and we would often go there for a delicious bread omelette and tea. Sometimes, Tau even gave us free tea without asking for any money. We had become so carefree that we stopped caring about the rules and regulations of our school. We would often sneak out to go to places like Priya and Connaught Place, making it a regular occurrence on weekends. Despite my challenges with physics, life was still full of fun and adventure with my friends by my side.

Over time, my bond with Ashish and Mamita grew stronger through our shared passion for horse riding. However, our friendship took a new turn when Mamita joined us for badminton. Ashish and I were selected to represent our school in a badminton tournament, but Mamita's name was not on the list due to her average playing skills. But I didn't want her to miss out on the experience, so I requested our coach, A. N. Singh, sir, to pair her with me in mixed doubles. After some convincing, he finally agreed, and we had a few days to prepare for the match. We even took a break from horse riding to focus on badminton training with an instructor from Hyderabad. Sir paid extra attention to me as I was representing in both men's singles and mixed doubles. On the day of the match, we were filled with excitement and nerves as we played at Manav Bharti School. Some of our classmates and friends came to cheer for us, but unfortunately, we didn't win a single game due to pressure and playing on an unfamiliar court in front of a large audience. Our coach was disappointed with our performance but encouraged us to practice more as we had another tournament in the winter. The host school even arranged a dinner for all participants, and we were happy to return to our hostel with our friends and teachers after a long day. This experience brought the three of us even closer and strengthened our bond as teammates and friends.

Despite our team's defeat, Ashish and I handled it with a positive attitude. However, Mamita was visibly upset and sat alone at the back of the bus. Seeing her in this state, I went over to her and sat beside her to offer some comfort. As she opened up about feeling homesick, I empathized with her and assured her that she was not alone in this journey. We chatted for a while, and by the end of the bus ride, Mamita seemed to have a more positive outlook and a smile on her face. It was heartwarming to see how a small gesture of friendship could lift someone's spirits.

As we reached the hostel, I saw Tarun and Sachin waiting for me. I immediately told them that we lost all the matches. Tarun, being a part of the cricket team, understood that it's just a game, and sometimes we win and sometimes we lose. They both consoled me and advised me to keep practicing for the next tournament. While lying on my bed, I couldn't help but think that if I had more stamina, I could have won as I lost all my matches in the last set. It was clear that I needed to start eating properly and incorporate running into my daily routine. It was a valuable lesson learned, and I was determined to work harder for the next tournament.

The next day, I had to inform my friends that I wouldn't be able to join them for dinner as I was invited by Mamita for dinner at the canteen. To my surprise, they didn't tease me or pull my leg like they usually do. They knew Mamita and I had become good friends, and they also felt sorry for her because she didn't have any friends. As I thought, I would meet Mamita at the canteen, but to my surprise, I saw her walking towards the mess. I was confused as she never ate at the mess, and today, after inviting me, she was going there for dinner. As I got closer, I saw her talking to Ranjit, who was standing outside the mess. When I reached there, Ranjit jokingly said, "**Kahan the be tum, kab se ye khoj rahi tumko.**" I explained that I was on my way to the canteen when I saw her going towards the mess, so I followed her. Mamita then invited Ranjit and Debashish to join us for dinner, but they declined as they preferred spending their mealtime socializing and pulling pranks on others at the mess.

As we made our way towards the main canteen, my friend Mamita told me that we weren't actually going there, but to the MBA canteen instead. I was a bit confused, but she explained that they offered a wider variety of items on their menu. When we arrived, I realized that she had already placed our order beforehand. We found a table near the counter, and within a few minutes, our food was served. I could tell from the aroma that Mamita had ordered chicken fried rice and chicken Manchurian, along with cold drinks. I couldn't resist trying the Manchurian as it looked and smelled amazing. I ended up eating more than I usually do and even went for seconds. Just when we thought our meal was over, the service boy surprised us with ice cream. Mamita had no idea that I don't eat ice cream due to my sinus problems and lack of interest in it. However, I didn't want to disappoint her, so I didn't say anything and ate it all. The entire experience at the MBA canteen was delightful, and I couldn't have asked for a better lunch outing with my friend.

After indulging in a big meal, Mamita and I decided to take a long walk around the campus. It was a Sunday, so we didn't have to rush for any prep. As we strolled, Mamita began talking about her family. She shared that she didn't want to come to Delhi for her 11th and 12th grades, but her parents insisted, as her cousins were studying in Delhi. She was homesick and longed to return home. During that time, she joined a horse-riding club and eventually became a part of the badminton group as well. Even though we only used to meet during those activities, she thanked me for being there for her. I couldn't help but feel bad for her struggles. I promised her that she could rely on me for anything now that we were friends. I knew she was finding it hard to adjust, being an innocent and pampered kid. It's tough for students like her to adapt to hostel life. Before parting ways, we went to the girls' hostel canteen for some tea. I reassured her that now that we were friends, she could rely on me for anything. It was a heartwarming moment to see her smile, and I couldn't help but feel bad for her struggles.

After a long day, I finally returned to my room. I was happy that I met a group of amazing people in the hostel who welcomed me with open arms: Piyush, Ranjit, Debashish, Abhishek, Tarun, Sachin, Manish,

Ashish, and Mamita—all of them were my closest friends. I remember how we bonded over our shared interests and sense of humour. We would spend hours talking, laughing, and making memories that I will cherish forever. Although I had many other friends, these people hold a special place in my heart. They have been there for me through thick and thin, and I am grateful for their presence in my life. Even though we may not see each other as often now that we have graduated and moved on to different paths, I know that our friendship will remain strong. These nine individuals have made a significant impact on my life, and I am thankful for the memories we have created together that will always bring a smile to my face.

CHAPTER 4

FROSTY FIGHTS AND BHAGALPUR DELIGHTS

Growing up in a diverse environment, I was always taught to embrace and respect differences among individuals. However, during my high school years, I was completely unaware of the prevailing tension between two sections of students in school. It all started when our seniors, who were having some issues with each other, were further fuelled by an action done by Amit, a student from Bihar studying commerce in my batch. This action transferred the tension to our batch, and I had no idea about the differences and their intensity. Being a newcomer to the school, I had no knowledge of the ongoing dispute between the two groups. In 5-6 months, I had befriended many students from both sections, still completely unaware of the tension between them. However, things took an unexpected turn when the situation escalated into a wild fight between the two groups. It was then that I realized the severity of the issue and how it had affected not just the students involved but also their peers who were caught in the middle.

As the days passed, the senior section of our school became divided into two separate camps, each vying for power and control. However,

I remained neutral in the midst of all the school politics. My close friends and I had no interest in participating in these power struggles. Instead, we were content with enjoying our boarding life on our own terms. One night, before a big fight between the two camps, Atul, a member of one of the groups, came to my room to meet my roommates. I had a friendly relationship with him, and we often met and talked. To me, we were friends. So, when he asked to go to the canteen for some tea and Maggie, I agreed and even ended up paying for him, which I now regret. On our way back to our block, I noticed a large group of students talking at midnight, which was an unusual sight. However, I didn't think much of it and went back to my room. It was there that I saw Manish and others from one of the camps talking in a group outside my room. Little did I know that this was just the beginning of a larger conflict that would soon unfold in our school.

As I stood there for a few moments, I couldn't help but overhear the intense conversation between my batchmates. It was clear that in the coming days, there would be a brutal fight on campus. They were discussing the potential pros and cons of the situation, trying to find a way to avoid direct conflict. However, it was also evident that if the opposite camp were to create any trouble, they would not hesitate to fight back with all their strength. Feeling like I had no part in this altercation, I started to walk towards my room. But just as I was about to leave, my friend Manish called me over and asked me to wait for a few minutes as he wanted to talk to me. I grabbed a cigarette from the window where I usually kept them and waited for Manish, curious to hear what he had to say about the situation. As I was about to finish my cigarette, my friend Manish came and took the remaining one from my hand. He then proceeded to brief me about the tense situation on our campus. Being from our side, he warned me that I might be targeted by the opposing camp. He advised me to stick with my friends and never wander alone. I was taken aback as I had never considered myself a part of any specific group. However, upon returning to my room, I overheard my roommates discussing the same matter. They too were concerned, and Tarun wanted to shift to a different room for safety reasons. This incident made me realize the gravity of the situation and the need to be cautious and aware of the existing tensions on our campus.

Like me, he was also labelled as a member of the opposite camp. Sachin and I reassured him not to worry and reminded him that we are all friends and will back each other. The conversation between us was intense, and I never wanted him to leave and go to another room. We had no interest in the ongoing politics or fight, and all we wanted was for everyone to coexist peacefully. I asked him to go back home until the situation calmed down, and he agreed. However, he did pack his luggage, and we helped him with it. We were filled with fear and sadness, knowing that our friend had to leave because of the tense situation. But we promised each other that we would stay connected and support each other no matter what. Despite being labelled as members of opposing sides, our friendship remained strong.

The night was filled with an eerie atmosphere as, for the first time, we locked our room from inside and closed the window, which was near my bed. Despite our efforts, we could not seem to fall asleep. From Tarun's window, we could see the students from the opposite camp still in a group, seemingly planning something. Even on our side of the camp, we could hear discussions still going on. As time passed, more students arrived, and they too were engaged in conversation. Despite the noise and commotion, we somehow managed to drift off to sleep. However, our peaceful slumber was short-lived as we were abruptly awoken in the morning by a knock on our room door. It was

A N Singh, sir, signalling the start of a new day at the campus. It was a restless night, filled with curiosity about what was happening on the school campus.

Ranjit came to my room and warned me not to go take a shower alone. He suggested that I go with him and our group of 7-8 friends instead. As we made our way to the shower, I couldn't help but feel a sense of unease and tension in the air. It was clear that most students were sticking together in groups, seeking safety in numbers. As we walked, I noticed many eyes staring at us, some with curiosity and others with suspicion. I even greeted a few people, assuming they were my friends, but to my surprise, they did not respond. It was then that I realized I was officially part of one of the groups or "camps" that had formed within the school. In a time of uncertainty and turmoil on campus, it seemed wise to stick with this group for our own safety. It was a strange feeling, knowing that we were all in this together but also feeling a sense of isolation from those who were not part of our group. But for the time being, it was better to stick together and have each other's backs.

While returning from breakfast, I met my friend Amit Singh near his hostel. He seemed worried and told me that there is tension in his hostel as well. It was disheartening to hear that the hatred and violence on campus had spread like a wildfire. When I reached my room, I was shocked to see rods and bamboo sticks lying outside my room. This further escalated my fear, and I found out that my roommate Tarun was planning to go home after lunch. Exhausted from the events of the previous night, I asked Sachin to lock the room from outside and give me the keys through the window. I desperately needed some rest and went to sleep around 8:30 AM. The current state of affairs on campus was unsettling, and I prayed for things to calm down soon.

I was suddenly jolted awake by loud shouts and curses outside my room. My heart started racing as I heard the sound of someone forcefully trying to break the lock on my door. Fear and panic consumed me as I realized that someone was trying to enter my room. In an attempt to protect myself, I lay still and pretended to be asleep, hoping that they would think there was no one in the room. But to my horror, they managed to break the lock and barged into my room. I could feel my entire body trembling as they shook me awake with a rod. In that moment, all I could think about was how I had nothing to do with any kind of politics or fight, and yet, here I was, caught in the middle of a potentially dangerous situation.

I saw Atul standing with a group of students, all carrying rods and sticks. But what caught my attention was Atul holding a cycle chain in his hand. Suddenly, they started shouting, "Here is one of them!" More students began to enter the room, making me feel increasingly uneasy. I tried to reason with Atul, reminding him that I had nothing to do with their fight, but he continued to shout and raise his voice, getting closer to me. Outside my room, the commotion only seemed to escalate with fighting and abuses being hurled back and forth. Before I could even explain myself, Atul started punching me on my chest with the cycle chain wrapped around his wrist. The blows were hard and relentless as others joined in. Feeling overwhelmed and scared, I closed my eyes, pretending to be unconscious in hopes that it would all soon come to an end.

As I lay on the floor of my room, my body numb from the repeated hits, I couldn't believe the sudden silence. They had finally stopped hitting me and left the room. I slowly stood up, feeling no pain anymore. My fear turned into a desperate determination to get to safety. I looked out of Tarun's window and saw my friends standing across the building. Many teachers were there, trying to stop them from coming towards the hostel. But they were armed with rods and sticks, ready to strike. I knew I had to cross the distance between us at any cost to be safe. However, Atul and his friends were still outside my room, making it impossible for me to make a move. Suddenly, I heard my friend Manish's voice, shouting and cursing in pain. My heart sank as I saw them hitting him with tube lights. Two more students from our side had been caught by them. It was a horrifying sight as I could see blood flowing from Manish's body. He was shouting for someone to go and inform others about what was happening. In that moment, I realized that I was the only one there who could help. With trembling hands and a racing heart, I made my way out of the room, determined to save my friends from the brutality.

The sense of fear and desperation consumed me as I stood facing the door that led to the staircase. On the right side of my room was Manish's room, and to the left was the staircase, the only way out of this nightmare. I knew that if I could gather enough courage to open the door and run towards the stairs, I might have a chance at rescue. But I was also aware that I had no idea how many students were near the staircase or below it, ready to capture me again. With my heart racing and hands trembling, I took a deep breath and opened the door in silence. As soon as I began running towards the stairs, they spotted me and started chasing after me, hurling abuse and shouting for others to catch me. But I didn't stop; my only focus was on getting out of this dangerous situation and seeking help. The adrenaline rush and fear pushed me to run faster, ignoring their threats and screams. In that moment, all I could do was hope for a miracle and pray that I reach safety soon.

As I was making my way down the stairs, my heart skipped a beat when I saw a group of students standing near the bottom. I was so scared that I almost jumped over their heads in an attempt to get away from them. Without a second thought, I started running as fast as I could, dodging other groups of students in my path. My only thought was to reach my friends, who were standing across the building, approximately 50 meters away. As I ran, I realized that the group of students behind me was also following me, unaware that they were running towards an opposing gang. Among my friends, Ranjit and Debashish were also present across the building. Finally, I reached my friends, and it was a close call, but I managed to escape unharmed. I told them to go and help our other friends Manish and two others who were alone and struggling at the North Block hostel. Without hesitation, all of my friends ran towards the North Block hostel to provide assistance to Manish and the others. It was a heartwarming sight to see my friends putting their safety aside to help those in need. In times of danger, they showed great courage and loyalty towards our friendship. My friends Ranjit and Debashish immediately took me to the MI room for medical inspection. On the way there, I explained to them what had happened—Atul had attacked me with a chain, resulting in cuts on my face and hand. I speculated that I must have been injured while trying to dodge his blows. My friends were carrying rods and sharp objects, ready for revenge. Soon, our other friends Amit Singh and Vinod arrived at the scene with sticks upon hearing about the attack on me. We were all enraged and determined to seek retribution against Atul and the two other individuals involved in the incident. For better or worse, I was engaged in a physical altercation and ultimately became actively involved.

After receiving first aid, my friends and I headed back to our hostel. However, the scene that greeted us was shocking. The clash between the two groups had escalated, and there was an open fight near the basketball court. We could see students from both sides wielding rods and sticks, creating a chaotic and violent scene. More than 100 students were involved in the fight, and we could feel the tension and anger in the air. As we got closer, we saw that a student from our side was being held captive and beaten up by 5-6 students from the opposing camp. Our blood boiled with rage, and we couldn't stand idly by. We quickly jumped into action to help our friend and put an end to the violence. It was a scary and overwhelming experience, but we were determined to do whatever it takes to keep our friend and ourselves safe. Ranjit and Amit, along with 3-4 more students, rushed to the rescue of a boy who was bleeding badly. The sight was gruesome, and it sparked a sense of urgency in them to help the boy. As they tried to stop the bleeding and assess the situation, I frantically looked around for a rod or stick. Not finding any suitable object, I grabbed two bricks and joined them in their efforts. However, as soon as the students from the opposing camp saw me with just two bricks in my hands, they started hitting me. I managed to dodge most of their blows but was still hit multiple times. In a moment of desperation, I threw one of the bricks at a student who had attacked me, causing him to fall and get injured. Taking advantage of the chaos, I snatched a rod from his hand and hit another guy on his legs, causing him to lose balance and fall to the ground. My actions may not have been conventional, but they were necessary in that moment of chaos and danger.

While in the midst of a heated fight, I suddenly spotted Piyush, my first roommate and my first friend in school, standing outside the warden's office. Piyush was the most innocent and sweetest boy in school, and I knew he was not one to get involved in any kind of conflict. However, seeing him there made me worry for his safety. I immediately asked him to sit inside the warden's office until things calmed down. When we entered, we found a few teachers already inside, mostly female teachers. They had locked themselves in the room for safety.

As we made our way towards the North Block, the adrenaline pumping through my veins, I couldn't help but feel a mixture of fear and anger. We knew that the situation was dangerous, but we couldn't back down now. As we approached the stairs, we saw a group of students from the opposite side. Without hesitation, they charged at us, and we were forced to defend ourselves. In the middle of the chaos, there was no option for us to retreat or surrender. We fought bravely, but it was clear that we were outnumbered. Just when it seemed like all hope was lost, a few students from our side joined the fight, showing their support and giving us the strength to continue. It was a fierce battle that raged on, but we refused to give up. We caught one of the boys from the opposite group, and I immediately asked him about the whereabouts of Atul. However, he refused to answer, so I hit him with my fist in anger. We were a group of twenty students who had gone together as we were certain that the boys from the opposite group were upstairs. As we reached the first floor, I saw some students from our side who informed us that the opposite group had already escaped to the South Block after causing chaos. Despite our efforts to catch them, they had managed to flee and avoid any consequences for their actions.

As I walked down the corridor on the first floor, I couldn't believe my eyes. The once pristine floors were now covered in pools of blood. My heart raced as I quickly made my way to Manish's room, which was locked from inside. I knew something terrible had happened, and my suspicions were confirmed when I heard voices coming from inside the room. I knocked on the door, and Manish opened it for me and my friends. As we entered, I could see the anger and determination in his eyes. He explained that they were having a meeting to discuss a strategy for revenge against those who had attacked them. Manish was still bleeding from his wounds, but he didn't let that stop him from planning their strike. Looking around the room, I saw over 20 students who were injured and bleeding, all ready to fight back. Manish turned to me and said, "I heard you were attacked too." I nodded, and he replied, "Don't worry; we will take revenge today itself." We will make those responsible pay for their actions.

My heart started racing as he placed a rod with sharp edges in my hand and asked me to be prepared. However, I had no intention of getting into a fight; I just wanted to catch Atul. He was the one who had started thrashing me along with his friends. He said to seek revenge, we had to get inside South Block, where Atul was also hiding. R M Singh, a fellow student, suggested that we strike them before they could call for help from the locals, as most of them were from Delhi. It was a risk, but we couldn't let Atul and his friends get away with what they did to us. The fact that Atul was also from Delhi, like most of his friends, only fuelled my desire to attack South Block. We had to act quickly and take matters into our own hands before it was too late. We knew we needed to change into proper clothes, so we all went to our respective rooms to put on some shoes and comfortable clothes. For me, comfortable clothes meant wearing two pairs of jeans and a couple of t-shirts. I had this belief that wearing two layers of clothing would protect me in case of any accidents. We were supposed to meet in 10 minutes, and everyone arrived except for Ranjit. When he finally showed up, he looked strange and different. As he got closer, I noticed that he had placed a steel plate on his chest and stomach and said it would protect him from any rod strikes. However, since it was making him uncomfortable, he eventually took it off. As we all marched towards the South Block, we were armed with rods and sticks. I proudly carried a special rod given to me by Manish. We were a group of around 100 students, and from the looks of it, the opposite side seemed to be of the same strength. All the male teachers and other staff tried to stop us, but our anger and furiousness made them take a step back. The vice principal threatened us and ran towards the chairman's office to call the police. However, before he could do so, 5-6 students went with him to try and stop him. They claimed they would negotiate with the chairman instead of resorting to calling the police. It was a simple plan to buy us some time. Meanwhile, our group would attack the South Block and make our voices heard. When we all came down, I saw Amit and his friends, who had also joined us. For the first time, Amit and I, along with our group of friends, decided to break the rules and openly smoke on the school campus. As we walked, passing around a pack of cigarettes, I couldn't help but feel a sense of camaraderie with my friends. We were all in this together, breaking the rules and feeling like we were invincible.

As we arrived at the South Block, we noticed that all the tough and strong students had already gathered in front. My friends and I were trailing behind. However, when we reached the main entrance, we were shocked to find it locked. It was a heavy iron gate, and there was no way we could break it open. Our only option was to enter through the terrace. But to our dismay, we saw that the students on the terrace were throwing bottles and stones down at us. Even on the main gate, they were hurling stones to prevent us from trying to put a rod in and break the lock. The situation was getting intense, and it seemed like they didn't want us to enter the building at any cost. We had to think of a different plan to get inside without getting hurt. We divided into three groups; it was clear that we all had one goal in mind—reaching the terrace of the South Block. The first group decided to take their chances by using the wall near the main gate to reach the terrace, while the second group opted for a safer route through the prep room terrace. The third group was determined to try their luck at the backside near the teacher's quarter. Meanwhile, I and several others stood near the main gate, carefully choosing a spot where we would be safe from any potential projectiles such as stones or bottles. We were all determined to reach our destination and ready to face whatever obstacles may come our way.

Our side had successfully managed to reach the terrace from all three sides, despite facing fierce fighting along the way. As they reached the terrace, we could hear loud shouting and curses coming from both sides. We knew that our plan was to wait for someone from our team to break the lock and open the front gate for us to enter. However, to our surprise, we saw students from the opposite camp opening the door instead. As we saw them coming out, our group immediately ran towards them, relieved to see that they were not carrying anything dangerous. We could tell that they were innocent and had nothing to do with the ongoing fight. Some of my friends escorted them to a safe area while the rest of us headed back towards South Block. My heart was pounding as we entered the large corridor that led to South Block. The scene that greeted us was horrifying—students were fighting everywhere, and there was blood all over the floor. Many students from South Block had locked themselves inside their rooms in a desperate attempt to stay safe. My friends and I frantically searched for Atul and his friends in this chaos. South Block was a four-storey building with over 100 rooms, making it incredibly difficult to find them in the midst of the turmoil. I couldn't help but feel afraid and nervous as we continued our search, unsure of what we would find. When someone shouted that Atul was on the 3rd floor, we knew it would not be an easy task to reach him. As we made our way up the stairs, we were met with a chaotic scene—students from the opposite camp were standing on the stairs, engaged in a heated fight. We had to sneak past them to reach the 3rd floor. However, our efforts were not in vain as we managed to make it to that floor. Just as we were about to search for Atul, some students from the opposite group noticed us and ran towards us. Thankfully, my friends were able to stop them and told us to continue our search for Atul. With over 20 rooms on that floor, it was a challenging task to locate his exact whereabouts. But we persevered and eventually found Atul and his group of friends. After struggling for what seemed like hours, my friends and I were finally able to break the room door and enter. The students inside the room initially protested and even tried to attack us, but upon seeing our anger and strength, they eventually calmed down and surrendered. We immediately caught hold of Atul and three of his friends who were involved in attacking me. This was the first time I had ever used such harsh language, using every mother and sister abuse that came to my mind. I grabbed Atul by his collar and tried to take him to the ground floor, as the room was too small for us to use a stick to beat him and his friends. We ended up taking him to the tennis court outside the hostel, where I don't even remember how many times I slapped him. However, upon reaching the court, Atul showed his strength and tried to run towards the warden's office in an attempt to escape. In a fit of rage, I pushed him to the ground and kicked him in the face, causing him to bleed. Despite Amit's warning not to hit him on the face, my anger was uncontrollable, and I started hitting him on the leg with a stick. I was so furious that I kept hitting him multiple times, convinced that I had broken his legs. It was only when Ranjit intervened and stopped me from causing further harm that I realized the severity of my actions. At this point, Atul was lying on the ground, close to fainting. Without a second thought, I left him there and joined my friends in bashing others. However, our violent outburst was soon interrupted by someone shouting that the school authorities had called the police and they would be arriving any moment. In a desperate attempt to escape punishment, we abandoned Atul and his friends and ran towards the South Block hostel to warn our fellow students. In a state of panic, we gathered in the centre corridor and communicated in loud voices about the impending arrival of the police. This caused chaos, and everyone returned to their rooms in fear of the consequences.

When I came to my room, my roommate Sachin informed me that our friend Tarun had left for his home. But before leaving, he had left some snacks for us. Being hungry, I ate some of the snacks. From my window, I could see that there was a commotion near the tennis court. As I looked closer, I realized that there were police officers, and they were carrying sticks. All the teachers and staff members were also gathered there. The police and teachers were taking some injured individuals to the medical inspection for first aid and bandaging. Just then, my friends Ranjit and Debashish came to my room and told me to act normal and innocent and go to the tennis court where the police were standing. It was clear that they wanted us to pretend to be innocent among the group of people standing there, most of whom were not involved in whatever had happened earlier. We quickly followed their instructions and joined the group, trying our best to act innocent and blend in with the others. After changing my clothes, I headed down to the tennis court where I joined the other students. We noticed a group of students from the opposite camp leaving the hostel after receiving first aid. Suddenly, Amit appeared and joined us. We then saw Atul walking towards the car parking lot with his bags. The sight of him made me furious all over again. Determined to confront him for the last time, we followed him to the parking lot. His friends were helping him walk as he was unable to do so on his own. We stopped him, and he started shouting for help upon seeing us. In a fit of rage, I slapped him hard, and we quickly ran towards the MBA hostel when we saw the police approaching the parking area. We went to Amit's hostel and changed our clothes before grabbing some books from his room and heading to the library to hide and let things settle down. As we returned from the library before dinner, my friends and I made our way to our room. However, on our way, we couldn't help but notice a group of students gathered near the warden's office, deep in conversation with the principal and other staff members. Curiosity led us to approach the warden's office, where we saw a list of students on the notice board who were expelled from the school and were asked to leave the campus immediately. It was then announced that the school bus will transport them to Hauz Khas, and from there they will go to their respective local guardians. This news made me feel tense, as my local guardian was my brother-in-law, who worked in the Navy as a doctor. He was known for his strict discipline, and I did not want to go and impose on him. I hoped that I would not be on that list of students expelled and have to face the consequences of staying at my brother-in-law's house. It was a worrisome thought, and I hoped that my name would not be on that list, but unfortunately, my name was on the list given by the school administration. We were given only 30 minutes to pack our bags and board the bus waiting near the main gate. I tried to talk to the principal, but the warden didn't allow me, claiming he saw me carrying a rod and confronting Atul and his friends earlier that day. With no choice left, I packed my bag and joined around 100 other students who were also leaving the campus. Three buses were waiting for us, and it was already getting dark. Although I have left campus in the dark before, this time it felt different and uncertain. As I packed my bag and checked my wallet, I realized that I only had a few hundred notes, probably around 400-500 rupees. Sachin's name was not on the list, and he had given me some money for emergencies. As I and the others came down and started walking towards the main gate, I noticed Shalini, Rachika, and Mamita standing outside my hostel. However, I decided to ignore them as I had done something that was not acceptable. But they called out my name, and when I turned to them, I saw that they wanted to talk to me. I hesitantly went up to them, and to my surprise, they gave me a few thousand rupees and told me not to show it to anyone. They said it was only for emergencies and for me. I wanted to hug them in gratitude, but instead, I just shook their hands and went to the parking lot to take the bus. Ranjit, Debashish, and I all boarded the same bus together. As the bus conductor informed us, we were to be dropped near the Uphaar cinema in Hauz Khas, and it took us around 30-45 minutes to reach there. Our bus happened to be the last one to arrive at the destination, and as we stepped out, we could see the entire area swarming with students from our school. My friend Manish came up to me and shared that instead of going to the local guardian house, we were going to GK, as Goenka's brother would be picking us up. While waiting for him, we decided to explore the area around Uphaar cinema. I was feeling quite hungry, and so were my friends. Although I had some money with me, there were about twenty-five students left, and if I were to pay for myself, I would have to pay for others too. So, a few of us decided to go to a nearby tea stall and bought a packet of Navy Cut cigarettes and some tea. I discreetly hid the packet inside my bag as it was just for me, Ranjit, and Debashish. Goenka's brother went out of his way to accommodate our group of twenty-five students. He came along with his friends in five different cars to make sure we had enough space for the journey. Fortunately, Goenka's house was a large bungalow with three floors, and the entire house was vacant as his family lived in Assam, making it the perfect place for us to stay. The ground floor was fully furnished, but the upper floors had no furniture. However, Goenka's brother had ordered

Dunlop's and pillows from a tent house to make us comfortable. The cook prepared a delicious dinner for us while his brother gave us lectures on the importance of our career and life choices. It was clear that we were not making the right decisions, and his words hit home for all of us. Despite knowing that we were wrongdoers, we were grateful for their hospitality and guidance during our stay at Goenka's house. After a satisfying dinner, our group decided to spend the rest of the night on the first floor of our building. What was supposed to be a form of punishment and stress for breaking hostel rules turned into a fun picnic for us. We laughed and chatted for hours, making tea multiple times in the kitchen on the first floor. As the night went on, we finished an entire packet of cigarettes. We were shameless, breaking rules and enjoying every moment of it. We ended up staying on the first floor for three days, and during our time there, we pooled our money together and gave it to Amit, who was also from Bihar, to buy a weapon in case the other group that had attacked us before would come back for revenge once we returned to the hostel. We waited for Amit for two days, but he never returned. Throughout the three days we spent away from the school hostel, we were constantly in touch with the school administration. Thankfully, after four days, we received permission to return back to the hostel. The school bus would pick us up from the same location near Uphaar Cinema in Hauz Khas. We were lucky enough not to have to spend any money during those four days as Goenka's brother took care of everything. Just before leaving for Hauz Khas, I bought a packet of cigarettes, but my mind was filled with worry about the consequences we would face upon returning to the hostel. Negative thoughts were racing through my mind—what would the school do? Had they already informed our parents? With so many questions and fears, I boarded the bus. The bus driver and conductor informed us that the school administration was very annoyed with our actions and would be taking strict action against us. The weight of uncertainty and fear only grew heavier as we made our way back to the hostel. We finally reached our hostel in just 30-40 minutes. As we entered the main gate of our school, we were greeted by the unexpected presence of our principal, Ma'am, the vice principal, and the warden. Their serious and angry expressions surprised us all. We were then instructed to stand in line and sign the attendance register one by one. It was already 4-5 in the evening, and we were exhausted, but we followed their instructions. Soon, we were asked to go to the chairman's office. As we entered the building, we were served with snacks and tea. It was heartwarming to see how much our school cared for us. Despite being tired, we felt happy and grateful. However, little did we know that something significant was about to happen. As we were sitting and enjoying our snack, we were suddenly interrupted by the presence of our principal, Ma'am, the vice principal, and Warden Sir. They sternly reminded us to finish our food quickly and gather in the chairman's office. We were all taken aback and worried as Chairman Sir only called students to his office when there was a serious issue to address. We hurriedly left our unfinished snacks on our plates and made our way to his office. As we entered, Chairman Sir's anger was evident on his face. We greeted him with a "Good evening," but he did not even acknowledge us. He went on to say that what we had done was unprecedented in the history of the institution, and we were solely responsible for it. The tension in the room was palpable as we waited for him to reveal what we had done. He ended by saying that we would have to face the consequences of our actions. Our hearts sank as we realized the severity of the situation. The news was shocking and devastating—he said we all were expelled from school and wouldn't be allowed to return until after the winter break. It was hard to believe that our actions had resulted in such a severe consequence. Just when we were supposed to go on vacation in 10 days, it seemed like our break had already begun. We were instructed to carry a letter for our parents and get it signed before joining school again after the vacation. To make matters worse, he asked us to sign a paper with a self-declaration and acceptance of our involvement in a fight that had caused tension on the campus. We were left with no choice but to sign the paper, knowing that it would reflect poorly on us. We were given a railway reservation form to book tickets for our hometown. The school administration was responsible for getting our tickets for the earliest available day. We all completed the form and handed it over to the warden, who then instructed us to stay in the hostel and only come out for meals. Essentially, we were under house arrest until it was time for us to leave for the train. As I entered my room, I was pleasantly surprised to see Sachin there. He gave me a warm hug and welcomed me back. I told him that I had to leave for my home, and he informed me that many students had already left the hostel and would only be returning after the winter break. The hostel occupancy had drastically reduced to only 20-30 percent. For dinner, I went towards the mess with my friends. As we were walking, I noticed Shalini and Rachika coming out of the girls' hostel. I asked my friends to go ahead and that I would join them shortly. Shalini and Rachika saw me and greeted me with big smiles. They could sense the worry on my face, and I told them that a few of us had been expelled from school and were being sent back to our hometowns until after the winter break. They said that it was good that I would be leaving 10 days before the scheduled break. I mentioned the letter that needed to be signed by our parents, and they replied that it was obvious the school administration would inform our parents. They added that I should have thought about the consequences of being a part of the conflict before getting involved. I felt uncomfortable as my closest friends were preaching to me when I needed their support. I walked with them to the mess and joined my friends at their table. Everyone looked worried, but there were also some students who were still able to enjoy the normal hostel life. It was a bittersweet feeling as I realized that soon, I would have to leave this place and say goodbye to my friends.

After finishing dinner, I immediately began packing my bag. It was winter, and I knew that I needed to bring my warm clothes, which would take up a lot of space. I had to pack tonight because I wasn't sure when we would be able to secure a reserved seat on the Indian railways. While packing, I chatted with my friend and ended up going to sleep at an odd hour in the middle of the night. As I drifted off to sleep, I couldn't help but notice that the warden, sir, was inspecting the hostel, specifically the North Block, multiple times. This was unusual as the North Block had never been under such scrutiny before. We were also informed that we were not allowed to visit other students' rooms, making me wonder about new rules and strictness.

The next morning, I woke up later than usual and quickly took a shower before heading to the mess hall for breakfast. To my surprise, we were informed that all classes had been cancelled, and instead, we were asked to sit for prep, a designated study time for students. As I made my way back to my room, I realized that I had nothing to do. It was incredibly boring, and I couldn't think of any productive way to spend my time. Eventually, I ended up falling asleep and only woke up when my friend Sachin came to my room for lunch. It was a lazy and uneventful morning, but at least I got some much-needed extra rest. While heading towards the mess for lunch, the warden approached me and asked me to meet him after lunch. He instructed me to inform all those whose names were on the list. As I relayed this message to my fellow classmates in the mess, Ranjit and Debashish questioned what more the warden could possibly do to punish us, as we were already being disciplined. They questioned what more could be done to us. With heavy hearts, we finished our lunch and made our way to the warden's office, wondering why we were being summoned. The uncertainty and apprehension hung in the air as we approached the warden's office, unsure of what was to come. As we reached the warden's office, we were greeted by the sight of Principal Ma'am and Warden Sir talking to a group of students. Intrigued, we joined them, only to find out that today's conversation was not as serious as we had anticipated. It was more of a counselling session, where the school authorities were giving the students some guidance and advice. Principal Ma'am was especially kind and understanding during this session. It went on for about 30-45 minutes, and it was a comforting and positive experience for all of us. Towards the end, Warden Sir announced that our tickets were booked and ready for collection. Principal Ma'am wished us good luck on our journey and left. We all collected our tickets, and as I looked at mine, I realized that I would be taking the Magadh Express at 8 PM the next day.

I was exhausted and ready to relax in my room. As I was unwinding, Manish came to me with exciting news. He told me that we were among thirty students who would be taking the Magadh Express tomorrow. I was thrilled because this train would take us through all the major cities of Uttar Pradesh, such as Aligarh, Kanpur, and Allahabad, before reaching Bihar. In Bihar, we would have 8-9 stoppages, including Patna, Begusarai, Kiul, Jamalpur, and our final stop, Bhagalpur. The thought of travelling with so many students on a train filled me with excitement as I knew it would be a memorable experience. I quickly checked my bag and was relieved to see that I only had one rucksack, which I had recently bought from Palika Bazaar. It was a stylish bag, and I couldn't wait to use it for the first time on our trip. I went to bed that night with a sense of anticipation for the adventures that awaited us on the Magadh Express. Ranjit came to my room before lunch to inform me that they will be leaving tomorrow at 2 PM by school bus as their train is scheduled to depart at 4 PM. He mentioned that around forty students will be going together, making it a fun and exciting journey. We chatted for a while, and later on, we headed to the mess for dinner, where we shared our excitement and anticipation for the trip. I couldn't wait to embark on this adventure with my classmates and create unforgettable memories together.

At mess, I had an encounter with Shalini and was surprised when she brought up the incident of my expulsion from school again. I nearly forgot about giving back the money to her. I retrieved my wallet and gave her the money. She mentioned that she didn't require it. She requested that I hold onto the money and return it in Bhagalpur. Shalini was insistent and promised to meet me in Bhagalpur, where she would be visiting in 10 days. Her kind gesture touched me, and I promised to meet her there. It was heartwarming to see how our friendship had withstood the test of time and how Shalini was always there for me, even after all these uncertainties.

After returning to my room, I found myself unable to fall asleep and ended up spending the entire night awake. As a hostel resident, I was not allowed to visit my friends' rooms, and it was a struggle to sneak out without getting caught by the warden. The constant fear of being inspected made it even more difficult to meet my friends. The next morning, I woke up early and headed to the shower area. To my surprise, I found Ranjit and Debashish already there taking a cold winter shower in Delhi. Despite the freezing temperature, we stayed in the shower area for about an hour. The warmth of our friendship helped us forget about the chilly water and made the experience memorable.

It was moments like this that made me appreciate the bond we shared and the importance of having good friends in life. As we sat down to have breakfast together, I couldn't help but feel a sense of sadness knowing that this would be the last time we would all be together for a while. However, during our breakfast, Debashish informed me that he would be going to Ranchi with Ranjit and would be staying there for 2-3 days before heading to his hometown, Asansol, in West Bengal. They wouldn't be joining us for lunch today, and we bid our farewells as we returned to our respective rooms. I quickly double-checked my bag and changed into more comfortable clothes before attempting to meet them before their departure. However, the warden denied my request to leave my room, so I had to settle for saying goodbye and wishing them a happy journey from my window. As I watched them leave the North Block hostel with smiles on their faces, I couldn't help but feel grateful for the memories we had shared and eagerly await their return after the break.

Our group was asked to gather near the warden's office with our luggage at 5:30 in the evening. I made sure to arrive promptly at the designated time and signed the attendance register. However, some of my classmates, including Manish, arrived about 5 minutes after me. After everyone had arrived, we boarded the school bus that would take us to the railway station. It was a little past 5:45 when we finally settled into our seats on the bus, excited for the journey ahead. The anticipation and eagerness in the air were palpable as we chatted and laughed while the bus made its way to the station. We were all looking forward to a memorable trip filled with fun and learning experiences. Little did we know that this trip would be one of the most unforgettable experiences of our lives.

As I reached the train station, I was informed that our seats were scattered across three different bogies. It was a relief to find out that my friend Manish and I were assigned the same bogie. Exhausted from the journey, I quickly settled into my upper berth and tried to get some rest. However, around 11 PM, Manish woke me up to inform me that we would be reaching Tundla Junction shortly and that we would be buying dinner there. As soon as we reached Tundla, a hawker came to our bogie, and everyone started ordering food. I decided to order a veg thali. It was pleasant that all my fellow passengers in the compartment were students from our boarding school. Eating with them felt like having dinner at our mess back at school. As we shared meals and stories, I couldn't help but miss my friends Ranjit and Debashish, with whom I used to always have dinner at school.

After a delicious dinner, I decided to relax and watch other students play cards. I sat in the lower berth of my train compartment, observing them intently. It was the first time I had seen a card game, and they were playing a game called twenty-nine. As the game progressed, I started to get bored as I had no knowledge about it. Eventually, I went up to my upper berth to sleep but was woken up early in the morning by a hawker selling chai. I checked the time on my trusty Timex watch; it was 8:30 AM. However, I couldn't go back to sleep as the sleeper class bogie was getting crowded with daily passengers in North India. It was difficult for long-distance travellers like me to find comfort. So, I sat back down on my berth, and my friend Manish called me to come down and sit before the seats were taken by the daily passengers. I joined him and bought two cups of tea for both of us. It was going to be a long journey ahead in the company of chatty daily passengers.

As our train made a stop at Patna junction, I realized that the stoppage was longer than usual. Knowing that we had some time to spare, I decided to ask one of my batchmates to look after our luggage while we got down at the station. It was around 12 noon, and hunger pangs had already started to kick in, so we decided to buy some lunch. My friend Manish and I went to the adjacent bogie where some of our other classmates were sitting. Upon seeing us, they got excited, and we all started chatting outside their bogie. When the train started moving again, we quickly jumped into their bogie as it was connected to ours. We continued our conversation outside the toilet area for a while before finally heading back to our own bogie. When my friend and I finally returned to our bogie after 15 minutes, our batchmates were visibly annoyed. They thought that we had missed the train and were worried for our safety. Despite having lunch, they were not eating as they were so concerned about us. We apologized for our delay and tried to adjust in the overcrowded train, but it was becoming difficult with passengers from Patna also boarding. We requested a local passenger to vacate a seat for us, but he refused to do so, resulting in an ugly altercation. One of our batchmates went to the adjacent bogie and called more students for help. Seeing our increased numbers, the local passenger finally gave in and vacated the seat for us to sit. Finally, we all had the opportunity to have lunch together. As students were getting off the train at their respective stations, our group was getting smaller, and our strength was reducing. However, I couldn't help but feel excited when we reached Jamalpur station. This was because I had been eagerly waiting to taste the delicious tea sold by the hawkers there. Once we reached Jamalpur, we had tea and recharged our energy levels before continuing our journey. By this time, only four students were left in our group, as the rest had reached their destinations. Finally, as our train entered Bhagalpur station around 5 PM, our journey came to an end.

As I got off the train, I could feel the excitement building up inside me. I had come back home after a long time, and I couldn't wait to see the surprised look on my parents' faces. I quickly hopped on a rickshaw and headed towards my home, which was just a kilometre away.

The ride only took 15 minutes, but it felt like hours as I was eager to reach home. To my delight, my family was completely taken aback by my sudden arrival. They had no idea that I was coming and were overjoyed to see me. As we sat down to catch up, my parents told me that they would have sent someone to pick me up from the station and made my favourite food if only I had informed them beforehand. They were curious to know why I came back ten days earlier than planned.

During my 20-day stay in Bhagalpur, I had the opportunity to indulge in all my favourite foods. As a boarding school student, my parents always complained about my weight and how I had lost so much during my time there. However, during my stay in Bhagalpur, I was able to eat to my heart's content without any worries. I also had the chance to catch up with all my friends from boarding school, and we even planned our return journey together. The atmosphere in Bhagalpur was a refreshing change from the stress and chaos of boarding school life. The peaceful and relaxing environment allowed me to unwind and recharge before heading back to school. Overall, my stay in Bhagalpur was a much-needed break from the hectic routine of boarding school life.

CHAPTER 5

SURVIVING FINALS

Life after returning from the winter break was a stark contrast to the previous semester. As I walked back into school, it was clear that almost everyone had returned from their break and was ready to dive back into their studies. The atmosphere was not as tense as it was before the break, but it also wasn't the same carefree and lively environment that I had grown accustomed to. However, one thing that stood out to me was how much closer I had become to my classmates. Perhaps it was the shared experience of being away from school for a few weeks, or maybe it was the newfound appreciation for each other's company. Whatever the reason, I was grateful to have formed stronger connections with my peers. It made returning to school after the winter break a little less daunting and a lot more enjoyable. Overall, life after the winter break may have been different, but in some ways, it brought us all closer together.

Atul and I crossed paths many times, whether it was in the hallways or during classes. However, despite our frequent encounters, we never spoke to each other or even exchanged a simple greeting. A new development in our school was the increased strictness of the teachers and the warden. They were always on high alert and quick to punish any students who misbehaved. To add to their watchful eyes, a few more guards had been hired to assist the warden in maintaining order within the school. With this heightened level of discipline, it was no wonder that Atul and I never dared to interact to sort out our differences, as we were both afraid of getting into trouble with the authorities. Our school had become a place of strict rules and regulations, making it difficult for students to form friendships or even engage in simple conversations after dinner.

With the installation of more street lights and the construction of guard rooms at every hostel block, the atmosphere on campus had changed. Regular inspections of rooms were conducted to ensure that no items such as rods and sticks were present. Post-prep students were strictly prohibited from visiting others' rooms, and we were under constant surveillance 24/7. In fact, we were even asked to surrender our door lock keys to the warden so that they could make duplicate keys and have access to our rooms even in our absence. Our once carefree hostel life had become a distant memory as we struggled to maintain any sense of privacy. Bunking classes and staying in our rooms was now next to impossible with the watchful eye. The newfound strictness on campus had made our lives difficult and left us longing for simpler times.

The height of the boundary wall in the school was recently increased, making it difficult or even impossible for anyone to jump over it. This measure was taken to ensure the safety and security of the students within the school premises. However, this new strictness was suffocating for me as I had never experienced such measures in school before. We were also required to wake up early for exercise and jogging, adding to the already strict routine. Furthermore, weekly tests were conducted to keep us busy and productive, leaving little room for leisure or relaxation. The past few weeks have been tough for me as I missed hanging out with my friends Ranjit and Debashish. Due to the strict rules of our hostel, we could only interact during school hours or while we were at mess. It felt like our bond was slowly fading away as we were not able to spend quality time together. Even something as simple as visiting the canteen for tea was not possible anymore. To make things worse, our teachers were taking attendance multiple times a day, even after our prep sessions. It has been two weeks since I came back from home, but I haven't had the chance to meet my other friends Shalini, Rachika, and Mamita. I have seen them a couple of times near the girls' hostel, but due to the strict and rude new warden, they were not able to come and meet me. It was disheartening to see how the new warden accompanied the girls to mess and made it difficult for us to socialize and catch up with each other.

Despite the strictness enforced by the school, one positive aspect was that all students were encouraged to participate in extracurricular activities. Fortunately, I was part of both the Badminton and Horse-Riding clubs. Every evening, students were required to play games, with cricket, football, and basketball being the most popular choices. However, I found my passion for badminton and horse riding and became a regular participant in these activities.

Ranjit and Debashish recently joined a lawn tennis club, and I would often visit them at their court. I was always fascinated by the sport and would try my best to play, but unfortunately, I never seemed to get a good grasp on controlling the ball. Despite this, I still enjoyed spending time with them and cheering them on when they played. My bond with Mamita, my horse-riding partner, who also enjoyed playing badminton with me, grew stronger. However, as much as I loved these activities, my daily routine had become quite mundane and repetitive, except for Sundays when we would have a break from our classes. Every day, I would wake up early in the morning, attend classes, play badminton in the evening, and then attend prep classes after dinner.

As days and months passed during my time in school, the strictness only seemed to increase. With numerous rules and regulations in place, it became increasingly difficult for me to focus on my studies. Despite my best efforts, I ended up scoring poorly in almost all of my tests, especially in the subjects of Physics and Chemistry. As a result, I started regretting my decision to take admission in the PCB (Physics, Chemistry, and Biology) stream. The pressure to perform well and the constant scrutiny from teachers only added to my already mounting stress. I found myself struggling to keep up with the rigorous academic demands and began to doubt my abilities. I wish I had chosen a different path that would have allowed me to pursue my interests and passions instead of being confined to a strict educational system that only caused me distress and disappointment. After struggling with physics for months, I have finally given up on the subject. Even my physics teacher has given up on me, as he started scolding and shaming me in class for my lack of understanding. I struggled especially with numerical problems, and it seemed like no matter how hard I tried, I just couldn't grasp the concepts. I wasn't alone in my struggles, as my friend Ranjit was also facing a similar situation. However, Debashish seemed to be managing to pass the exams somehow. The only subjects I found easy were English and Biology. With some effort and intense studying, I was able to comfortably pass in biology tests. It's disheartening to give up on physics, but I have come to terms with the fact that not everyone is good at everything. Perhaps I'll have better luck with other subjects in the future.

As the end of the first year approached, the looming final exams were the talk of the campus. It was a given that they would be held in the same month, and all the diligent students had already begun their preparations. However, I was not one of them. While my peers were studying diligently and making study schedules, I found myself unprepared and not ready for the upcoming exams. The thought of facing these important exams filled me with anxiety and dread. I couldn't help but feel overwhelmed and unsure about how I would perform. Despite knowing that I needed to start studying, I found myself procrastinating and avoiding the subject altogether. As the days passed by and the exams drew closer, I realized that I had to pull myself together and start preparing if I wanted to pass. It was a race against time, but I was determined to make the most of what little time I had left before the dreaded finals began.

The anticipation and stress levels in the school have risen as it was announced on the notice board that exams will be starting at the end of this month. The specific starting date of 7 March has been set, and the students have begun to take their preparation seriously. With the impending exams, the atmosphere in the school has turned serious and focused. Everyone has started to organize their study time according to the schedule of the exam date, making sure to cover all the necessary topics and revise thoroughly. The library and study areas are now filled with students, each one determined to do their best in the upcoming exams. The teachers too have intensified their efforts, providing students with extra study materials and conducting review sessions to ensure that they are well-prepared for the exams. The notice board announcement has served as a wake-up call for everyone, reminding us of the importance of these exams and the need to put in their best effort. As the days pass by, the school is abuzz with a sense of determination and motivation, all in preparation for the upcoming exams.

I can feel the pressure mounting with only two weeks left to prepare. However, I have come to the realization that trying to focus on all subjects might actually result in poor performance in each one. After thoroughly analysing the syllabus and schedule for the exam, I have decided to skip studying Physics. With so much material to cover in physics, I am afraid it will consume most of my time and leave me with little for other subjects. Therefore, I have made the decision to only study the physics theory and leave out all numerical. This will give me enough time to adequately study and perform well in the other subjects. While it may seem like a risky move, I am confident that by properly allocating my time and focusing on the subjects where I can excel, I will be able to achieve a better overall result in the final exam.

The schedule of final exams this year was a welcome change from the previous half-yearly exams. The school administration had carefully planned the exam schedule, allowing for adequate gaps between each exam. This gave students like me enough time to revise the syllabus and prepare thoroughly for each subject. What's more, I was delighted to find out that there was no exam scheduled on 11th March, which also happened to be my birthday. While my friends may have expected me to throw a party, I will have the perfect excuse of having an exam. However, I have already made up my mind to give a party for my friends at a restaurant near Qutab Minar after the exams are over. I have decided to host it on a Sunday so that my close friends Shalini, Rachika, and Mamita can attend. I will also invite them to take a day off and visit their local gurdwara before joining us at Qutab Minar for a fun and memorable celebration.

The long-awaited exam was finally approaching, and it was starting on 7th March with Chemistry as the first exam. The tension and anxiety among students were palpable for the first challenge. For the next few days, the schedule included Physics on 10th March, Biology on 13th March, English on 15th March, Hindi on 17th March, and Physical Education on 18th March. However, we were given a slight breather as there was a gap of three days between each subject's exams. This break will allow us to revise and prepare for the upcoming exams. Moreover, it will give us some time to relax and rejuvenate our minds before taking on the next subject. The practical exams were scheduled separately, with Chemistry on 21st March, Physics on 24th March, Biology on 26th March, and Physical Education on 28th March. This gave us ample time to focus on our practical skills and perform well in the exams. Overall, the exam schedule seemed well-planned and provided us with enough time to prepare and perform to the best of our abilities.

Preparing for exams can be a daunting task, and I found myself in a similar situation. With my exams around the corner, I knew I had to give my best effort to excel. However, I had to focus on three subjects: Physics, Chemistry, and Biology. English was always a strong subject for me, and it didn't require much of my attention. But for Hindi, I had to put in some extra effort to ensure I was well-prepared. As for Chemistry and Biology, I gave my best effort and spent hours studying and revising. However, physics proved to be the most challenging subject for me, and it was giving me sleepless nights. But with determination and perseverance, I continued to work hard and prepared myself to face the exam with confidence. For preparation for the physics exam, I focused solely on learning and memorizing the theories. I completely neglected the numerical, despite my friends' suggestions to focus on them as they cover 70% of the syllabus. However, this proved to be a mistake as I soon realized that I had only prepared for 30% of the exam. Even if I gave my best, I knew that I would not be able to score more than 15%. With this realization, I was already aware that I would perform poorly in the exam. The maximum I could hope for was fifteen marks out of 100. It was a tough decision, but with all these calculations in mind, I decided to leave the physics numerical untouched and focus on other subjects instead.

With just one week left before the exams were set to start, the pressure and anxiety were at an all-time high. After having lunch at the mess, I bumped into Rohit bhaiya, who worked in the administrative section of our school. He was a friendly and approachable person, and I had formed a good rapport with him. As he inquired about my preparations for the exams, I confidently told him that I was sure of passing with good marks except in Physics. I shared my fear of the subject with him, not knowing why he asked me to meet him alone after dinner. As I made my way back to my room, I couldn't help but wonder how Rohit bhaiya could possibly help me with my physics struggles. Little did I know that his guidance and support would make all the difference in my performance during the exam.

As I was deeply engrossed in studying for my upcoming physics exam, I suddenly heard my name being called from downstairs. It was Ranjit and Debashish, my hostel mates, asking me to join them for dinner at the mess. On my way there, I spotted Rohit bhaiya, and knowing that it was against the strict rules and regulations to leave the prep area during study hours, I decided to skip dinner and catch up with Rohit bhaiya instead. When Ranjit questioned me leaving dinner, I quickly made an excuse, saying I was already full and not in the mood for a meal. He reminded me that it was Saturday and the mess would be serving my favourite dishes—paneer and chicken. But I had to make a tough choice between a delicious dinner and passing my physics exam. With the fear of failing looming over me, I chose the latter and stuck to my decision. Passing in Physics was just as important as enjoying a nice dinner. I met Rohit bhaiya, and he kindly took me to the MBA canteen and ordered bread omelette and tea for me. While we waited for our food, he reassured me not to worry about the upcoming exam. He said that whatever he was about to tell me would be kept strictly between the two of us, and I should not disclose it even to my closest friends. However, I couldn't help but mention my two other reliable and close friends, Ranjit and Debashish. Rohit bhaiya then asked me about their ability to keep secrets and advised me not to say anything to them for the time being as he would talk to them first.

As I rushed towards the mess, I could see my classmates sitting and eating dinner. But as soon as I entered, they all looked at me with concern, noticing my heavy breathing. They all seemed worried, thinking that something tragic had happened on campus once again. I quickly reassured them that everything was fine and that I had just come running as Ranjit had received a call from his home. This news had stressed Ranjit out, as he never received calls from his family. It was unlike him, as he usually called home once a week, just like me. I went closer to him and whispered in his ear about Rohit bhaiya. Ranjit was someone who loved chicken, and he had promised to finish his dinner before coming. However, I reminded him that we didn't have time after dinner, as we couldn't afford to miss our prep session. Debashish, being the wise one, suggested that we finish our meal quickly and go meet Rohit bhaiya instead.

As the three of us, Ranjit, Debashish, and I, made our way to the MBA canteen where Rohit bhaiya was waiting for us. He warmly greeted us and asked us to sit down. As we settled in, he ordered tea for Ranjit and Debashish too. We were curious as to why he had called us here. Rohit bhaiya then began talking, and we had no idea what he was going to say. He said it was a secret and that he might lose his job for sharing it with us. We assured him that we would keep it between us. He then revealed that he was responsible for printing the question papers for our upcoming exams. Our jaws dropped in shock when he said that he could give us the question paper for the physics exam tomorrow, five days before the actual exam. He asked us to meet him at the horse-riding ground tomorrow evening and requested we bring a notebook and pen to copy the questions as he couldn't give us a printed copy. We were thrilled and couldn't believe our luck. We promised to keep this secret and finished our tea before heading straight to our prep session. During our prep session, Ranjit and I talked slowly about the physics paper, expressing our concerns and worries. The main concern was regarding the numerical problems, as none of us had a strong understanding of them. Debashish, an optimistic member of our group, reassured us that we would figure it out once we had the question paper in our hand tomorrow. However, we were not convinced that we would be given the question paper in advance. Despite our doubts, we continued to discuss and plan our study strategy. Following our conversation, we began to study, and I took out my chemistry book and notes to revise. After finishing the prep session, I headed back to my room. However, I couldn't contain my happiness and excitement that was bubbling inside me. I didn't want to show my roommates my elation, so I decided to sneak out and visit my friend Ranjit's room. Unfortunately, his roommates were also present, so we couldn't have a proper conversation. We chatted briefly about general topics before I had to return to my room. On my way back, I was spotted by a guard who questioned me about my whereabouts. In order not to raise any suspicions, I quickly made up an excuse and said that I had gone to the toilet located behind Ranjit's wing. When I finally reached my room, I saw that my roommates were fast asleep. With a glimmer of hope for receiving the exam papers tomorrow, I too went to bed and drifted off into a peaceful sleep.

The next day, as I woke up with a sense of happiness, I couldn't help but feel a tinge of fear in the pit of my stomach. My friends and I had planned to do something that was completely unacceptable—we were going to cheat by getting the question paper leaked. This was something I had never done before, and the uncertainty and fear of getting caught weighed heavily on me. Despite these mixed emotions, I managed to attend my classes in the academic block. But as soon as school ended, I rushed back to my room. I was supposed to meet my friends Ranjit and Debashish at 4:30 to go horse riding to meet Rohit bhaiya, but I couldn't shake off the feeling of unease. What if we got caught? What if this was all a big mistake? These thoughts plagued my mind as I waited for my friends to arrive. As we headed towards the ground, the fear was apparent on our faces. We were dead scared of being caught for copying the question paper. Mamita, my horse-riding partner, was already at the ground, and her presence only added to our discomfort. We knew that we could not copy the paper in her presence, and this added to our nervousness. When Mamita saw me, she seemed happy and asked if my friends were also joining the horse-riding club. I replied, saying that they were just there to watch, and if they found it interesting, they might join as well.

While we were in the midst of our conversation, I noticed Rohit bhaiya approaching us. However, upon seeing Mamita with us, he appeared slightly annoyed. Ranjit, noticing the tension, immediately went up to him and explained that she was already with us when we arrived. He also mentioned that she was a friend of Asif's and he would be taking her to the canteen. After their conversation, Ranjit came over to me and requested that I take Mamita to the canteen. I asked her if she would like to join me for a cup of coffee at the MBA canteen, as I was suffering from a headache. Being the kind friend that she is, Mamita agreed to come along. We went to the canteen and ordered two cups of coffee. To my surprise, she also ordered Yum Yum, a Nepali noodle. I was glad that Ranjit and Debashish would have enough time to copy the question paper while we were away at the canteen. It was a win-win situation for all of us.

Since the MBA canteen was located near a horse-riding ground, I could see Ranjit and Debashish from there. I could see that Rohit bhaiya had given them a question paper and was discussing something with them. Ranjit and Debashish were sitting on the ground, copying the questions from the paper. It seemed like they were in a hurry as they finished copying within just 10 minutes. However, as other people approached them, they quickly hid the paper to avoid getting caught. It was quite amusing to witness their clever tactics of copying the paper without getting caught. Our sports teacher walked by the canteen and spotted me and my friend Mamita sitting there. He approached us and inquired about our presence in the MBA canteen. Our teacher was usually friendly, but after a recent fight, he had become stricter, like other teachers. I explained that I had a headache and needed some coffee, while Mamita had missed her lunch and was feeling hungry. He waited for us to finish and then accompanied us to the ground. Meanwhile, Ranjit had returned the question paper to Rohit bhaiya, and Rohit bhaiya left in a hurry. Ranjit and Debashish went to the lawn tennis court to mark their attendance. Mamita and I stayed back for a horse ride. It was nice to have a caring teacher who understood our needs and took the time to make sure we were okay.

During dinner at our mess, I met Ranjit and Debashish. As we were eating, Ranjit mentioned that he had torn a page from his notebook where he had written down the questions for an upcoming exam. He explained that he was afraid of being caught with the question paper as we had successfully leaked it beforehand. Our mess was not designed for secret conversations, as there were 8-9 students sitting at each table. We decided to save our discussion for the prep session, which was held in a spacious hall where we could talk comfortably without the fear of being overheard.

After dinner, our group met at the prep room and settled at the last bench in the corner. We were all nervous about the leaked physics paper, which consisted of fifteen challenging questions. As per our plan, each of us copied 5 questions in our notebooks to ensure that we had all the questions covered. We also made a strategy to divide and solve the paper among ourselves to make sure we had all fifteen questions solved. However, our next challenge was to solve the paper without getting caught, so we had to rely on our batchmate's help. To avoid any suspicion, we marked some of the questions in our textbook as if we were solving them normally.We decided to approach Anmol, who was known as the brightest student in our batch. I showed Anmol some questions from our textbook. He tried to explain the concepts behind the questions, but I told him I didn't have enough time to understand them in depth. Instead, I decided to memorize the important questions and their answers. He solved two questions and three questions were solved by some other student. With their help, we managed to solve all fifteen questions within a span of 1.30 hours. After completing the session and feeling confident about our preparation, I asked Ranjit and Debashish for copies of their solved questions so that we could each have our own set to review before the exam.

After finishing my prep session for the day, I headed back to my room to make three copies of solved physics questions for myself, Ranjit, and Debashish. After that, I took out our biology textbook to revise. Remembering the advice of my biology ma'am, I focused on memorizing the important questions that she had highlighted as potential exam topics. My roommates Tarun and Sachin were also busy studying, creating a peaceful and productive study environment. However, as the night went on, I couldn't help but feel the weight of impending exams looming over me. Before finally going to bed late at night, I took a moment to look at the calendar and realized that in just three days, our final exams would begin.

The next day, I woke up early and went for my usual morning jogging and exercise routine. As I returned to my hostel, I noticed our warden sir asking every student to provide their details for railway reservation. Being a summer month, there will be a rush of people wanting to travel, and our school had a system in place where they would book tickets 45 days in advance and one month after the final exams ended. This was to ensure that all students could travel together safely and avoid any last-minute hassle. I walked into his office and took a seat to fill out the necessary details. I wrote down my name, age, sex, and the name of my boarding station as well as our hometown station. As I was filling out the form, I caught a glimpse of Manish inside the warden's office. He smiled at me and informed me that we were going home together with more than 100 other students. The thought of having the entire bogie to ourselves filled me with excitement and anticipation. It was hard to believe that I would finally be heading back to Bhagalpur for my summer vacation. With the form completed, I made my way back to my room to grab my towel and soap before heading to the shower area. The thought of going home and reuniting with my family after a long time made me feel warm and happy inside.

After having a fulfilling breakfast, I headed to the academic block for some self-studying. The syllabus for all subjects had been covered, and the teachers were present in the class to offer assistance to students who had any doubts or needed clarification. I had already revised Biology, Chemistry, English, and Hindi once and was confident that I would be able to score decent marks. However, for physics, I still had to memorize fifteen solved questions. I took out the solved questions and started memorizing the theory part. By lunchtime, I had managed to memorize 3-4 questions. After finishing lunch, I began my studying routine for the day. However, as the hours passed, I found myself staying back even after school hours to memorize the questions for my physics exam. It was a daunting challenge for me, especially since I already had a leaked copy of the question paper in my possession. Despite this advantage, I knew that I still needed to study and understand the concepts to do well on the exam. The pressure of not getting caught with the leaked paper and the fear of failing the exam weighed heavily on me.

At around 4:30 in the evening, I finally decided to take a break and went to my room to rest as I was feeling exhausted and tired from a long day. I quickly fell asleep, but at around 7 PM, my roommates woke me up for dinner. We went to the mess, and I sat at our usual table with Ranjit and Debashish. While having dinner, I asked them about their preparations for the upcoming exam. They mentioned that they were currently focusing on memorizing numerical problems and planned to study the theoretical concepts a day before the exam.

During the prep session, I focused on revising both English and Hindi. The chemistry exam was on March 7th, just two days away.

Realizing the importance of a solid study plan, I created a schedule to cover all my subjects for a final revision. After returning to my room, I immediately started revising Chemistry from the very beginning. Setting an alarm for 7 AM, I knew I would have the entire day to focus solely on Chemistry.

The next day, on 6th March, I was determined to make the best use of my time before the final exam. I spent the whole day revising all the important questions and made sure to go to bed early so that I could wake up at 5 AM for a final round of revision. On 7th March, I stuck to my routine and woke up at 5 AM. I began revising the important questions again before heading to the mess for breakfast. The examination was scheduled from 9 to 12, and being the final exam, there was a sense of tension and fear among all the students, including myself. Everyone was busy revising important topics and trying to calm their nerves. At 8:45, when I arrived at the academic block, I saw the seating arrangement and noticed that Abhishek and I were placed in the same room as in the previous exams. As soon as the Hindi teacher arrived, she handed out the question paper and answer sheet, and I braced myself for what would be a challenging but important exam. Seeing the question paper, I was relieved as most of the questions seemed manageable except for 2-3 of them. I started writing confidently, knowing that I would be able to score good marks. As I looked around, I could see a mix of emotions on the faces of my classmates. Some seemed stressed, while others were focused and determined. I noticed that even Abhishek was busy writing, which gave me reassurance that he also knew the answers. Taking a quick water break, I stepped outside to clear my mind and came back to finish the paper by 11:45 AM and handed it in to our teacher. As I stepped out of the academic block, I saw groups of students discussing the paper and sharing their thoughts. However, I preferred to leave the academic block as discussing the question paper after writing the exam was something I didn't enjoy. Heading back to my room, I was joined by my roommates Sachin and Tarun within a few minutes. The three of us were relieved that our first exam was over.

I went to sleep and woke up at 5 PM after a long and much-needed rest. Despite feeling well-rested, I still felt tired and decided to take a shower to refresh myself. After my shower, I stayed in my room and checked the leaked physics question paper. However, even with the leaked paper, I struggled to memorize the numerical. Frustrated, I marked the questions that I needed to focus on again. Later, I went to the mess for dinner, and Ranjit informed me that his chemistry paper went well. After dinner, we both went to our rooms to grab our notebooks with solved answers and headed to the prep room. Unlike other subjects, memorizing physics numerical was proving to be a challenge. During the prep session, I tried my best to study the theory part in hopes of understanding it better. It was clear that I needed more practice and focus to do well in my physics exam.

After returning to my room from prep, I decided to take a break and asked permission from the warden to go to the canteen for a cup of tea. He granted me permission but reminded me to return quickly. I grabbed my Milton bottle and headed to the canteen, where I asked for ten cups of tea to fill my bottle. When I returned to my room, I shared the tea with my roommates Tarun and Sachin. However, even though I was trying my best to study for my upcoming physics exam, I couldn't seem to remember the numerical problems. I was feeling anxious and stressed about failing the exam despite having access to a leaked question paper. But I refused to give up and continued studying until late at night before finally going to bed. I was determined to do my best and not let my fears get the best of me.

I woke up at 7 AM and went straight to the mess for breakfast. With only two days left before my exam, I was determined to make the most of my time. I put in all my efforts throughout the day, studying and revising physics. During prep, my friends and I chatted the entire session to relieve the stress and tension. It was a much-needed break from the intense studying. After prep, I went back to my room and spent some time revising a few important questions before going to bed. Despite the pressure and anxiety of the upcoming exams, I was confident that I would be able to manage and do well.

On 9th March, just a day before the Physics exam, we came up with a desperate plan—to hide solved answers in the academic block toilet for cheating. I was nervous and afraid that I might forget everything I had studied, so I needed this backup plan. We quickly made small chits of solved answers and hid them behind the pipes in the toilet. This was our second attempt to cheat in order to pass the exam. I felt relieved knowing that I had a backup plan in case things didn't go as planned. However, I still studied with full concentration that day and went to bed early, determined to wake up at 4 AM and start revising the numerical problems. Despite our desperate attempts to cheat, I was determined to do my best and not rely on dishonest means to pass the exam. The next morning, I woke up early and revised the numerical problems, feeling confident and prepared for the exam.

On 10th March, after finishing breakfast, I spent some time revising the theory part before heading to the academic block at 8:45 AM. As I entered the classroom, I noticed that the seating arrangement was the same as usual. Just then, Ravi sir, our English teacher and my favourite teacher, walked into the class. I was relieved to see him, as his presence always brought a sense of positivity and motivation. However, there was still a lingering tension and confusion regarding the leaked question paper. What if we had gotten the wrong one or if the paper had been changed? My worries were put to rest when Sir started distributing the question paper, and I saw that it was indeed the same one we had leaked. Relief washed over me as I knew I had prepared for this exact paper and would be able to perform well. As the clock struck 9, I took a deep breath and started writing the theory part first. Within 30 minutes, I had finished it and moved on to the numerical section. The first few questions were a breeze, but as I delved deeper into the paper, I realized that I had forgotten a few answers. In a panic, I asked Ravi sir for permission to go to the toilet. As I was about to enter, I saw Ranjit coming out. We exchanged nervous glances but couldn't talk as the warden was sitting close by. Inside the toilet, I quickly jotted down answers on my handkerchief and returned to finish the remaining questions. However, to avoid getting too high marks and raising suspicion from the subject teacher, I intentionally left out two questions worth five marks each. With an hour left on the clock, I pretended to be engrossed in my paper as other students started submitting their answer sheets. As soon as it was 12 o'clock, I submitted my paper and breathed a sigh of relief.

When I came out of my room, I saw Ranjit waiting for me with a huge smile on his face. As soon as I joined him, Debashish also came, and we could all feel the happiness radiating from each other. We were all relieved and delighted that we had successfully pulled off our cheating plan. Both Ranjit and Debashish had managed to solve all the questions without getting caught. In a playful tone, I joked that they would surely be the toppers of our class. We all laughed and then went to our own rooms. I was so exhausted that I fell asleep in my school uniform and didn't wake up until 5 PM. After changing into comfortable clothes, I headed to the canteen to grab a bite to eat, as I had missed lunch and was hungry.

This physics exam was by far the toughest one I have ever taken, but I managed to get through it. I felt a huge weight lifted off my shoulders as if I had finished all my subjects. I bumped into my friends, Ranjit and Debashish, at the mess and saw the exhaustion on their faces. It was evident that they were tired. Ranjit and Debashish suggested that we go to Tau's canteen for a change. It was a great way to unwind after the intense exam and spend some quality time with friends. After the fight on campus, it became difficult for students to cross the school boundary. However, we heard that some students have started going there. They asked me to ask Manish for the safest place to jump from the boundary wall and go to Tau's canteen. Manish suggested that the best place to go is from the auditorium side. Our school had three auditoriums, and one of them was an open auditorium. From there, students could easily go to Tau's canteen.

We decided to go to the prep room without our books so that we could quickly finish attendance and head out one by one. We knew a shortcut from the North Block to the auditorium, which seemed like the best option. We made a plan to meet behind the North Block and head towards the auditorium. Ranjit went first, followed by Debashish, and I was the last one to go. As we reached the auditorium, we saw that it was a bit dark, and some dogs were barking outside the wall. We could also see Tau's canteen about 100 meters away. Without wasting any time, we jumped from the auditorium and made our way towards the canteen.

As we reached the canteen, we were taken aback by the sight of it. It was completely different from how it used to be before. The lights were dimmer, and there were fewer students around. Suddenly, I saw Tau, who used to call me Asif Ali, walking towards us. He greeted us and asked me, "Where were you, Asif Ali?" expressing his disappointment for not seeing me lately. We told him about the campus fight we were involved in and how we had been staying away from the canteen. Tau assured us that this canteen was a safe haven, even safer than our own school campus. After a brief conversation, he left and sent his son to take our order. We ordered three cups of tea and three Navy Cut cigarettes. As we sat there smoking and sipping our tea, we couldn't help but feel a sense of nostalgia. It had been a while since we had come to the canteen, and it felt great to be back, even if it was just for a few moments. We sat there for some time, enjoying our tea and cigarettes, before deciding to repeat our order. Around 11:45 PM, we left Tau's canteen, and my friends Ranjit and Debashish followed me to my room. I expressed my concern about the warden's frequent inspection and how it was not safe for them to be in my room. However, they assured me that they could handle it. As I entered my room, I was surprised to see it beautifully decorated. It was 12 AM on March 11th, my birthday. Little did I know, my friends Tarun and Sachin had asked Ranjit and Debashish to keep me occupied while they planned a surprise party for me. This explained why they had taken me to Tau's canteen earlier. They had even arranged a cake for me. Just as we were about to cut the cake, the warden unexpectedly showed up. To our relief, he wished me well, and we even offered him a slice of cake. I asked him for permission to call my next-door neighbour, Manish, and he agreed on the condition that we finish quickly and go to sleep. I felt overwhelmed with joy to have such amazing friends who went through all this trouble just to make my birthday special amid the pressure of exams. As everyone bid me goodbye, I thanked them from the bottom of my heart before finally calling it a night.

The next day, I woke up feeling incredibly blessed. It was my birthday, and even with strictness, they still managed to make my day special by arranging a cake at 12 AM. As I made my way to the mess for breakfast, I decided to make a quick call to my family back home. However, when I saw the long line at the booth, I decided to head straight to the mess instead. As I finished my breakfast and was leaving the mess, I spotted my friends Shalini and Rachika standing outside. As I approached them, they both hugged me and wished me a happy birthday. It was a pleasant surprise as I hadn't mentioned my birthday to anyone. Shalini told me that Ranjit had informed her about it. Just then, our friend Mamita joined us, and they excitedly told her to wish me too. Mamita wished me well and then surprised me by inviting us to a lunch party at the MBA canteen. She asked me to inform our friends Ranjit and Debashish as well. We all decided to meet at the canteen during lunch hours. I quickly caught up with Ranjit and Debashish and informed them about the lunch plan. All of us met at the MBA canteen during lunchtime. Mamita and I had been to this canteen several times together, so she knew exactly what I liked. To my surprise, she had ordered all of my favourite food for my birthday, which made me feel guilty as I should have been the one paying for it. I insisted on paying, but Mamita was firm in her decision. I then promised to treat everyone after the exams were over, and we could go to a restaurant near Qutub Minar. The girls were worried about taking leave from school to go out, but I assured them that they could use the excuse of visiting their local guardian. After lunch, we stayed at the canteen instead of going back to class. The girls were feeling scared about bunking class for the first time, but we told them to relax and enjoy this little break from our hectic exam schedule. We continued our conversation over a cup of coffee. As the day progressed, we eventually made our way back to our rooms. With my biology exam just two days away on the 13th of March, I immediately checked my syllabus to see what needed to be revised. My roommates were diligently studying, which motivated me to also start revising for the exam. After dinner at prep, I dedicated my time to studying biology. Even when I returned to my room after prep, my roommates and I still found time for a small chit-chat. As I opened my book, I realized that biology was not a difficult subject but rather very lengthy. To make the most out of my revision, I went back to the beginning and even marked down important questions that I needed to revise on the day of the exam. Knowing that tomorrow would be a day full of studying, I made sure to get enough rest and went to sleep early.

The biology paper, as expected, was easy but lengthy. Our biology teacher had always given us important questions to prepare for the exam. With the biology exam now over, we were finally free from all major subjects like physics, chemistry, and biology. During the lunch break, I met my badminton partner Ashish, and he suggested that we should meet at the badminton court in the evening to play. I also invited Mamita to join us. I was feeling happy and relieved as all my exams had gone well so far. After playing badminton, I returned to my room and took a refreshing shower. It was a great day, and I felt rejuvenated after playing my favourite sport.

After dinner at prep, my friends and I decided not to study at all. The day after tomorrow, on the 15th of March, we have our English exam. We took permission from our warden, sir, to go to the canteen for a cup of tea. However, we ended up staying longer than expected and came back to our rooms later than planned. As I entered my room, I saw my roommates studying diligently as they had their accounts paper the next day. I had nothing else to do but go to sleep. I knew I had to make up for the lost study time the next day.

As I entered the academic block on 15th March, I noticed a new update on the notice board: railway tickets for all the students had been booked and could be collected from the warden's office after our exams today. Excited at the prospect of going home for a break, I made my way to the class and waited for our teacher to arrive. As soon as she entered the class, she distributed the question paper, and I was relieved to see that the questions were relatively easy. I started writing and finished the paper with an hour to spare. However, when I approached my teacher to submit my answer sheet, she asked me to revise it. Confused and nervous, I looked through my answers but found nothing that needed correction. As I sat there, unsure of what to do, my restlessness started to disturb my classmates. Finally, my teacher took notice and asked me to step out of the class. Even though I had nothing to revise, I couldn't help but feel embarrassed and uncomfortable as I waited outside while my classmates finished their exams. I noticed the warden sitting with a few other teachers. I immediately made my way towards him, feeling a bit anxious. I had come to inform him that I wouldn't be able to collect my railway ticket right now as the boarding day was still 45 days away, and I was afraid of misplacing it. Being familiar with my carefree nature, the warden understood my concern and reassured me that it was okay. He kindly advised me to collect the ticket one week before my departure date, ensuring that I wouldn't lose it in the meantime.

The exams of Hindi on 17th March and Physical Education on 18th March went smoothly for me. These papers were just a formality, as they were relatively easy compared to other subjects. I only needed passing marks in these exams. I appeared in all the practical exams except for Physics. I was weak in physics and was always scared of Vivas. To avoid the dreaded Vivas, I pretended to have stomach pain on the day of the physics practical exam and got admitted to the medical inspection room. Since I had already cheated in the physics theory paper, missing the practical did not bother me as I was confident of passing the exam.

With all exams now completed, the school administration has given us a much-needed break of two days before starting the new session. It is a refreshing change after all the hard work and stress of studying for exams. We are eagerly waiting for our results, which will be announced in ten days. However, for now, we are making the most of our two days off. We can finally sleep in and wake up anytime we want, without having to worry about studying or attending classes. The canteen has become our go-to spot, even after dinner. We have been visiting Tau's canteen multiple times a day to satisfy our craving for cigarettes and tea.

As promised, I had invited all my close friends for a special lunch to celebrate my birthday, which was on 11th March. However, due to exams, we were unable to celebrate on the actual day. On Saturday night, I happened to meet three of my closest friends, Shalini, Rachika, and Mamita, at the canteen outside the girls' hostel. They were hesitant to leave campus the next day for our lunch plans, but I convinced them to take a day off and pretend to visit their local guardians. The following day at the mess, Shalini excitedly informed me that their leave had been approved and wanted to know where we would meet. I instructed her to meet us on the main road. After meeting Shalini, I came back to my room. I quickly changed into my favourite jeans and white shirt, wanting to feel comfortable and relaxed. As I was getting ready, my friends Ranjit and Debashish also stopped by, looking sharp and ready to go out. We had not applied for leave, but that didn't stop us from going out. We were used to jumping the boundary wall of our campus to go out for some fun. We managed to get a lift from a villager to the main road, and from there, we walked almost half a kilometre to our designated meeting spot with some girls. We arrived 10 minutes early and waited for them to come. Since they were officially allowed to leave the hostel, they took a lift from some parents who were there for their child's admission. They seemed happy but also a bit afraid to be outside the safe confines of our campus. We convinced them to take a bus instead of a taxi, as it would only take 10-15 minutes.

CHAPTER 6

FROM SUMMER BREAK TO SENIOR YEAR

I have recently returned to Delhi after spending more than a month in Bhagalpur, and the feeling of leaving behind a place that I had grown to love was bittersweet. The summer break had been a refreshing change from the hustle and bustle of city life, and the thought of going back to my routine was daunting. However, as I boarded the train back home with my friends Manish, Shalini, and Amt Singh, all the sadness faded away. We were all excited and chattering away, looking forward to the journey ahead. As we passed by different towns and villages, we couldn't resist trying out the local street food like Jhali Muri and pakodas at Jamalpur. We also enjoyed some peanuts (known as Chinia Badam in Bihar) and tea, sharing stories and laughter along the way. Each one of us had brought home-cooked meals for dinner, and after the train departed from Patna station, my friends and I decided to share our food with each other. As Shalini and I were close friends, we spent the entire night talking and catching up. She even offered me some snacks that she had brought from her home. As the train arrived at New Delhi railway station, we were greeted with heavy rain, even though the monsoon season had not officially arrived in Delhi. We quickly booked two taxis to take us to Chattarpur in Mehrauli, where our school was located. However, due to rush hour traffic and heavy rain, it took us almost two hours to reach our destination. Finally, we arrived at our school and made our way to our respective rooms with our luggage, exhausted but excited for the adventures that awaited us at our boarding school.

As I entered my room, I couldn't help but feel a sense of loneliness. My roommates had not returned from summer break yet, and it felt strange to be in our room without them. After dropping off my luggage, I headed to the warden's office to mark my attendance. The warden, noticing that my roommates were still absent, sent a helper with me to clean my room. The helper did an excellent job of cleaning and organizing the room, so I decided to tip him for his hard work. With the room now spotless, I went to take a refreshing shower. As I walked around the hostel, I noticed that there were only a few students who had returned so far. It seemed that most of them would be returning today or tomorrow, and I couldn't wait to catch up with them and hear about their summer break. It felt good to be back at the hostel, and I was excited for the new semester ahead.

I was feeling quite hungry, so I walked into the mess. I noticed that the usual seating arrangement had changed. Now, we were allowed to eat anywhere we wanted. To my surprise, the girls' and boys' sections were merged together. I saw my friend Shalini sitting with the girls, and as soon as she noticed me, she waved me over to join them. At first, I felt a bit uncomfortable sitting with the girls, as it was not something I was used to. However, Shalini made me feel at ease, and we started chatting and laughing while enjoying our meal together. After having lunch, I returned to my room feeling exhausted from the long train journey the previous night. As soon as my head hit the pillow, I drifted off into a deep slumber. The next thing I knew, it was already 6 PM. Curious, I went to Ranjit's room to check on him, and his roommate informed me that he would be coming back tomorrow. Disappointed but understanding, I headed back to my room to relax for the rest of the evening.

As I was walking towards the dining hall to have my dinner, I caught a glimpse of Debashish carrying his luggage. Excitement rushed through me as he had just returned after his summer break. It had been months since we last saw each other, and I was overjoyed to see him again. Without wasting a moment, I hurried towards him, and we embraced each other tightly, expressing our happiness at being reunited. I offered to help him carry his luggage to his room, and he gratefully accepted. As we walked, we caught up on each other's lives and shared stories about our summer break. After settling his luggage in his room, Debashish went to wash his hands and face, leaving me with a feeling of warmth and contentment knowing that my friend was back.

We went to the dining hall for dinner, but unfortunately, we were late. By the time we arrived, most of the students had already finished their meals and left. Luckily, the kind service bhaiya arranged a table for just the two of us. Upon our arrival back at the hostel, we sat near the basketball court to chat about the vacation. Since the warden's office was close by, I asked him to mark his attendance there. I continued sitting, patiently waiting for him to return. However, as my roommates had not yet returned, I asked Debashish to sleep in my room for the night.

The next day, I woke up to a knock at the door by Tarun. I was pleasantly surprised to see him, and he seemed equally happy to see that the room was clean. It was always Tarun who took care of keeping the room tidy and organized. I had woken up quite late and had missed my breakfast for the first time. It was already 10 AM, and I could feel my stomach grumbling with hunger. As Tarun unpacked his belongings and started arranging his clothes in the almirah, I couldn't help but feel grateful for his presence.

I went to the washroom, and on my way back, my friend Tarun surprised me with sweets and snacks. As I was feeling hungry and had not eaten breakfast, I thoroughly enjoyed the treats. Tarun also informed me that our friend Sachin would be joining us in the afternoon. Later, I went to Debashish's room, and from there we went to the canteen to have tea. Since we chose to go to the main canteen near the main gate, we were able to see students returning from their holidays. Many new faces, accompanied by their parents. It was evident that these were the students who had joined 11th grade and were now our juniors. As I looked at them, I realized that we were now seniors and there would be many more juniors joining our school in the coming days. As mischievous thoughts crossed our minds about ragging them, I was reminded that our school had a strict policy against it. These new students had no idea what their life at our school would be like once their parents left. It was their first day, and we knew we would have plenty of opportunities to rag them in the name of introduction.

During a conversation with my friend Debashish, he excitedly informed me that he had recently picked up his passion for boxing again. Before joining our current school, he had studied at St. Paul in Darjeeling, where he used to actively participate in boxing tournaments. However, upon joining our school, he realized that there were not many opportunities for boxing as the school focused more on other sports. Therefore, I had assumed that his desire for boxing would soon be short-lived. As we were chatting in the canteen, I noticed Sachin getting down from a taxi with his parents. Excited to see him, I went up to him, and he greeted me with a big smile. He then introduced me to his parents as his roommate, which made me feel a sense of belonging in this new environment. I offered to help him with his luggage, but he politely declined, saying that his younger brother would assist him. His parents seemed in a hurry and wanted to meet the principal, so they left soon after our brief encounter. I went back to the canteen where Debashish was waiting for me. We chatted for a while before heading to the dining hall for lunch.

After finishing lunch at the dining hall, I returned to my room and found my roommates Sachin and Tarun chatting. Sachin had brought homemade Ladoo's and snacks, which he offered to us. He kept the box in his almirah and said we could have them whenever we had cravings. Exhausted, Sachin went to sleep after taking a shower, and Tarun and I followed suit. However, my sleep was interrupted by Ranjit, who had just returned from his holidays. He excitedly woke me up, and I couldn't believe he was actually there. I hugged him instantly, overwhelmed with joy to see him after so long. In the one year of our friendship, our bond had grown from being friends to becoming like brothers. Ranjit then told me he had come straight to my room after keeping his luggage in his room. He said he just wanted to meet me and would come over again after taking a shower. After half an hour, I decided to go to his room. He had taken a shower and changed his clothes. We both then decided to go to our friend Debashish's room, as Ranjit hadn't seen him since he returned. Debashish was filled with excitement and joy upon seeing Ranjit. It was a reunion for all of us, catching up on each other's lives and reminiscing about old memories.

We reminisced about our old days as we walked to the dining hall, just like we used to before the holidays. Ranjit was taken aback by the new seating arrangement when we entered. As we settled down, we couldn't help but notice the large number of new faces in the hall. They were all our juniors who had just joined the boarding school. They were sitting together in a row, eating silently without even raising their heads. Our table was just two tables away from theirs, but they were too intimidated to even look in our direction. It seemed like they were eating slowly, hoping that we would finish our meals quickly and leave. After we were done, Ranjit stopped by their table and kindly reminded them to eat properly as they would need the energy to survive in a boarding school. He also asked how many of them were from the North Block hostel, to which a few raised their hands. I saw Mamita sitting in the next row with a group of girls, waving at me enthusiastically. I made my way to her, and she immediately asked when I had returned from my holiday. I replied that I had arrived yesterday afternoon. She then informed me that she had come back this morning and questioned why I hadn't come to meet her. I explained that I had no idea she had returned. She then mentioned that Rachika would be arriving tomorrow morning before class. As we chatted, I couldn't help but notice the uncomfortable and scared expressions on the faces of the other girls. Mamita also noticed this and suggested I catch up with her later so that the girls could eat comfortably. As I left, I saw my friends waiting for me outside the dining hall, and we decided to go for a long walk before calling it a day and heading back to our rooms.

The next day marked the end of my summer holidays and the beginning of the classes. As I was still adjusting to being back, Warden Sir came to our room to wake us up for our morning exercise. Despite my reluctance, I knew I couldn't make any excuses on the first day. However, to my surprise, Ranjit and Debashish didn't show up. After jogging around the football field, I sat down in the middle of the field with Manish. The morning routine was nothing short of pathetic, and I couldn't find any motivation to continue. I promised myself that I would not be participating in this routine from the following day and would find ways to hide from the warden.

After breakfast, my friends and I made our way to the academic block to attend our class. We arrived late and could hear the faint sound of our school anthem being sung by the students. We quickly made our way to the corridor and patiently waited for the anthem to end. Once the anthem ended, we quickly made our way to our designated assembly line, joining our classmates in formation for the day's activities. Since it was the first day after the break, we were greeted by Principal Ma'am with a warm smile. She gave a speech, welcoming us back and also extending a warm welcome to the new students joining our school. It was heartening to see her ask the seniors to treat the newcomers as family members and not to engage in any form of ragging. She made it clear that any complaints of ragging would be taken seriously, and strict action would be taken against those involved. As I listened to her words, I couldn't help but smile inside, as I had heard the exact same speech last year when I was a fresher. I knew that this strictness would only last for a couple of days before the freshers were left on their own to handle any ragging that may occur. After Principal Ma'am's departure, we all made our way to our respective classrooms for lectures.

In the evening, I went to play badminton. To my surprise, our warden, who was also our sports teacher, came to watch us play. It had been a few months since I last played badminton, so it was challenging for me to get back into the flow of the game. As our warden watched us play, he gave me some pointers and tips on how to improve my game. He reminded me that there would be an inter-school tournament next month and I needed more practice if I wanted to perform well.

However, in the past few months, I had started smoking, and it had greatly affected my stamina. As a result, I found it difficult to play the entire match as I was constantly short of breath. Warden sir suggested that I should practice for mixed doubles. I realized that my only option for a partner was Mamita. However, she was absent today, so I decided to talk to her during dinnertime. I headed towards the lawn tennis court, and I was pleasantly surprised to see that Ranjit and Debashish had really improved their skills in tennis. They were playing with great technique and precision. After their game was over, we all went to take a shower as we were sweating profusely.

At the dining hall, I was excited to meet Mamita. As I approached her, I saw that she was sitting with Shalini, Rachika, and a few other girls, most of whom were freshers. I immediately shared with Mamita about the upcoming interschool badminton tournament, which was just a month away. I told her the warden had asked me to participate in the mixed doubles category, and I wanted you to be my partner as we had played well together. Mamita was happy and agreed to participate in the tournament for the first time. We both felt a rush of adrenaline as we eagerly looked forward to representing our school. While talking to Mamita, I couldn't help but notice a beautiful girl sitting nearby. She was a fresher, and she was the most beautiful girl I had ever seen. Her big, deep eyes met mine for a few seconds, and I was mesmerized. Her hair was long and wet, and it seemed like she had just taken a shower before coming to dinner. She was wearing a pink nightdress that perfectly complemented her fair skin. I couldn't take my eyes off her, and it seemed like she was aware of my gaze. Just then, suddenly, Shalini interrupted, reminding me that my friends were waiting at the dining table. Giving a serious look to the girl, she asked me to join my friends at their table. But my mind was still fixated on the mesmerizing beauty in front of me.

As I went to eat with my friends, I couldn't help but feel curious about the girl. Who was she and what was her name? These thoughts consumed me as I made my way to our table. I couldn't shake off this feeling; it was something I had never felt before in my life. Even as I started eating, I found myself turning to look at her a couple of times. My friend Debashish noticed my behaviour and asked if I was okay. I reassured him that I was fine, but I knew there was something I needed to tell them both during prep time. My mind was racing with questions about this girl and what she could possibly mean to me. I was feeling both excited and scared at the same time. I couldn't wait for prep time to come so I could finally share my thoughts with my friends.

As I walked back to my hostel after having dinner at the dining hall, my mind was preoccupied with thoughts of the beautiful girl I had seen there. The way she looked at me had captivated me, and I couldn't shake off the feeling of wanting to know more about her. As I walked, the cold breeze blowing against my face only added to the magic of the moment, making my heart race even faster. I longed to know her name and meet her, to have a chance to talk to her and maybe get to know her better. Her face kept replaying in my mind, and I couldn't shake off the feeling that she was someone special. I couldn't wait for another opportunity to see her again.

With all this going on in my mind, I couldn't concentrate in my prep session and ended up sitting with my friends at the last bench. Noticing my distracted state, Debashish and Ranjit asked me what was bothering me. I hesitated at first, but then decided to confide in them about the girl I saw earlier. They both laughed it off, and we didn't discuss it further. However, as time passed and they saw me still feeling down, they reassured me that they would help me find her.

They suggested asking for help from Shalini and Rachika, who were from the same hostel as the girl. But I wasn't ready yet, as I feared this crush would fade away soon. We continued talking, and when the prep session was over, we went back to our room. Despite their support, I couldn't shake off the thoughts of that girl and wondered what could have been if I had talked to her.

After returning to my room, I didn't reveal anything to my roommates about my encounter with the girl from yesterday. It was too early, and I wasn't sure how to approach her. Instead, I went to bed and spent the night thinking about her. I eagerly awaited the next day, hoping to see her again. When I woke up, I headed to the shower and put on my school uniform. For the first time, I used hair gel to style my hair and even polished my shoes to look perfect. Usually, I would just hang my tie around my neck, but today I made sure it was perfectly tied. Ranjit and Debashish noticed my efforts and gave me a sly smile. I went to the dining hall, hoping to catch a glimpse of her, but she wasn't there. Desperately searching for her, I saw Shalini and Mamita eating. I went to them, and they were surprised to see me there, as I rarely meet them in the dining hall. Shalini's suspicion arose from my behaviour yesterday, and she asked if I was looking for someone. To avoid any suspicion, I simply said that I came to meet them. Deep down, however, I was disappointed that I didn't get to see her again.

As I walked towards the academic block, my heart felt heavy with disappointment for not being able to find that beautiful girl I had seen the previous day. I was determined to find her and had even considered going to every classroom, but I knew it could cause chaos among the juniors, and I didn't want to intimidate her. Even during lunch, she was nowhere to be found. Our school was one of the largest boarding schools in India, with over 8000 students, making it nearly impossible to locate someone without knowing their name. So, I patiently waited for dinner time, hoping to catch a glimpse of her and perhaps strike up a conversation.

My batchmates have started taking part in ragging under the guise of introducing juniors. I couldn't help but feel a sense of excitement wash over me. For months, I had been eagerly waiting for this moment since I passed my final exams in 11th grade. Despite my eagerness to participate, I found myself not in the mood for ragging. When my friends Ranjit and Debashish came to my room, I told them that I was tired and needed to rest before going for dinner.

Before heading to dinner, I decided to dress up and wore a nice pair of jeans and a t-shirt. As I approached the dining hall, I saw my friends Ranjit, Debashish, Mamita, Shalini, and Rachika standing outside. I could sense that they were discussing me, so I pretended not to notice and kept walking towards the hall. However, Ranjit called out my name, and I had no choice but to stop and meet them. Without any exchange of greetings, Shalini bluntly asked, "Who is that girl?" I shot an angry look at Ranjit for disclosing everything to them. In a casual tone, I replied that there was nothing like that, and when they insisted, I told them that I didn't even know her name. I explained that she was eating with them yesterday when I came to talk to Mamita about the badminton tournament. Rachika then mentioned that there were many girls present, and they themselves had not befriended any of the juniors. As we all eagerly entered the bustling dining hall, I scanned the room for the girl I was searching for. But she was nowhere to be found. Shalini noticed my disappointment and reassured me not to worry and suggested that they would bring some juniors to the canteen outside their hostel after prep, and that I could come and identify her.

The prep session was only supposed to be 1.30 hours, but on that particular day, it felt like time had almost stopped. I was eagerly anticipating meeting this girl, and spending that seemingly never-ending 1.30 hours in class felt like an eternity. After the session ended, I rushed back to my room to put on some cologne, wanting to make a good impression on her. My mind was racing with thoughts and doubts—what if she was already in a relationship? What if she refused to meet me? Despite my anxieties, I joined my friends, and we made our way to the canteen. I couldn't shake off the feeling of nervousness, but I knew I had to take a chance and see what would happen.

Mamita was waiting outside the canteen area for me, Ranjit, and Debashish. As we entered the canteen, I could see Shalini and Rachika inside sitting with some junior students. My heart began to race with excitement and nervousness as I entered. Mamita noticed my nervousness and reassured me that all our friends were there to support me. She advised me to act normal and pretend that our meeting was not planned. Ranjit and Debashish went ahead and greeted them as if their presence was a pleasant surprise. They then called me over as I was talking to Mamita near the entrance. With Mamita by my side, I walked over and joined them at the table.

Mamita ordered tea for us and then asked if we needed anything to eat. I was feeling incredibly anxious, so much so that I didn't even notice the junior students in the room. It was Rachika who introduced us to them and caught my attention. As I looked up, I saw that girl sitting quietly, looking tense and scared. When she introduced herself as Shreya from the commerce department, her voice was surprisingly calming to me. I could sense her fear through her voice and immediately wanted to make her feel comfortable. I tried my best to act normal and avoided revealing that she was the girl we had been searching for over the past two days. I didn't want to add any more fear or stress to her already troubled state. Rachika leaned in close to me and whispered in my ear, "Is your girl here?" I felt my heart race and my palms sweat as I quickly responded with a lie, "No, she's not here." I kept talking to Mamita, trying to avoid the topic of my girl. But just as I thought I was in the clear, Shalini started questioning the new students about their hobbies. When they asked Shreya about her hobbies, she replied that she likes to read and play badminton. This caught Ranjit's attention as he mentioned that Mamita and Asif also play badminton and are part of the school team. Shreya nodded, saying she had heard us talking about a tournament just two days ago in the dining hall. I couldn't help but feel relieved that at least one thing we had in common. She then expressed her interest in playing with us, and though I didn't say anything, Mamita quickly invited her to join us.

Shalini asked Shreya to sing, but she hesitantly replied that she didn't know how to sing. However, Shalini was insistent, and Shreya was on the verge of tears. I couldn't bear to see her in this state and interrupted, telling Shalini not to force her now and that she will sing some other time. I started talking to Shreya, hoping to distract her from the pressure to sing. As I spoke to her, I couldn't help but notice how innocent she was and how her voice was truly magical. When she looked at me while we talked, my heart skipped a beat. It wasn't infatuation, but rather I was falling in love with her. Shreya seemed to feel comforted by my presence and our conversation, and I couldn't help but feel an instant connection with her. I knew that I wanted to get to know her more and perhaps even explore a romantic relationship with her in the future.

It was getting late for the girls, and they realized that it was time to return to their hostel. As they were preparing to leave, I went to the canteen counter to pay, only to find out that it had already been paid by Mamita. She was always such a darling friend to me. Just as we were about to leave, Shreya came up to me and thanked me. I asked her for what she was thanking me. She said that I had saved her from having to embarrass herself by singing in front of everyone. I simply smiled and told her not to worry, and that if she ever found herself in a similar situation, she could just mention my name. My friends and I had a bad reputation in school, especially among the girls. It wasn't because we had done anything wrong, but rather because of our carefree lifestyle and regular habit of bunking classes. Nevertheless, Shreya smiled and left with the rest of the girls.

As we walked back to our hostel, Ranjit and Debashish suddenly started talking about Shreya. They both said that she was the girl I had been looking for. I was taken aback by their statement and asked how they could be so sure. They replied that it was evident in the way I looked at her and the fact that I had saved her from being forced to sing, while I hadn't done the same for other girls. I couldn't help but feel touched by their observation and told them that they were true friends for noticing my emotions. Debashish teasingly told me to save my emotions for Shreya, and I playfully told them to shut up before heading to our respective rooms with a smile on my face.

The next day was a struggle for me as I couldn't concentrate in my class. My mind was occupied with thoughts of Shreya, and I couldn't wait to see her at lunch. I constantly scanned the dining hall, hoping to catch a glimpse of her, but she was nowhere to be seen. I started to wonder what time she usually goes for lunch and where she preferred to sit. During my return from lunch, I saw her heading towards the academic block for her classes. Our eyes met, and she gave me a warm smile. Seeing her in her school uniform made her look even younger and more beautiful. I longed to talk to her, but she was surrounded by her friends. As she entered her classroom, I noticed that she turned back and looked at me. She caught me staring at her and smiled again before entering the classroom.

I couldn't wait for the evening, as I was eagerly anticipating going to play badminton and finally getting the chance to meet Shreya. We never really had the opportunity to talk much. The thought of playing alongside her. As I was walking towards the badminton court, I saw Ashish walking in the opposite direction. I called out to him and asked if he was coming to play. He replied that his leg was hurting and he needed to take a break from playing for a couple of days. I was disappointed because I used to love playing with him. Unlike other games, in badminton, you always want to play with better players in order to improve your skills. Now, I had to play with Mamita and with the warden sir if he was available. I made sure to carry an extra racket to the court so that my friend Shreya could use it if she didn't have one. Our school had three badminton courts, and one of them had a wooden floor, which was always reserved for us as we were part of the school team. As I entered the badminton court, my eyes were met with a flurry of activity and the sound of shuttles being hit back and forth. Most of them were high school students, engrossed in the game and determined to win. As I made my way towards the court, they greeted me warmly and invited me to join them in a game. However, I politely requested they wait for a few minutes as I needed to do some stretching before playing. Being an athlete, I knew the importance of warming up to prevent any injuries. As I finished my stretching routine, I glanced over and saw Warden Sir, as usual, dressed in his shorts and carrying his racket. He didn't spend much time stretching and immediately asked me to play. Despite being in his 50s, he had impressive stamina and some decent skills, and on the other hand,

I was proud of my superior technique, but my smoking habit had taken a toll on my stamina. As we played the second set, I noticed Mamita approaching, but she was alone. This made me feel sad as Shreya was not with her. When I finished the second game, I sat down on the ground to catch my breath. Mamita came and sat beside me. She could see that I was exhausted, and she gently suggested that I quit smoking as it was clearly affecting my performance. In a nonchalant manner, I replied that I had already reduced my smoking and would be quitting completely in the near future. Warden sir had asked me to start the third game, and I was more than happy to do so. Mamita asked me to take some rest after the third game as she was expecting Shreya to join us any moment. Mamita also mentioned that she had no idea about Shreya's playing style and requested that I play at least two games with her as we needed to build coordination for our upcoming mixed doubles tournament.

I went to the water dispenser to quench my thirst. On my way back, I saw Shreya standing with Mamita. She was wearing comfortable track pants and a t-shirt paired with white sports shoes. I went up to them, and Shreya greeted me with a cheerful "Hi!" I nodded in response, and she told me that she was running late because she went to the sports shop on campus to buy a racket and shuttle. She had bought the Yonex Carbonex series, which used to be my favourite until I got the Muscle Power series, which was much lighter in weight. Curious about her purchase, I asked her why she bought a shuttle as well. She explained that her hostel mate had informed her that she needed to bring her own shuttle to play. Mamita and I shared a smile, and I told Shreya that since she would be playing with Mamita, she didn't need to worry about bringing her own shuttle, as the school provided us with everything we needed since we were on the school team.

I asked Mamita and Shreya to do some stretching exercises before starting their game. Mamita had been under my guidance for quite some time now, but Shreya was new and needed my help. To my surprise, Shreya showed great skills in playing. Her selection of shots was impressive, but she had two major drawbacks: her movement on the court was slow, and her shots lacked power. Despite this, Mamita enjoyed playing with Shreya. After their first set, they took a rest and came over where I was sitting. I gave Shreya some feedback on her game, and she humbly requested that I guide her. She also asked me to play with Mamita so she could observe my footwork. I could see that Shreya was enjoying my game, especially my surprise drop shots and powerful smashes. Today, I played with the intention of impressing Shreya, and it seemed to have worked. She was thrilled with my performance, and it motivated her to improve her own skills. As usual, Mamita asked me to go to the canteen for some lemon water. She also invited Shreya, but she seemed hesitant. When questioned, Shreya revealed that she had heard from some hostel friends about Mamita and me being romantically involved. Smilingly, she said she didn't want to disturb us. Mamita clarified that we love each other very much, but only as friends. She mentioned that I was actually in love with a junior girl whom I saw in the dining hall two days ago. Shreya's curiosity was piqued as she asked which girl it was. Mamita explained that, unfortunately, I haven't seen her since, and I don't even know her name. All I remember is that she was wearing a pink nightdress that day. Mamita then shared that we, all friends, are on a mission to find this mysterious girl who has caught my attention.

As I sat there, chatting with them, I couldn't help but feel my nerves getting the best of me. Shreya, the girl that I had been searching for, was sitting with me. However, when both of them got up to leave, Shreya didn't smile or say goodbye. My heart sank as I worried that she may have somehow sensed that I was interested in her and she was the girl I was looking for. I continued sitting there, feeling tense and anxious, until suddenly Shreya turned back and looked at me. I waved at her, and, surprisingly, she waved back. Instantly, a sense of relief washed over me, and I headed home to take a much-needed shower.

While making my way to the dining hall, my friends Ranjit and Debashish bombarded me with questions about Shreya. They wanted to know if I had spoken to her or even proposed to her. Irritated by their constant pestering, I curtly replied that we had just played badminton together. As I walked into the dining hall, I noticed Shreya sitting with her group of friends. However, despite passing by their table, she didn't bother to look up or acknowledge me. This behaviour of hers left me feeling annoyed and frustrated. It seemed like she was intentionally ignoring me.

As I made my way to the table where my friends were sitting, I could hear the buzz of excitement in their voices. It was Saturday night, also known as ragging night in our hostel. For Ranjit and Debashish, it was a night of excitement, and they eagerly asked me if I would join them in taking part in the ragging activities. Without any hesitation, I replied that I had been looking forward to this night for a whole year, ever since my seniors used to rag me. Despite facing a lot of ragging in the past, I was not going to miss out on the opportunity to pass it on to the juniors. As we sat down at our table, we noticed a few juniors next to us who were nervously eating their dinner. Ranjit wasted no time in inviting them to his room after prep for some introduction sessions. The juniors were visibly scared upon hearing this and could not even finish their meal properly.

After finishing my dinner, I informed my friends Ranjit and Debashish that I would meet them at prep. While washing my hands, I noticed Mamita standing with Shreya outside the dining hall. However, I chose to ignore them and began walking towards my hostel. Suddenly, Mamita called out my name, and I turned around to see her. I politely told her that I had some important work to attend to and promised to meet her tomorrow.

I was having a terrible headache and knew I needed to take some medicine to alleviate the pain. Our medical inspection room was located right next to the girls' hostel. I quickly made my way there and took the necessary medication. However, knowing that it was a night notorious for ragging the junior students, I decided to make a quick stop at the canteen to grab a cup of tea before heading back. I saw Mamita having coffee, and I went to her. I saw Shreya entering with girls from my batch. They sat next to my table. Girls from my batch were trying to rag Shreya and her friends. I immediately told them to stop as Shreya was close to me, and they should not make her uncomfortable. However, one of the girls in a low voice said that I couldn't always be there to save her. I firmly told them that if they catch her 100 times, I would come 100 times to save her. I even threatened to make their hostel life hell if they continued to disturb her. Just then, Mamita intervened and asked me to stop shouting and sit down at my table. She assured me that she would talk to them about it. Shreya was visibly upset and scared, and she even requested that I leave as I was causing more problems for her. After speaking with Mamita about Shreya, the girls allowed her to go. I expressed my gratitude and apologized to my batchmates for my behaviour. Mamita then invited Shreya to join us for some tea and relaxation, but she declined and returned to her hostel. Confused by her behaviour, I asked Mamita what could be wrong with Shreya. Instead of showing gratitude, Shreya seemed angry and refused to join us. Mamita explained that Shreya was afraid and did not want to get into any trouble. Mamita was curious about my constant concern for Shreya and asked me if she was the same girl I had been in love with. After much hesitation, I admitted that she was indeed the one. Mamita then questioned why I hadn't told her earlier. I explained that Shreya seemed very nervous when we were at the canteen together yesterday, and I didn't want to make her uncomfortable by confessing my feelings. I asked Mamita to keep this information to herself and specifically not tell Shalini and Rachika. I assured her that I would personally inform them in a few days. I also requested that she keep this secret from Shreya as well, as I feared that she might stop talking to me after knowing my intentions. Finishing my tea, I left for Ranjit's room, hoping that Mamita would keep my secret safe. When I entered Ranjit's room, I noticed that he was not there. Upon asking his roommate, I found out that he had gone to Debashish's room. Without wasting any time, I made my way towards Debashish's room, only to find out that they were not there either. I assumed that they must have gone to Tau's canteen. I decided to head back to my own room, hoping to catch up with them later.

After a few minutes of sitting in my room, I heard a knock on the door and someone calling out, "Asif sir, can I come in?" I instantly knew it was one of the juniors from school. As he entered, I could see that he was a well-built young boy. He informed me that Ranjit sir was looking for me and asked if I could come to the terrace.

As I approached the terrace, I noticed that it was locked. Frustrated, I realized that I would have to use the wall to climb up and reach the terrace. I knew that my batchmates, including Ranjit, Debashish, Abhishek, and Manish, had taken this route to avoid getting caught by Warden Sir. As I reached the top, I was taken aback by the scene in front of me. My batchmates were indulging in ragging of juniors, smoking, and drinking tea. Despite having a severe headache, I sat there quietly. Manish even offered me a cigarette, but I politely refused. To my surprise, one of the juniors served me tea, and I thanked him for it. However, Abhishek quickly pointed out that there was no need to thank them as they were here to serve and entertain us. However, I was not feeling well and decided to leave. Ranjit asked me to wait for five more minutes as everyone would be leaving together. I returned to my room and went to sleep.

The next day started off on a positive note as I woke up feeling well with no signs of the headache that had bothered me the previous day. However, I couldn't shake off the annoyance I felt towards Shreya for her behaviour in the canteen. As I was having lunch, Mamita approached me and informed me that she wouldn't be able to join me for our regular badminton practice session as she had made plans to go horse riding. Knowing that we needed to practice for an upcoming tournament, I requested that she prioritize badminton and take a break from horse riding for the time being. After some convincing, she finally agreed and even asked me to come a little earlier so that she could fit in her horse- riding session after our practice.

I went to the badminton court for my usual practice, but this time Mamita was already waiting for me. Surprisingly, there were no other students in the court as we had arrived an hour before our scheduled time. We decided to utilize this extra time and started with some stretching exercises. As we were about to begin our first game, I noticed a few high school students entering the court. Since Mamita and I were playing singles, I suggested that they join us so that we could practice mixed doubles. However, I wasn't really in the mood to play that day. As we were playing our third game, I saw Shreya entering the court and standing near us. I purposely avoided looking at her, and after finishing the game, I told Mamita that I wasn't feeling well and didn't want to continue playing. But she insisted on playing more, so I suggested that she play with either the boys or Shreya. I packed my kit and bid them farewell without glancing at Shreya even once that day.

I headed to the lawn tennis court where my friends Ranjit and Debashish were playing. They greeted me with smiles as I walked in holding a bottle of Thumbs Up. I sat and watched their game while sipping on my drink. After they finished, we walked towards our hostel. As we were about to enter the North Block hostel, I saw Shreya approaching from the opposite direction, with a badminton racket in her hand. Ranjit and Debashish deliberately slowed down their pace, but I continued walking and entered the hostel. They came up to me and asked why I didn't talk to Shreya. I explained that I didn't even notice her coming, and even if I did, what would we talk about? We were not friends, just seniors and juniors. Debashish then asked if everything was okay between us, to which I replied that we don't talk much.

As I entered my room, I was surprised to see Tarun and Sachin waiting for me. Sachin excitedly informed me that Tarun was taking us to the MBA canteen. I couldn't help but ask what the occasion was. Tarun simply replied that we didn't need a special reason to enjoy a meal together at the canteen. Just as we were getting ready to leave, Ranjit and Debashish called out my name, asking me to join them for dinner at the dining hall. I quickly informed them that Tarun had already made plans to take me to the canteen, so I wouldn't be joining them for dinner at the dining hall.

When I met Ranjit and Debashish at prep, they excitedly told me about their encounter with Mamita and Shreya at the dining hall. They were surprised to see how well the two girls had bonded even though they were from different grades. Ranjit and Debashish couldn't help but wonder how senior Mamita and junior Shreya had become such good friends in such a short period of time. I explained to them that Mamita didn't have many friends and Shreya was new to the school, so they naturally gravitated towards each other. They also shared a common interest that brought them closer. In the midst of our conversation, Debashish mentioned that Mamita had asked about me, why I am acting strangely lately and wasn't talkative like before. Debashish replied that he has noticed the same behaviour from me as well. He then shared that I used to be the naughtiest one in their group, always looking for fun. But now, I have changed. Despite their efforts to cheer me up by making a plan to go to Tau's canteen, I was not in the mood and refused their offer. However, my friends were determined to lift my spirits and suggested going to the girls' canteen after prep. I declined again, explaining that I wanted to sleep early. My friend Debashish pleaded me not to isolate myself and reminded me that we were falling apart. He even suggested that I could just come along and not drink tea, but at least spend some time with them. He assured me that they would not take much time and would return early so I could still get enough rest. Despite my initial hesitation, their persistence and genuine concern convinced me to join them.

After prep, my friends insisted that I join them at the canteen. Reluctantly, I followed them, and we settled down in the garden area where chairs were placed. Soon, they went inside to get some tea and returned with three cups, offering me one as well. They mentioned that it would make me feel better. However, they failed to mention that our other friends Shalini, Rachika, Mamita, Shreya, and her friends were inside the canteen. Shalini noticed us sitting in the garden and came to join us. She suggested that we all go inside as it was hot outside. But my friend Debashish insisted that we were comfortable where we were. However, Shalini persisted and said she would call the others so we could all sit together. However, none of us replied, and there was an awkward silence between us. I couldn't understand why I was so irritated with Shreya that I couldn't bear to look at her or even talk to her. As the group had become larger and there were only a few chairs available, everyone sat on the ground, but I chose to remain seated on a chair, pretending to have a leg pain. My friends Mamita, Shalini, and Rachika were sitting close to me. Rachika noticed my sadness and asked if it was because I couldn't find the girl whom I had seen in the dining hall a few days ago. She held my hand and reassured me that we would find her. I glanced at Ranjit, Debashish, and Mamita, knowing that they were aware that Shreya was that girl who happened to be sitting there. I suddenly felt uncomfortable and made an excuse about having an assignment to complete, using it as an opportunity to leave as it was getting late. I stood up abruptly and said goodbye to them; everyone looked at me with confusion. It was a sudden and unexpected departure, leaving them all feeling a bit uneasy. Mamita followed me as I started walking and stopped me near the dining hall. She asked me what had happened and why I was acting this way. She even mentioned if something had occurred between Shreya and me. I assured her that there was nothing wrong between us and that we simply didn't talk because she was my junior. Mamita then revealed that Shreya had come to her room after prep and was curious as to why I had stopped talking to her. She mentioned how I had always been friendly towards her and even stood up for her when she was being ragged. Shreya wanted to thank me, but I hadn't even looked at her. Mamita tried to cheer me up, but my emotions were too overwhelming. I longed to hug her, but I knew it would only cause gossip amongst the students. As I said goodbye and headed back to my room, I made a decision to close the chapter on Shreya and focus on the friendships that truly mattered to me. I promised myself to avoid any encounters with Shreya and not engage in any conversation with her. With time, everything would fall back into place.

CHAPTER 7

THE STRUGGLE OF JUGGLING STUDIES, TOURNAMENT, AND ROMANCE

Life at the hostel was becoming interesting again as the rules and regulations of the school were being compromised. The students were finally able to have some freedom and were no longer under constant scrutiny. The warden, who used to be strict and would do surprise inspections after 10 PM, had stopped coming altogether. It was like old times when the students were left to do as they pleased, without any fear of getting caught. This newfound freedom had brought a new energy to the hostel, with students staying up late, playing games, and bonding with their roommates. The atmosphere was lively and carefree, and everyone was enjoying this change. It seemed like the students were finally able to make the most of their hostel life without any restrictions holding them back. We were able to smoke in the school toilets without any consequences, and we didn't have to go to Tau's canteen for that. We also had the freedom to bunk classes and stay inside a room that needed to be locked from the outside. The door lock in my room has also been changed because the warden has the keys to the previous one. Additionally, staying in the canteen after prep for a long time has become a regular occurrence for us.

Me, Ranjit, and Debashish were living our best lives, enjoying every moment and making the most of our school years. One day, during lunch at the dining hall, Mamita came to us with an excited look on her face. She told us that she had been dying to go to a concert of her favourite band, Parikrama. However, none of us had ever heard of this band before. Mamita explained that the concert was going to be held on Saturday night at Feroz Shah Kotla Stadium. We were all curious about how she was planning to attend the concert, especially since it was going to be late at night. But Mamita reassured us that she had it all figured out and would even manage to get tickets for us. However, she didn't want to go alone in the night, and so she invited us to join her. I couldn't help but smile at her and jokingly said that she was taking us as her bodyguards. Mamita pleaded with us not to ditch her on the day of the concert as it meant a lot to her. We promised to confirm the following day as we also needed to take leave to go to our local guardian's house. We had to stay outside that night as it was not possible for us to come back to the hostel late at night or early in the morning. However, during our prep time, we were given a new topic to discuss and plan. We were not particularly interested in attending a concert but rather just wanted to go out and have some fun. None of us had any knowledge about the band performing that night, Parikrama. Personally, I had no interest in English songs and was not familiar with genres like heavy metal, rock, hard rock, or jazz. However, I noticed Abhishek sitting with his friends. He used to be a part of our group, but now we only talk when necessary or come face to face. I approached him and asked if he knew about the Parikrama band since he was into English songs. He had heard of them but hadn't really listened to their songs. In those days, cassettes were the only option for listening to music, and everyone had their favourite songs with them. Abhishek suggested that I ask Tenzing as he was more into

Indian rock bands. Although we had only met a few times and were not close, I found myself going up to Tenzing and asking him about Parikrama, feeling a little awkward about it. Ranjit's questioning the need to research Parikrama was quickly followed by his request for me to inform Mamita that we were all set for fun. However, our excitement was momentarily dampened by the realization that we needed to get approval for leave from the warden. Knowing that he would not grant leave to all three of us on the same day, we came up with a plan to get approval signatures from three different teachers. As I had a good relationship with the warden, I would approach him for approval while Debashish and Ranjit would seek approval from the principal and vice principal, respectively. With three days before our trip, we could each take permission on a different day and then submit the approved leave in the administrative office for our gate pass. We also had to submit another copy to the warden's office so that he would be aware of how many students are not in the hostel.

The next day, I met Mamita at the badminton court, and we discussed our plans to go on a trip outside the campus. Shreya, who was also playing at the court, asked Mamita if we were planning to go outside. Mamita shared our plan with her, and she expressed her desire to join us. Mamita happily agreed and told her that she just needed to take leave to go to her local guardian's house. Shreya had some concerns about her parents being notified, but Mamita assured her that with over 8000 students on the campus, it was unlikely for them to track our movements. They only kept track of students up to 9th grade. I didn't interrupt their conversation and left to meet Ranjit for his match at the lawn tennis court.

I decided to take a refreshing shower before heading to the canteen for a chat with Mamita. The canteen was conveniently located next to the girls' hostel, and as I was walking towards it, I saw one of our batchmates and asked her to send Mamita to meet me. Within a few minutes, Mamita arrived and gave me a warm hug, mentioning that I was the first person to come looking for her in the hostel. It was also the first time I had ventured into the girls' hostel to meet someone. Overjoyed to see me, Mamita insisted on treating me, and I suggested we save it for another day. I asked her for a walk with me. As we were heading towards the ground, I mustered up the courage to tell my friend Mamita that I would prefer if she didn't bring Shreya along for the concert. I explained that her presence would make me uncomfortable, and I would not be able to enjoy myself. However, my words seemed to irritate Mamita as she had grown close to Shreya and considered her a friend and younger sister. I tried to reason with her, reminding her that I too was her friend and deserved the same consideration. She then took my hand and reassured me that I was dear to her and no one could come between us. I reminded Mamita of how Shreya had not even thanked us or joined us for tea after we had saved her from being ragged. But Mamita simply replied that she had already explained the situation to me before and I was not willing to understand, so there was no point in discussing it further. When we walked towards the MBA canteen, we spotted Shalini and Rachika sitting at a table, sipping on coffee. We decided to join them and jokingly mentioned how we were not invited. They playfully asked us what we were doing there, to which Mamita replied that Asif had come to the hostel looking for me and had invited me for a walk. Shalini teased Mamita, saying how lucky she was, as Asif never came looking for me. I chimed in, mentioning how I had even gone to Shalini's home in Bhagalpur during our summer holidays, looking for her.

Mamita informed them that we needed to finalize our plan for the upcoming concert. She mentioned that we were all going out for a concert, and I quickly added that there was a Parikrama concert on Saturday night. Mamita didn't want to go alone, so she had asked me, Ranjit, and Debashish to join her. Rachika immediately questioned why she didn't ask her to come along. I added that Shreya was also planning to attend with them. On hearing this, Mamita's expression turned to anger as she declared that Shreya was not coming, and neither were we. It was clear that Mamita no longer wanted to attend the concert.

Mamita was a little on the chubby side. I couldn't resist teasing her by calling her "Bhalu" (Bear) and playfully pulling her cheeks. I pulled her cheeks and said that Bhalu was angry. However, Mamita quickly responded and asked me not to call her Bhalu. Shalini intervened and advised her not to take any boys with her. She suggested that we all go together, and after the concert, we could go to Rachika's home to sleep. I was worried that Ranjit and Debashish would tease me for ruining the trip, but I looked at Mamita and knew she wouldn't go without me, as I was dear to her. As we finished our coffee and headed towards the dining hall, Mamita asked what she should tell Shreya if she asked about our plans. I suggested we tell her the truth and not take any risks by bringing her along as she was a junior. But Mamita refused to do so and said she would instead say that I am not ready to come if Shreya is also coming. I didn't care what she would say to Shreya. I asked her to say what she wanted.

As I entered the dining hall, I saw Shreya walking in, and she immediately made her way to sit with Mamita. Throughout their meal, Shreya kept turning her head towards my table, but I avoided making any eye contact with her. It seemed as though she wasn't eating properly and left within ten minutes. I finished my dinner and went to wash my hands, but as I was about to leave, Mamita approached me. To my surprise, she didn't speak to me about anything except for saying that I was "cold-hearted." Confused, I stopped and asked her what I had done to make her think that. She replied, saying that I was unnecessarily hurting Shreya. Not wanting to continue this topic, I simply said that if she believed that, I couldn't help you understand otherwise. Despite not wanting to engage in this conversation, it saddened me to think that someone could perceive me in such a negative light. Ranjit and Debashish also joined our conversation and urged me to work out the differences with Shreya. They pointed out that there is nothing but misunderstandings between us because we haven't been talking to each other. I promised to talk to her but also made it clear that I don't want to be friends with her. Mamita suggested that she would bring Shreya to the canteen after prep and asked me to talk to her in a polite manner. Despite my reservations, I agreed to her request and hoped that this conversation would finally put an end to our differences.

I was at prep; my friends reminded me to be polite and mindful of her innocence. It made me realize that perhaps my previous interactions with her had been too brash and careless. I went to my room and changed into a fresh t-shirt, and I even put on some deodorant, wanting to appear presentable. However, as I sat in my room, I couldn't help but feel nervous and unsure of what to say to her. Just then, my friend Ranjit came to my room and suggested that I go alone to speak with her. Despite my request for his support, he insisted that I handle the situation on my own, promising to join me after thirty minutes. It was clear that he wanted me to take responsibility and sort things out with her directly.

I made my way towards the canteen and sat in the peaceful garden outside the canteen area, purposely avoiding the crowded and noisy atmosphere inside. I wanted to have a comfortable conversation with

Shreya, and the garden seemed like the perfect place for it. After a few minutes, I saw Mamita approaching with Shreya by her side. I was surprised to see Shreya in a traditional salwar suit, instead of her usual western attire. She looked absolutely stunning in her black salwar suit with a bright red dupatta. They both came and sat next to me on the chairs, and there was a brief moment of silence. It was Mamita who broke the silence by asking me to buy tea for everyone.

I went inside and grabbed three cups of tea for myself, Shreya, and Mamita. Mamita soon stated that she would finish her tea and leave, leaving Shreya and me to sort out any differences between us. We both remained silent, unsure of what to say. As Mamita was leaving, she told Shreya that I had been looking for a girl from her batch whom I had seen in the dining hall. Shreya nodded her head in understanding, and Mamita continued to say that she shouldn't be revealing this information, but it was actually you that he had been searching for. At that moment, Shreya looked at me with surprise in her eyes.

After Mamita left, there was a heavy and awkward silence between us. In an attempt to break the tension, I asked her how she was doing. She responded with a simple, "I am fine," and asked me the same question. I replied with the same answer, but Shreya could see through my facade. She told me that my friends had mentioned how full of life and happy I used to be before meeting "her.". I denied any truth to her words and reassured her that there was nothing wrong. But Shreya persisted, asking me why I avoided her and what she had done to deserve such treatment. She even went as far as saying that I didn't even look at her anymore. She said, "I asked you to leave while the seniors were raging at me because you were very angry." She told me that she was not sure if I would believe her. She trusted me and confided in me that ever since she joined this school, she had been feeling lonely as it was the first time she was staying away from her family. She wanted to leave, but her parents were not ready for her to do so. That's when she met me and my friends. Despite being a junior, she enjoyed our company and started enjoying hostel life and playing badminton with us. When I stood up for her during the fight, she was happy but at the same time worried for me. That day, she didn't sit for tea with Mamita and me because she was scared of my anger.

This conversation was getting difficult for both of us. She said she wanted to thank me for saving her from raging, but I wasn't ready to talk. She looked sad and on the verge of tears as she expressed her feelings. Seeing her like this made me feel terrible, and I realized that it was all my fault. In that moment, I asked if I could hold her hand and apologized for everything I had done. Her tears only intensified as she begged me not to hurt her like this again. It was then that she reminded me that even though she was my junior, she treated me like a friend. I reassured her that I would never repeat my actions and promised to always be there for her. We shook hands, and she said, "We are friends now. You will treat me like you treat your other friends." I assured her, "Don't worry; you are very special to me and will remain special all my life." She replied, "You are equally special to me." Our friendship was off to a great start, and she wasted no time in setting some ground rules. "Now you have to practice badminton with me, and we'll go to the canteen very often," she said with a mischievous grin. As we were chatting, Mamita suddenly returned and asked if everything was sorted between us. Shreya replied with a big smile, saying that all the confusions had been cleared, and we were now friends who were very happy. I could see the happiness radiating from Shreya's face every time she looked at me, and I couldn't help but fall for her even more. Soon, Ranjit, Debashish, Shalini, and Rachika joined us. Ranjit had already told Shalini and Rachika about my feelings for Shreya, and they were all aware of it. Mamita suggested that from tomorrow onwards, we should all sit together in the dining hall at the same table to make sure we could meet at least three times a day. We all agreed to this plan as we often missed each other during our busy days. It seemed like everything was falling into place, and I couldn't wait to spend more time with Shreya and my friends.

As the night grew darker, my friends and I decided to call it a day and head back to our rooms. I walked alongside Ranjit and Debashish, who were chatting about how relieved they were that everything had been sorted out between Shreya and me. I glanced over and noticed Shreya heading in the opposite direction towards her hostel. To my amazement, she turned around and waved goodbye before continuing on her way. Once I reached my room in North Block, I lay on the bed and couldn't help but think about Shreya. The way she smiled, the sound of her laugh, and the warmth of her hand—everything about her had captured my heart. After much contemplation, I finally accepted that I had fallen in love with her. As I drifted off to sleep, I couldn't wait to see where this journey of love would take me.

With all the various distractions and developments happening in my life, I found myself completely lagging behind in my studies. I became increasingly irregular in attending classes, especially in my physics class. My lack of motivation and focus caused me to almost completely stop studying. Even during prep time, after marking my attendance, my friends and I would sneak out to go to Tau's canteen for a cigarette. This became a daily routine for us, sometimes even happening two or three times a day. In the evenings, I would practice badminton with Shreya and Mamita. However, with an upcoming interschool tournament just a few days away, I became very focused and determined to do well this time, as I did not perform well in the previous tournament.

In just two days from now, on Saturday, we have to go to the concert. Thankfully, everyone's leave was approved, so we can all go together. But the biggest surprise of all was when Mamita told me Shreya was coming with us. I see her every day at the badminton court and dining hall, but she never mentioned that she was also planning on going. I was thrilled to have her join us. Knowing that I needed to dress perfectly at the concert, I borrowed a black t-shirt from my Nepali friend. The shirt had a picture of Kurt Cobain, the lead singer of Nirvana, on it, which perfectly paired with my Pepe jeans. A good choice to attain a live musical concert.

We all met at the canteen. I asked Shreya to join me inside the canteen to bring some tea for our friends. She happily followed me to the counter, but we were met with a rush of customers, causing us to wait for a few minutes for our turn. As we waited, I confided in Shreya that I was about to cancel my plan because she was not coming. However, her response filled me with happiness and relief as she smiled at me and said that I didn't need to cancel anymore. She expressed how much she appreciated and admired it when I showed care and concern for her. Even though I mentioned that I care for all my friends, she insisted that I cared for her more. When I asked her to elaborate, she didn't finish her sentence and instead asked me to guess. She smiled again and said that I already knew what I wanted to say.

We returned with tea for our friends. They had already made a plan for the evening, which involved leaving the hostel at 10 AM and taking two taxis to Palika Bazaar and Janpath market for some shopping. We would then have lunch there before splitting up for a few hours. The girls would go to Rachika's house to change clothes while the boys would meet them at 7:30 PM at gate number 1 of Feroz Kotla stadium, where Mamita's cousin would give us our tickets for the evening concert. Luckily, we didn't have to pay for the tickets as Mamita had purchased them for all of us. I asked what we would do during that time, and Debashish suggested that we roam around Connaught Place and change our clothes in the toilets at Palika Bazaar. Shalini pointed out that the boys had an advantage as they could change anywhere and didn't need to worry about makeup like the girls did. After the concert, we would all go to Rachika's house, where her mother would meet us and even prepare dinner for us. It was going to be a fun and eventful evening with our friends in Delhi. As we were talking, I noticed Shreya staring at me and asked if she needed anything. She replied with a no.

After dinner at Rachika's house, the boys will go to Mukherjee Nagar, but I reminded them that we didn't know what time the concert would be over. It would be too late to go to Mukherjee Nagar at that time. I suggested we go directly to Mukherjee Nahar. However, Mamita assured us that the concert would end by 11 PM and we could reach Rachika's house by 11:30 PM. After meeting her parents and having dinner, we could then go to Mukherjee Nagar. Shalini suggested that we finish our meeting so she could select three outfits for the next day. I was curious why she needed three outfits, and she explained that she wanted to keep a western dress for the concert, a night dress, and one for the next day when we returned to the hostel. Debashish decided to only bring one t-shirt for the concert because he was comfortable sleeping in jeans. He also planned to wear the same outfit on our way back the next day. I couldn't agree more with his decision. As we were leaving, Shreya came up to me and offered to keep my clothes in her bag if I didn't want to carry them. Her gesture showed how much she cared for me. I politely declined and said I would keep my bag. We all left the canteen together, but I couldn't take my eyes off Shreya until she reached her hostel. Right before entering, she gave me a smile that felt like it would stay with me forever. Her smile is something I will always remember in my life.

The next day, I woke up early, filled with excitement for the day of outing with my friends and Shreya. I quickly packed my bag and cleaned my Nike sneakers, eager to start the day. After taking a refreshing shower, I headed to the dining hall for breakfast, hoping to see my friends there. However, none of them were present, either because they had already eaten or they were busy getting ready for the outing. Disappointed, I returned to my room, where I found Tarun and Sachin getting ready for their classes. Since I had an official leave, I decided to skip my classes and changed into comfortable clothes for the outing. I went to the administrative block to collect my gate pass and informed the warden about my plans. As luck would have it, I bumped into Debashish there, but we avoided speaking in front of the warden. Upon submitting my gate pass, the warden asked me where I was going and when I would return. Without hesitation, I lied and said that I was going to my local guardian's house for a family function and that they would drop me back at the hostel by tomorrow evening. Living in the hostel for a year had taught me how to come up with convincing lies effortlessly. By 9:30, I was all set to leave. As I made my way towards the main gate, I saw my friends Ranjit and Debashish heading in the same direction with their bags. I went to the warden's office to inform him that I was leaving and then headed towards the gate. There were over 50 students leaving for their breaks, and as I reached the gate, I spotted Ranjit and Debashish waiting under a tree. They informed me that they had already booked two taxis for us. It was already 10 AM, and the girls were still nowhere to be seen. Feeling a bit restless, I decided to head to the nearby canteen and have some tea. While I was at the canteen, I noticed the girls joining our friends and looking around in search of me. I waved to catch their attention and saw Shreya, wearing a beautiful dress and looking absolutely gorgeous. She kept turning back towards the canteen as if she was waiting for me. Just then, two black and yellow taxis pulled up at the gate. I quickly went to my friends and hopped into one of the cars. It seemed that one car was for the girls and the other for the boys.

As our taxi approached the main road, my friend Ranjit and I requested the driver to make a quick stop at the nearest cigarette shop. The driver, however, took one look at us through the rearview mirror and pointed out that we were too young to be smoking. But he still obliged and pulled over to the shop, much to our relief. As Ranjit went in to buy a packet of cigarettes, even the taxi carrying our female friends stopped alongside us. I noticed Shreya signalling me not to smoke. I couldn't help but wonder if she was annoyed with me for smoking, especially since we had always been such good friends. But then a thought crossed my mind: What if our relationship turned into something more than just friendship? Would Shreya be able to accept me as a smoker? As I lit my cigarette and took a drag, I couldn't help but worry about the potential consequences of my habit on our friendship. Would she try to change me, or would she understand and accept me for who I am?

As we arrived at Palika Bazaar, I noticed how crowded it was and immediately suggested that we stick together. Shalini and Rachika, however, were too excited about the shopping possibilities and couldn't resist stopping at every shop. To make things easier, we split into groups: Shalini and Rachika, Mamita and Shreya, and myself, Ranjit, and Debashish. While the first two groups went off on their shopping spree, my group decided to just roam around. However, my enjoyment was cut short as my leg started to ache. I had been experiencing pain for a few days now, but it seemed to have worsened. Seeing people taking breaks on the staircase, I asked Ranjit if I could sit there while they continued to explore. They agreed and mentioned they were going out for a smoke and would be back soon. Shalini noticed me sitting down and immediately made her way over to me. She asked what happened and where the other boys were. I told her that they had gone outside to smoke and I was just taking a break as my leg was hurting. After a few minutes, Mamita and Shreya joined us, having been informed by Shalini about my condition. They sat beside me until Ranjit and Debashish returned. Not wanting to disrupt their plans, I suggested that the girls continue their shopping while I rested. However, Shreya silently expressed her desire to stay and keep me company. Debashish suggested that I may have pulled a muscle while playing and advised me to do some stretching exercises. I followed his advice and started feeling better.

After spending some time shopping, the girls returned with their bags and decided to go to Janpath, a popular flea market located about 400-500 meters from Palika Bazaar. I was feeling much better now and walked towards Janpath along with my friends. Mamita, Shreya, and I walked together behind our other friends, and I couldn't help but want to hold Shreya's hand while walking. Upon reaching Janpath, we split up, and I ended up sitting next to a bookseller. He was an interesting old man who seemed to be well-versed in all the books he had on display, as if he had read them all himself. I struck up a conversation with him, and he shared his knowledge and insights on various books with me. It was a pleasant experience, and I was glad to have found a new companion in the form of the bookseller at Janpath.

After a few minutes, Shreya came to me and said she was thirsty. We decided to go to a nearby stall that was selling water and cold drinks. I bought a bottle of water for her and even asked if she wanted a cold drink, but she refused. As we were walking back, she asked me how my pain was. I couldn't resist giving her a flirty reply, telling her that I was feeling much better after she came to see me. She smiled at my response and seemed like she wanted to say something, but she kept silent. It frustrated me when she would hide her emotions like that. She then went back to continue her shopping. After almost an hour, everyone came back with even more bags. It seemed like they had bought the entire market. I took a few bags from Shreya, and she smiled and handed them to me. That's when Ranjit, seeing me take her bags, gave me a sly and cunning smile.

Mamita had kindly offered to treat us to lunch, and she suggested we go to Narula's. It was my first time visiting this popular restaurant, and I was excited to see what they had to offer. The food was delicious, and we all ordered our favourite dishes. As we finished our meal, the girls decided to take a taxi to Rachika's house. Before leaving, Shreya whispered to me that she had a surprise for me. While leaving, I could see sadness in her eyes, as if she was about to leave permanently. As they left, my mind couldn't help but wonder what the surprise could be. Was she going to confess her feelings for me? With these thoughts racing through my mind, my heart started beating erratically, eagerly anticipating what was to come.

Ranjit, Debashish, and I went to Central Park in Connaught Place. As soon as we entered the park, we could feel the lively and energetic atmosphere around us. Families were enjoying their time together; children were running around and playing, while couples were taking romantic walks. We noticed that many people who had come to Connaught Place for shopping were also using the park to take a break and relax. We couldn't resist the delicious snacks and lemon tea being sold by vendors in the park. After refreshing ourselves, we headed to

Palika Bazaar and went straight to the restroom to freshen up and change into clean t-shirts. I even sprayed some perfume to smell good. I was excited as I was going to attend my first concert that evening.

Our evening started off around 6:30 as we took an auto-rickshaw to head to the Feroz Shah Kotla stadium. As we arrived, I couldn't help but notice the large crowd of young people from all over Delhi who had gathered there. It took us some time to navigate through the crowd and find gate no. 1. Thankfully, this gate wasn't as crowded, as the entrance for the concert was through gate no. 3. Just as we were settling in, our female friends Shalini, Rachika, Mamita, and Shreya arrived in a taxi at around 7:15. They were all dressed in skirts and tops, looking absolutely stunning. I couldn't help but compliment all of them, especially Shreya, whom I couldn't compliment alone. As we entered through the gate, I wanted to talk to Shreya and let her know how incredibly attractive she looked. Her makeup enhanced her beauty, making her eyes look even bigger. It was a great start to what promised to be an amazing evening filled with music and fun.

As I walked into the crowded venue, my eyes were immediately drawn to the stage. The bright lights and electrifying music stunned me, and I couldn't help but feel a rush of excitement. However, due to the large crowd, it was impossible to get close to the stage. My friends and I found a comfortable spot in one corner and made a pact to stick together throughout the night. Just then, Shreya came and stood next to me, pleading for me to stay with her. Without hesitation, I nodded in agreement and reassured her that I would always be by her side.

This place was unlike any I had ever been to before. The atmosphere was strange and unfamiliar, with people from all different backgrounds gathered in one place. It seemed that most of the people there were rock music lovers, as many were donning bandanas and some were even smoking. The scent of weed lingered in the air, something I had never experienced before. As we were standing, I could see musicians already on stage, tuning their instruments. The speakers were incredibly powerful, and the music was loud, causing the crowd to shout in excitement. Suddenly, the lead singer, Nitin Malik, and lead guitarist, Sonam Sherpa, appeared on stage, causing the lighting to change and the ground lights to dim.

The energy in the stadium was palpable as people were shouting and cheering loudly. The moment the band started singing their first song, "Till I Am No One Again," the entire crowd went wild. Everyone was jumping and banging their heads to the beat, and I couldn't help but feel like we were all caught up in a frenzy. Shreya was scared and held onto my hand tightly. As I looked at her, she pleaded with me to make her feel safe. So, I held her hand more strongly, trying to reassure her. The crowd only seemed to calm down when the band sang "Gonna Get It," and then they were back to jumping and headbanging. The lighting on stage was perfect for the situation, adding to the electrifying atmosphere.

I saw Ranjit lighting a cigarette and passing it to me after smoking half of it. I took a drag, but before I could finish, Shreya snatched the cigarette from my hand and threw it on the ground, saying that I didn't look good while smoking. Feeling a little bored, I announced that I was going to get some water and tea. Surprisingly, Shreya also tagged along. As we walked towards the entry gate, we came across some stalls selling snacks and tea. I bought a bottle of water and shared it with Shreya before getting us both some tea. We ended up talking for an hour, completely losing track of time. When we returned to our friends, we saw them having a great time. As the clock struck 11, the concert ended, and we all headed to the main road to book two taxis for Kalkaji.

We reached Kalkaji within 25-30 minutes and were warmly welcomed by Rachika's family. As soon as we entered their house, they greeted each one of us with genuine warmth and hospitality. However, I couldn't help but feel a little uncomfortable as we were running late to reach Mukherjee Nagar. Rachika's family lived in a beautifully designed two-storied house, which was a reflection of their affluent lifestyle. We were then served with a delicious spread of vegetarian dishes, which left us all satisfied and content. After dinner, we were treated to some mouthwatering desserts that truly melted in our mouths. Despite the rush to leave, we couldn't help but appreciate the generosity and kindness shown by Rachika's family towards us. Rachika's father was curious about our plans and asked where we were heading. We told him that we were going to Mukherjee Nagar, and from there, we would return to the hostel the next day. However, her mother expressed concern about us traveling alone at night and suggested that we stay there instead. While Ranjit wanted to continue with our original plan, Debashish and I convinced him to stay at their house. Rachika's elder brother generously offered us his room and even arranged extra bedding so that we could sleep comfortably.

The next day, we woke up to the delicious aroma of a wonderful breakfast. Her father and his elder brother kindly offered to drop us off at our hostel before lunch. We were all quite tired from the previous day's activities, so as soon as we reached our rooms, we took some much-needed rest. Later in the evening, we all gathered for dinner, and despite being exhausted, everyone seemed happy and content. After dinner, Mamita asked me to meet her at the canteen after our prep session. I was curious about what she wanted to talk about and eagerly agreed.

After finishing our prep, I asked my friends Ranjit and Debashish to join me at the canteen. But to my surprise, they had different plans and wanted to go to Tau's canteen instead. I ended up going alone and saw Mamita waiting for me. She informed me that our upcoming tournament was starting in a week and we were not adequately prepared as we had been practicing less. To make matters worse, she had not received any official confirmation that she was a part of the team. Worried about the situation, I assured her that I would talk to our warden, who happened to be our sports teacher as well. I knew that he would be able to help us with the official confirmation and also guide us in our preparation for the tournament.

She then asked me if I had proposed to Shreya. I hesitated and replied that I wasn't sure she would say yes. Mamita then encouraged me to go for it, saying that Shreya really likes me and often talks about me. She even mentioned that Shalini and Rachika have started speculating that we are dating. Mamita pointed out the way we look at each other and talk; it's obvious that there is something between us. Even Rachika's sister has noticed the connection between us. Feeling more confident, I promised Mamita that I would find the perfect time and way to propose to Shreya. After our conversation, I went back to my room with a newfound determination to make my feelings for Shreya known.

I went to attend class the next day, feeling nervous and anxious as I knew my physics teacher would be annoyed with my regular absence. As expected, he scolded me for missing classes and expressed his concern about my performance in the upcoming board exams. It suddenly hit me that I was in 12th grade and the boards were just a few months away. The thought of failing and having to repeat the class with younger students was humiliating. In a state of worry, I confided in my friend Ranjit during lunch. He advised me to focus on my upcoming tournament, which was just 4 days away, and then put all my efforts into studying after that. However, I knew that if I immersed myself in preparing for the tournament, I wouldn't have enough time and energy left to concentrate on my studies.

In the evening, I went to the badminton court, excited to play and practice for the upcoming tournament. I was pleasantly surprised to see our warden, sir, already there. I eagerly asked him when we would receive official confirmation that we would be participating in the tournament. He reached for his notebook and wrote down the names: Ashish for singles, Ashish with Rohan for men's doubles, and me with Mamita for mixed doubles. He assured me that he would get the signatures from Principal Ma'am and put up the names on the notice board by tomorrow. We then started practicing together until Mamita and Shreya joined us. After two continuous games, I was feeling tired and exhausted. Our warden, sir, noticed my fatigue and asked me to take some rest.

Mamita and Shreya started playing singles, and Warden Sir noticed the impressive skills of Shreya. Curious to know who Shreya was, he asked about her, and I informed him that she was a girl from 11th grade who had recently started playing with us. Warden sir then asked if both of them could form a female doubles team, to which I replied in the affirmative. He called out to them and asked Mamita if she could play with Shreya, but she declined as she was already playing mixed doubles with me. Shreya then spoke up, saying that she was not prepared for it and would participate in the next tournament instead. Sir wrote her name down in his notebook and said that he was registering her for the tournament and that she could play if she wanted to. He then asked Mamita and me to practice mixed doubles in the meantime. He promised to seek permission from Principal Ma'am for us to practice during prep time until the tournament was over.

I was thrilled by this news as it meant I could practice at night as well without worrying about missing my prep sessions. It was an exciting opportunity for all of us, and I couldn't wait to start practicing with Mamita.

After finishing dinner, I headed to the court for some practice. To my surprise, the lights were off, and the door was locked. I assumed that we would have to wait for permission to start practicing from the next day. Disappointed, I went to my prep class. However, my disappointment was short-lived as Warden Sir suddenly stormed into our class and started shouting at me. He reminded me that he had given me permission to practice, yet here I was, sitting with my friends. He sternly instructed me to report to the court in just 5 minutes.

I quickly rushed to my room, running and out of breath, and quickly grabbed my shoes and racket before heading to the court. As I arrived, I saw all my teammates already there, waiting for me. Mamita asked me where I had been and warned me that if I wasn't serious about practice, she would team up with Shreya for the female doubles. Shreya was also present, as our warden sir had gone to her class earlier to call her for practice. We began stretching when our warden sir informed us that the principal ma'am and her husband would be coming to watch our practice. However, I was in a bad mood due to the way Warden Sir had shouted at me earlier in the prep room.

I started playing with Mamita against Warden Sir and Shreya. Instead of relying on my favourite drop shot, I started playing aggressively and using powerful smashes. I even intentionally aimed my smashes at Warden Sir, which was a bold move. However, every time I hit him, I couldn't help but apologize. Mamita was taken aback by my new game style and asked why I wasn't playing my usual game.

I replied that I would switch back to my preferred style once Warden Sir is gone.

While playing our second game, I couldn't help but notice the staff from Principal Ma'am's office setting up chairs near our court. Suddenly, I saw Principal Ma'am and her husband walking towards us, both wearing sports shoes and carrying rackets. I was amazed and at the same time a little nervous, as I knew we would have to stop playing once our game was over. As expected, after our set was finished, Principal Ma'am approached us with a warm smile and praised our performance. She encouraged us to continue playing with full spirit in the upcoming tournament and to make our school proud.

Principal Ma'am and her husband started playing, although it was more like they were knocking rather than playing. We couldn't help but watch them for a while before we headed back to our hostel.

The next day, I made the impulsive decision to bunk all my classes and spend the entire day sleeping in my room. As evening approached, I headed towards the badminton court and noticed Shreya walking towards it alone. Curious, I asked her where Mamita was. To my shock, Shreya informed me that Mamita had fallen in the toilet and injured her leg, and she would not be able to join us for practice that day. My heart sank as Mamita was not only my best friend but also my partner in an upcoming badminton tournament that was only two days away. Shreya continued to explain that Mamita had been taken to the medical

inspection room and they would be taking her for an x-ray at a center in Mehrauli. My mind raced with worry and concern for Mamita's well-being. I knew I had to visit her as soon as I returned from the court, but Shreya informed me that she would be occupied with medical procedures for some time. I could only hope for the best and pray for Mamita's speedy recovery.

After a tiring game of badminton, we decided to visit the MI room to check on Mamita. The nurse informed us that she had not returned from her x-ray yet and would be back by 8:30. Frustrated, we stepped outside, and Shreya suggested going to the canteen, but I was not in the mood. I promised her that we would go after prep and even mentioned going to the MBA canteen as it was my favourite hangout spot. Shreya asked if we were allowed to go there, to which I replied that I wasn't sure, but we had never faced any trouble before. As we waited, I couldn't help but notice how much Shreya enjoyed spending time with me. I wondered if she had any romantic feelings for me, but she never showed any signs. She simply wanted to spend more time with me, which made me feel special and appreciated.

I returned to my hostel and made my way directly to Ranjit's room. As I entered, I saw him chatting with his roommates and Debashish. Without wasting any time, I shared the news about Mamita with them. They were all surprised and concerned for her well-being. They immediately suggested that we all go to the MI room to visit her after our prep time. Feeling a bit exhausted and sweaty from all the physical activities, I decided to take a quick shower before heading to Mamita's room. Knowing that my friends were equally worried about her, I felt grateful for their support and willingness to visit her with me.

Ranjit, Debashish, and I decided to go to the dining hall for dinner. As we were about to start eating, our other friends Shalini, Rachika, and Shreya joined us at our table. Shreya sat next to me and noticed that I was not eating and seemed worried. She asked me what was wrong, and I confided in her about my friend Mamita, who was going through a tough time. Shreya reassured me that Mamita would be fine and even served food on my plate. Everyone at the table smiled at her kind gesture. Shalini pointed out that Shreya had served me food, urging me to eat properly. Shreya blushed at the attention but continued to show her kindness and care towards me.

After our prep session, my friends Ranjit and Debashish and I decided to visit our friend Mamita in the MI room. As we walked in, we saw that our other friends Shalini, Rachika, Shreya, and a few other girls from the hostel were already there. I immediately got worried and asked if everything was okay. They reassured me that Mamita was fine and resting inside the room. We got permission from the nurse to go in and see her. As I entered the room, I saw Mamita lying on the bed. I asked her about the x-ray, and she told me that she had a hairline fracture in her ankle, and the doctors had advised her to take bed rest for a week. Despite being in pain, Mamita had a smile on her face, trying to make us feel better.

I went to the canteen and bought two bottles of juice. I placed the juice bottles on her side table where all her medicines were kept. She smiled at me and said, “I love you so much. No one cares for me as much as you do.” I replied, “Everyone cares for you.” But she shook her head and said, “You do a little extra to get noticed.” Just then, I saw Shreya, who didn’t seem happy with my gesture. Mamita told me she won’t be able to participate in the upcoming tournament now. She was feeling sorry for it, but I reassured her not to worry about the tournament and focus on taking care of herself. I promised to visit her every day and joked that I won’t bring any juice next time. We all smiled and realized the strong bond of friendship that we share. It’s not about grand gestures, but small acts of care and support that make our friendship special.

As we all gathered outside the MI room after meeting Mamita, I excitedly informed Shreya and me that we were heading to the canteen to discuss something important. My friends immediately understood that we wanted to spend some quality time together. As we reached the MBA canteen, the staff greeted me with warmth and asked where I had been. I replied that I had been caught up with other things and finally sat down with Shreya. She seemed a bit uneasy as most of the people there were MBA or BBA students who knew me personally. I reassured her to relax and feel at ease since this was the best place on campus. I promised her that she would start liking this place once she started coming here regularly. Without even having to place an order, the staff at the canteen brought us two steaming cups of coffee and cheerfully said, "Here is your favourite coffee." Confused, Shreya spoke up and said that we hadn't ordered anything yet. The staff member explained that this was the first thing "bhaiya" (brother) always ordered when he came here. I turned to Shreya and asked if she wanted anything else. She hesitantly declined, but I insisted she try the famous Yum Yum noodles. The canteen was bustling with noise and people, so we decided to go to the lawn behind it for a quieter and more peaceful setting.

Shreya suddenly remembered that she had forgotten something and needed to go back to her hostel. She promised to return in just 5 minutes. When she came back, she had a shopping bag with her and handed it to me with a grateful smile. She thanked me for everything I had done for her and for being such a special friend. As I opened the bag, I saw a stylish black shirt inside. Shreya said it would look great with my jeans, and I thanked her for the thoughtful gift. But she insisted that there was no need for thanks, as it was given out of love. Curious about where she got it, I asked her, and she replied that she had bought it from Palika Bazaar. Feeling a bit guilty for not having anything to give in return, I told her that all I could offer was my love. Shreya blushed and replied that it was the best gift I could give her.

As we continued our conversation over my favourite noodles, she brought up the fact that I wouldn't be able to participate in the upcoming tournament due to Mamita's injury. I confirmed her statement, admitting that I had been thinking about it. In a spur-of-the-moment decision, I asked her to be my partner in the mixed doubles event, replacing Mamita. She seemed hesitant at first and questioned if I was sure about it. I reassured her by reminding her of how well we had played together in the past. Despite her initial reluctance, she finally agreed to think about it and discuss it with Mamita. However, I urged her to make a decision quickly as the tournament was starting the next day, and our school needed to inform Manav Bharti School, who was organizing the event.

While saying goodbye to her, I couldn't resist the urge to tell her something important. However, with the tournament preparation, I decided to save it for later. As I mentioned this to her, I saw a spark in her eyes, and she declared that she wouldn't talk to me anymore if I didn't tell her now. Trying to calm the situation, I asked her to wait until the tournament was over. We walked towards her hostel and said our goodbyes. But even before I could leave, she pleaded with me to tell her what was on my mind. I couldn't help but smile at her persistence and promised to see her the next day at the court. Before entering her hostel, she whispered that I had the power to keep her awake all night just by not telling her. With a wave, I left for my hostel feeling grateful for our friendship.

The following day, while on my way to breakfast, the warden met me and told me that I didn't have to go to class that day. He said that after breakfast, all the participants had to go to the chairman's office for a meeting. I informed him about Mamita's injury, and he already knew about it. He then asked me to pair up with Shreya for the mixed doubles event. I told him that Shreya was hesitant about it. But he insisted and said that we would talk to her right away. We went to the girls' hostel and asked the female guard to call Shreya. In no time, Shreya arrived looking scared upon seeing me with Sir. He then explained to her that since Mamita was injured, she had no choice but to pair up with me. Shreya was wearing her school uniform, so Sir informed her that there was no class for us that day, and we had to go straight to the chairman's office after breakfast. He asked her to finish her breakfast quickly and report to the chairman's office.

As we walked towards the dining hall for breakfast, Shreya expressed her fear about participating in the upcoming sports tournament. I reassured her and told her to simply enjoy the game. After breakfast, we headed towards the chairman's office, where we saw a large group of students from various teams, such as cricket, football, basketball, swimming, badminton, and other athletic teams. The chairman was busy meeting with each team separately to discuss their strategies and preparations for the tournament. Seeing the determination and passion on the faces of these young athletes, I felt a sense of excitement and energy in the air. Shreya and I joined the crowd and eagerly waited for our turn to meet with the chairman. It was truly inspiring to see so many students coming together for their love of sports, and I couldn't help but feel proud to be a part of such a competitive and enthusiastic community.

When the badminton team was announced, we all eagerly went inside the school hall. Principal Ma'am and Warden sir were already seated inside as we took our seats on the chairs provided for students. Each of us was asked to introduce ourselves and mention the section we were representing in the upcoming badminton tournament. As a gesture of hospitality, we were offered tea and biscuits. The chairman shared with us that our school had been participating in badminton tournaments every year, but we had not been able to secure any medals in the past few years. A palpable silence fell over the room as we all listened intently. Warden sir then spoke up and said that we did not have to go to our classes that day, but instead, we had to change into our badminton attire and head to practice. He reminded us that during prep, we needed to rest and sleep early in preparation for the tournament. As we walked out of the meeting, Ashish, who was representing the school in singles and men's doubles, told me that he was afraid of not winning. I reassured him that it was more important to play for fun rather than just for winning.

After changing into our uniforms, we made our way back to the court for our first game. Shreya, who was new to the school and participating for the first time, seemed nervous. I could see it in her hesitant movements and the way she fidgeted with her racket. I didn't say anything to her at that moment, knowing that she needed some time to adjust. As we started playing, I could tell that Shreya was still unsure of herself. So, I decided to give her some suggestions and tips while we played. I reminded her to cover the net and to be prepared for any drop shots from the opposing team. She mentioned that she was scared of their powerful smash shots, but I reassured her and told her to just stay focused and try her best to return the shuttle back to the female player on the other team. I also suggested aiming for the third court, and if it's too close to the net, sending it back to a safe spot if needed. Leave the rest of the court for me to cover.

She said that I would get tired easily if I tried to cover the entire court because I smoke a lot. I reassured her that we would follow this arrangement, and if there were any problems, we could decide while playing the match. However, she then suggested that we divide the court into two sections and each of us would cover our own section. Warden sir, who was busy attending to all the sports activities, came to our court and instructed us to play five sets instead of three to improve our stamina. By lunchtime, we were both exhausted and dead tired from playing.

We were asked to come back at 5 PM for the last practice before the big competition. After a satisfying lunch, I went back to my room and set an alarm for 4:45 PM to ensure I wouldn't miss the practice. I woke up to the sound of the alarm and quickly washed my face before heading towards the badminton court. However, I noticed that Shreya was not there yet. After a few minutes, she arrived and told me she was feeling very tired. I advised her to rest and let the others continue practicing while we played just two games at the end. After the practice, we went back to our hostel and decided to meet after dinner to go and visit our friend Mamita in the medical room. Shreya expressed her fear of representing our school in the upcoming competition, but I reassured her that there was no reason to panic and encouraged her to stay calm and focused.

After dinner, we headed to the MI room where we found Mamita waiting for us since morning. As we entered, Mamita greeted us with a big smile and said that she had been waiting for us since morning. I couldn't help but feel guilty for keeping her waiting for so long. I shared the news that Shreya's name had been put in the mixed doubles by the warden, which made her panic unnecessarily. Mamita reassured her that it was just a game and advised her to play with confidence and her natural skills. Feeling exhausted, I excused myself and mentioned that I wanted to catch up on some sleep. Shreya walked me to the gate and mentioned that since there were no preparations for us, she would stay back and spend some time with Mamita.

The next day, as I was still dozing off in my room, the warden sir came knocking on my door and woke me up. He instructed me to take a quick shower, have breakfast, and report to his office at 9:30 AM with my bag packed and ready. He reminded me that the bus would leave for Manav Bharti School at 10 AM sharp. I quickly packed my bag with essentials like two extra t-shirts, trousers, jeans, a black shirt, and deodorant. After a refreshing shower, I headed to the dining hall for breakfast, where I saw Shreya and asked her if she could keep some extra t-shirts in her bag. She readily agreed and told me that she had already packed her bag with extra t-shirts. I requested her to meet Mamita before coming to the North Block hostel near the warden's office at 9:30 AM. Shreya promised to meet Mamita and join me on time.

I returned to my room feeling excited. As I entered, my roommates Ranjit and Debashish were waiting for me and wished me good luck for the upcoming match. I quickly changed into my sports attire and grabbed my bag and kit bag before heading to the warden's office. I made sure to pack an extra racket in case of any emergency. As I reached the warden's office, I noticed a few other players from different sports also waiting for their turn. I was standing when Shreya arrived with her own bag and racket. I offered to carry her racket and placed it in my kit bag. The excitement and anticipation for the match were palpable among all of us.

The school bus arrived, and we excitedly boarded it. Shreya and I sat together, and she held my hand tightly throughout the journey to Manav Bhart School out of nervousness. Upon arriving at the school, we were amazed to see more than fifty schools participating in various sports. The field was set up with tents for each school to keep their bags and belongings. Our warden, sir, instructed all the badminton players to grab their rackets and follow him to the badminton court. I could feel the anticipation and nervousness building up as we made our way to the court, ready to represent our school in the upcoming badminton tournament.

When we reached the badminton court, our excitement was palpable as we saw our names on the list for the first game. Shreya and I did some stretching and knocking to warm up before the match. Luckily, Shreya seemed to have gained some confidence and was more focused on the game. As we began playing, I couldn't help but notice the lack of coordination among our opponents. I quickly pointed out their weak spot to Shreya and advised her to return the shuttle between two players. This tactic worked like a charm, and we comfortably won our first game with a score of 9-21. It was a great start to the tournament, and we were both thrilled with our victory. This win also boosted our confidence for the remaining matches.

We have secured our spot in the second round, which was set to take place just an hour after the first. Shreya was beaming with happiness, and her confidence was radiating. As we were resting, Warden Sir came to us and praised our efforts, encouraging us to continue playing like this. He even brought us bananas to boost our energy levels. However, our school lost the men's mixed doubles match. But we didn't let this dampen our spirits as we headed into the second game with determination. With a score of 17-21, we emerged victorious and secured our spot in the finals. It was ecstatic, and we couldn't wait to give it our all in the upcoming match.

Ashish was representing our school in the men's singles category. Unfortunately, he lost his second game, but it was still a proud moment for us. With only 30 minutes of rest before the finals, we were feeling exhausted and nervous. However, our warden, sir, surprised us by bringing two bottles of water and encouraging us to stay hydrated and focused. He then informed us that our school had won a gold medal in the 100 meters race and a bronze in the relay event. He expressed his confidence in us winning gold in the badminton mixed doubles as well.

Unfortunately, we lost the second match in set of three. With 5 minutes of rest before the final match, Warden Sir gave us water once again. Ashish gave us some valuable advice to start playing our drop shots as the opposing team would have a hard time picking them up as they were also tired. Shreya looked at me with hope in her eyes, and I reassured her that we would give our best. I decided to start playing long shots to the third court, knowing that the other team would try to end the rally quickly with a smash. As expected, they started making mistakes, and we were leading with a good margin. But as the game progressed, I started to slow down due to a lack of energy. The opposite team took advantage and equalized the score to 14 each. That's when I told Shreya that we should switch to playing drop shots as they wouldn't be expecting it. We took the lead once again, and they started panicking and making more mistakes. It was exhilarating to see them struggle with my drop shots. Just one point away from winning, I was almost out of breath. Shreya suggested we stop the game as she was afraid, I might collapse, but Ashish motivated us by shouting that it was just a matter of one point and we were almost there. The referee asked us to continue the game after taking a break for me to drink water. Shreya was worried for me, but I couldn't give up now. I asked her to take charge for two points while I rested behind her. Unfortunately, Shreya made a mistake with her serve, and we lost a point, giving the other team a chance to serve. However, they made an easy shot towards Shreya at the net, and for the first time ever, she hit a powerful smash that won us the match. We were ecstatic and hugged each other tightly.

I was panting and struggling for breath, and my friends noticed my exhaustion. They immediately rushed me to a nearby tent, where they handed me a bottle of water, and Shreya gently washed my face with cool water. I was so out of breath that I couldn't even speak a word to thank her. After a few minutes of rest, I started feeling better, and my breaths became less laboured. About an hour later, we were informed by our warden that there was a lunch organized by Manav Bharti for all the participants. As we were getting ready to leave, the warden came up to me, hugged me, and blessed me with a pat on my back. He then instructed us to finish our lunch and collect our medals as our names were announced. After eating our lunch with excitement and pride rushing through our veins, we made our way towards the stage to receive our medals. Students from our school cheered for us, including our warden, who was also shouting at the top of his voice. It was truly a moment of triumph and pride for all of us.

After receiving our medal, Shreya and I decided to sit in the tent for a while to relax and celebrate our victory. I wanted to change my clothes, so I asked Shreya to wait for me, and I took my bag with me. In the washroom, I quickly changed into the jeans and black shirt that Shreya had given me and sprayed some deodorant on myself. As I was heading back, I came across a student and asked him if there was a canteen in the school, as I wanted to buy some chocolate. He kindly offered to show me the way, and we walked together to the canteen. I bought a Dairy Milk chocolate bar and, on my way back, I couldn't resist plucking a beautiful rose from the school's garden. I had been planning to propose to Shreya for a long time, and this seemed like the perfect moment. With the rose in hand, I walked back to the tent, ready to ask Shreya to be mine forever.

Shreya's face lit up with joy as she saw me entering the tent wearing the black shirt she had given me. We were both alone in the tent, as everyone else was busy exploring the school or watching some game. I could see the excitement in Shreya's eyes as she saw me wearing her gifted shirt. I pulled out a Dairy Milk chocolate bar from my bag and handed it to her. Her eyes sparkled with excitement as she exclaimed, "You have to give us a treat for our victory!" We both laughed, and she suggested that we share the chocolate bar together. As she carefully opened the wrapper of the chocolate, I nervously handed her a rose and professed my love for her. I explained that I had been in love with her since the first time I saw her and that I wanted to be with her always. But as tears started streaming down her face, I couldn't help but feel scared that I might have said something wrong. Quickly apologizing for any unpleasantness, I reassured her that I didn't want to lose her as a friend. However, to my surprise, she punched me and told me that she had been aware of my feelings all along. In fact, she had been waiting for me to express them. With a beaming smile, she confessed that she loved me. In that moment, as I saw how elated she was, I knew that my love for her was reciprocated and that we were meant to be together.

Our bus started around 5 PM, and we reached school around 6 PM. I was very excited as we had just won medals and won Shreya's heart. As soon as we reached the school, we went directly to Principal Ma'am's office to inform her about our victory. She was overjoyed and congratulated us all. From there, we went to the MI room to inform Mamita. She was very happy and gave us a big hug. I then told her that there was one more piece of news—I had proposed to Shreya, and she had said yes! Mamita hugged Shreya once again and told her to take care of me and that she could now call me by my name. We were all thrilled and couldn't stop smiling. After that, I went back to my room in the hostel, where news of our win had already spread. As soon as I entered my room, my roommates, Ranjit and Debashish, started shouting and screaming with excitement. They couldn't believe that we had won medals for the school. They also asked me for a party, but I told them that I would throw one after I received some money from my parents. It was a day filled with joy, success, and love, and I couldn't be happier.

In my life, everything seemed to be falling into place except for one crucial aspect—my studies. I had been neglecting my academic responsibilities, and as a result, I was struggling to keep up with my classmates. However, as the board exams were approaching, I realized the gravity of my situation and became determined to turn things around. I knew that I had wasted a lot of time, and now I had to make up for it by studying hard. Physics and chemistry were my weakest subjects, and passing them seemed like an impossible task. Therefore, I decided to seek help from my subject teachers to fully understand the concepts and improve my grades. I knew that difficult and hectic days were ahead of me, but I was willing to make the necessary sacrifices to succeed in my exams.

CHAPTER 8

FROM SCIENCE TO HUMANITIES: NAVIGATING THE SHIFT AND CONQUERING BOARDS

Ever since the badminton tournament and my new relationship with Shreya, my life has been completely transformed. People have started to recognize me, and I have been busy maintaining relationships with my friends and Shreya. Time seemed to fly by as I attended classes, except for Physics, which I was so scared of that I avoided attending those classes altogether. I managed to keep up with my other subjects, but deep down, I was always afraid of the looming board exams that were just a few months away. My friends Ranjit and Debashish were in the same boat as me, struggling with the same fears. However, Debashish had a sharper mind and was more regular in class and in studying, while Ranjit and I were completely hopeless. The pressure of the upcoming exams weighed heavily on our minds.

My other friends, Shalini and Rachika, were both from the commerce stream and were very studious. They always maintained a steady pace in their studies right from the beginning. On the other hand, Mamita belonged to the humanities stream and had a very relaxed attitude towards her studies. I remember asking her if she felt stressed about the upcoming exams, to which she confidently replied that she studies for two hours daily and that was enough for her. She also mentioned that she would go full throttle from December onwards. Shreya, my love angel, was a junior and didn't have to worry about the board exams this time. Looking at my friends, it seemed like everyone had their life sorted out. However, I couldn't help but feel a sense of hopelessness as I was struggling to keep up with my studies.

I made a conscious decision to work hard and put in extra effort in my studies. As the half-yearly exams approached, I was determined to do my best and not rely on leaked papers to pass. I wanted to truly understand my academic standing and work towards improving it. I spent hours studying and preparing for the exams, even sacrificing hanging out with my friends. I only met Shreya at the dining hall and rarely visited the canteen. When the internal exam results were announced, I was disappointed to see that I had performed poorly in Physics and Chemistry. However, my hard work paid off in other subjects as I scored good marks. Despite knowing that I would fail in Physics, the surprise of failing in Chemistry was a wake-up call for me. It made me realize that I needed to put in more effort and seek help in subjects that were challenging for me.

I couldn't shake off the worry that the school would send my results by speed post to my parents. I had not performed well in the exams, and I knew my parents would be disappointed. Desperate for a solution, I turned to my friend Ranjit and expressed my concerns to him. To my surprise, he was facing the same dilemma, as he too had not fared well in the exams. Together, we decided to seek help from Rohit bhaiya. He listened to our worries and assured us that he would help us this time, but only on the condition that we take our studies seriously from then on. He handed us a packet envelope containing our results, meant to be sent to our parents. However, he asked us to burn it and keep it a secret. Following his advice, we went to Tau's canteen, ordered tea and cigarettes, and burned the envelope there, leaving no trace of it. We returned feeling relieved but still anxious about our upcoming board exam results. Despite the temporary comfort, we both knew that we needed to start studying diligently if we wanted to do well in our boards.

I decided to discuss my results with Shreya. As I shared my disappointment and fears with her, she remained optimistic and showed unwavering support. She assured me that I still had time to turn things around and that if I put in all my effort, I could pass the exam. Shreya then questioned my decision to pursue science, mentioning that I could have taken admission in humanities instead. She reminded me that there are countless career options available for humanities students as well. In response, I explained that my parents had a specific plan for me—to pass the exam and study medicine in Russia. However, I confessed that I had no interest in medicine and did not want to endure five years of painful studies. Shreya empathized with me but reminded me that now my only option was to study and pass the board exams. As for medical studies, she advised me to discuss it with my parents after completing my board exams.

During prep, staff from Principal Ma'am's office came and asked me, Ranjit, and a few other students to come and meet with Principal Ma'am in her office. I knew immediately that we were being called because of our poor academic performance. As we entered her office, we saw ma'am working on some files. She asked us to take a seat and wait for a few minutes. After taking off her glasses, she started talking to us. Ma'am expressed her disappointment with our results and mentioned that she knew me personally since the day I brought a medal to school. She further explained that she was worried about our upcoming board exams and how our poor performance could reflect badly on the school. It was clear that ma'am cared about our academic success and wanted us to do well not only for ourselves but also for the reputation of the school. She further emphasized that school is there to support and guide us through our academic journey. Her words were reassuring and gave me hope that I would receive the necessary help to excel in my studies. She promised to ask the teachers to give us more attention, which made me feel relieved as I struggled with certain subjects. However, at the same time, I couldn't help but worry that the physics teacher might start giving me more attention, which would make my life miserable as he was known for ragging students in front of the whole class. To my surprise, she informed us that she had organized a special class for us during prep time. She reminded us that it's never too late to regret and make positive changes in our academic performance. From tomorrow onwards, the extra class will commence, and she will personally monitor our progress. Every week there would be a test. She emphasized the importance of dedicating our time and efforts to studying in order to achieve good marks. After her motivational speech, she dismissed the rest of the students but asked me, Ranjit, and Kamal to stay back. As she looked at me, she said, "I know you, Asif. Where are you lagging?" I was at a loss for words, but with a sense of fear, I managed to speak up and confess that I struggle with science. It's a subject that I have no interest in and fail to understand. She then said that I should have taken admission in the humanities stream and focused on performing well in extracurricular activities to groom myself into a decent young man. She advised us to start taking special classes, and if there was no improvement, we would have to meet again after 15 days to discuss further options. After the conversation, we returned to our prep class. Ranjit expressed his frustration, saying that everything was becoming difficult to manage. He regretted not being serious about our studies from the beginning. We started studying, and even after our prep class, I went to my room to continue studying.

I went to attend my class with a sense of unease. As soon as I entered the classroom, I noticed that all the teachers were paying close attention to us. Despite their efforts, I couldn't shake off the feeling of discomfort that had settled over me. The physics class was particularly challenging, and no matter how hard I tried, I couldn't seem to grasp the concepts being taught. As the class came to an end, I had to accept the harsh reality that no matter how hard I tried, I would not be able to catch up with the syllabus in time.

After the bell rang, signalling the end of the physics class, I couldn't help but feel overwhelmed and defeated. No matter how much effort I put into studying, I knew I wouldn't be able to catch up with the syllabus in time. Feeling troubled, I turned to my friend Ranjit for advice. He shared that he was considering quitting school and returning home to Ranchi. My heart sank at the thought of losing him as a friend and a support system in the hostel. I encouraged him not to make any impulsive decisions and suggested we start taking special classes together to see if we could improve our understanding of the subject. I promised him to put all our effort into studying hard if there was still a chance for us to pass.

During dinner, I met Shreya at the dining hall and shared with her the news about a special class that our school is offering to help us prepare for our upcoming exams. Shreya was happy to hear about this extra support and expressed her gratitude towards the school for always looking out for students. I also mentioned to her that if my class ended on time, I would love to join her in visiting Mamita at the MI room to check on her health. Before heading back to my room, I made sure to chat with my other friends Shalini and Rachika about their exam preparations. They both assured me that they would start studying seriously from next month. As soon as I got back to my room, I grabbed my physics book and notebook and went to the special class. When I reached the classroom, I saw that sir had already started taking the class. He noticed me coming in late and got visibly angry. He scolded me, saying that I am completely spoiled and not taking my studies seriously. He mentioned that he was putting in extra effort to help us all pass, but we were still not taking it seriously. There were 10-12 students, including Ranjit. I walked towards my seat next to Ranjit, but Sir asked me to sit in the first row, closer to him. He announced that he would start from the first chapter and complete it in just two days due to the shortage of time. However, as he began teaching the basics, I found myself struggling to understand as there were several concepts from the 11th grade that I was not familiar with. Despite his best efforts, the teacher's explanations were in vain, and I was left feeling depressed. He assured us that a test on the chapter would be taken the day after tomorrow. As the class progressed, it became apparent that the teacher had exceeded his allotted time, but he continued teaching diligently. Before dismissing us, he gave us a few questions to solve and asked us to show him our solutions the next day.

I was supposed to meet Shreya but ended up running late. I rushed to my room, and without wasting any time, I dived into solving them. Though I struggled with the numerical problems, I managed to understand and memorize the theory portion. Despite feeling tired, I pushed through and studied till late at night. Finally, I decided it was time to get some rest and went to sleep.

The next day, after a sleepless night due to an assignment, I went to breakfast and was greeted by my friends, including Shreya. As soon as Shreya saw me, she noticed the redness in my eyes and asked what happened. I explained to her that I had been up all night trying to finish my assignment. She expressed her concern and asked how I would manage such a routine for the next few months until our board exams. I replied, saying that I had no other option and had to push through. She wished she could be of any help to me. Shreya then informed me that Mamita, who had been in the medical room, would be getting discharged today, and we could meet her at dinner in the dining hall. I was relieved to hear this news as I had been worried about her well-being.

As I walked to class, my heart was pounding with fear and embarrassment. I was scared of facing my teachers' questions, knowing that I wouldn't be able to answer them. It felt like too much pressure to handle, and I started questioning my decision to unroll in this school. However, thoughts of Shreya came to my mind, and I realized that it was a good choice to come here, but maybe I had chosen the wrong stream. Even at lunch, I couldn't bring myself to eat as I was consumed by my worries. But Shreya's loving words and cheerful presence lifted my mood. She reminded me how lucky she was to have me, and in front of everyone, she came close to me and said those three magical words: "I love you.". Her comforting words gave me hope that everything will eventually work out, and I shouldn't be too upset about my current situation. Shreya's unwavering support made me feel grateful and blessed to have her in my life.

After lunch, I went back to the academic block to attend my class. As I walked towards the classroom, my chemistry teacher called out to me and informed me about a special class that he would be taking at 4:30 PM and asked me to inform other students who were also required to attend. After lunch, we had an English lecture. However, my mind was preoccupied with thoughts about how difficult and overwhelming my academic life had become. The constant pressure to perform and excel had taken a toll on me, and I found myself wondering how long I could handle it. I went to my room to take a rest.

After waking up, I needed a cigarette to feel good. I had hidden the packet on top of the almirah, and I climbed on the bed to reach for it. However, I forgot that the ceiling in my room was quite low, and as soon as I stood up, I was hit by the moving fan. The impact was so strong that blood immediately started gushing from my head, covering my face. In a panic, I saw the blood splattered on the walls and realized that I needed medical attention. Since there was no one else in the room, I quickly went to the next room where Manish was sitting with his friends. He immediately asked me what happened, thinking I might have been in a fight. I quickly reassured him that it was just an accident caused by the fan. With the help of Manish and a few other students, I was able to make my way to the MI room for treatment.

As I stumbled into the MI room with a deep gash on my head, the doctor immediately sprang into action. He took me inside and carefully inspected my wound, noting that the bleeding had not stopped. He quickly called for a nurse, instructing her to bring a needle as he needed to stitch up the wound. After cutting away my hair and expertly stitching up the wound, he bound it with dressing. The whole process took more than thirty minutes, and the doctor informed me that I would have to stay in the MI room for two days as I had lost a considerable amount of blood. As I was settling into a bed next to other patients, I asked if there was a possibility for a private room, but the doctor simply smiled and said that this was a school and they did not have such arrangements. Many students from my hostel came to visit me, bringing me comfort and support.

As I sat alone in my room, nursing my injury, I couldn't help but wonder why my friends Ranjit and Debashish hadn't shown up yet. Just as the thought crossed my mind, they burst into the room, panting and out of breath, explaining that they had been at Tau's canteen and someone had informed them of my injury. They scolded me for being careless and sat with me, trying to change the topic and act normal. I assured them that I was fine and urged them to go have dinner. However, they refused, stating that they were not hungry. Ranjit even went to the nurse to inquire about my dinner time and was told it would be served after some time. The nurse then asked them to leave so I could rest. As they were leaving, Debashish asked why our other friends, like Shreya, were not here. I explained that they might not be aware of my injury.

The MI room was conveniently located next to the girls' hostel, with one door opening directly into the corridor of the hostel. As I was lying on the bed, I could hear the familiar voices of Shreya and Mamita talking to the nurse. Their footsteps grew louder as they approached my room, and when they entered, I saw that they were both crying. Despite their tears, I couldn't help but smile at the sight of them. They looked at me with pity in their eyes as Mamita informed me that I had lost a lot of blood and had seventeen stitches. Mamita stood near my bed and asked Shreya to sit down on the bed, but she remained silent and continued to cry. Despite her sadness, I couldn't help but think how cute she looked while crying.

Mamita's words hit me like a bolt of lightning: "Stop living a carefree life," she said. I was taken aback by her stern tone but soon realized the truth behind her words. I had been injured, and it was causing pain to my friends. I couldn't believe it; how could I have been so careless? I had been living in this room for almost a year and had never once gotten injured. I used to be attentive about taking care of the ceiling fan, but I guess with my mind occupied elsewhere, I didn't notice that it was switched on. Mamita's words made me realize the gravity of the situation. She reminded me that I had friends and family back home who were worried about me, especially Shreya. She shared how Shreya had started crying in the dining hall upon hearing about my injury while they were waiting for us to start dinner. It was then that Shreya and I left our dinner and came to see me.

Shalini and Rachika also joined us in the MI room on hearing about my injury. Shalini explained that she was talking to her mother at a public telephone booth when Rachika came and told her about my accident. She also mentioned that her mother was concerned and would inform my family about it. Worried about my family's reaction, I requested Shalini call her mother and ask her not to convey the news. The nurse attending to the patient on the adjacent bed then informed us that it was their school's policy to inform parents in case of any injury. The nurse politely asked them to leave as I needed rest. Shreya, who had been quiet the entire time, looked at me with tears in her eyes. She asked the nurse for five more minutes.

Everyone bids their goodbyes and promised to return after prep. However, Shreya stayed back for five more minutes, expressing her sadness and concern for me. She took my hand and reassured me, urging me to keep my mind free from worry and stress as it could possibly lead to another injury. Just then, the nurse brought in my dinner, and Shreya eagerly took the plate, feeding me with her own hands. It was a heartwarming gesture that made me feel so good in that moment. After I finished my meal, Shreya apologized for potentially missing prep and attendance and having to explain her absence. With tears in her eyes, she left the medical room with a promise to return after prep. The nurse then administered my medicine and advised me to rest.

I was lying on my bed, feeling miserable, when I heard a knock on my door. Principal Ma'am, along with Warden Sir, came to visit me. I was surprised to see them, and one of the staff members came in carrying a glass of freshly squeezed juice for me. Principal Ma'am expressed her concern about me and assured me that this was the first time anything like this had happened in the school. She promised to look into the issue of the ceiling and relocate the fan to a safer place. I tried my best to act normal and not show my discomfort. Principal Ma'am told me to take a rest and not worry about anything. She also assured me that if I needed anything, all I had to do was let her know. She said that all the students were like her own children and that she loved and cared for them deeply.

After ma'am left, the attending nurse came to me and said that I was very famous. She explained that so many people had come to visit me in the MI room. She replied that even Principal Ma'am, who rarely visits the MI room, had come with the warden sir just to meet me. I couldn't believe it and felt overwhelmed with gratitude. I told the nurse that I love them all, and they have shown their love by taking the time out of their busy schedules to come and visit me.

As I was having a conversation with the nurse, Mamita, Shalini, Rachika, and Shreya returned from their prep. Rachika said that tomorrow, I would be getting some fruits as she had requested the canteen manager to bring them. However, I reassured her that it was not necessary. The painkiller medication I had taken earlier was wearing off, and I was starting to feel uncomfortable and agitated with my bandage. I couldn't even smile or talk properly. Seeing me in pain, Mamita couldn't hold back her tears, causing a chain reaction among the others. We all ended up in a group hug, and seeing how much they cared for me made me emotional, and I couldn't hold back my tears either. Just then, Debashish arrived with tea in a Melton jug and informed me that Ranjit couldn't make it due to a special class. Before leaving, Shreya promised to visit me the next morning and bring me some tea when she wakes up.

The next morning, Shreya arrived with hot tea, biscuits, and a towel. She kindly offered to clean my face with the wet towel as I was still recovering from the stitches on my head. I insisted that I could do it myself, but she reassured me that it was better for me to rest and not exert myself. She jokingly mentioned that there was no need for me to show my manliness in this situation. After I finished my tea, she left for her class, leaving me feeling grateful for her care and thoughtfulness. Her small gestures of kindness made me realize how lucky I was to have her. Despite the pain and discomfort from the stitches, I felt comforted and cared for by Shreya's presence.

Around 10 am, the doctor arrived to see me. He noticed there was swelling on my head and informed me that if it didn't reduce by evening, I would have to go for an x-ray. I reassured him that I was feeling better. Later in the evening, my friends came to visit me, and I informed them about the possibility of needing an x-ray. Shalini and Rachika offered to talk to the doctor on my behalf, and they left to meet him. Meanwhile, Mamita took the fruits that Rachika had brought and went to her hostel to wash them. I could feel myself getting better, and Shreya even commented that I looked better today. I agreed with her and mentioned that I needed to recover quickly as I was missing a special class. However, Shreya assured me not to worry about it and that my health was more important.

Shalini and Rachika came back with the doctor. The nurse removed the bandage from my wound, and the doctor carefully inspected it. To my relief, he said that it looked fine, and he would check on it again tomorrow morning. He also mentioned that if everything continued to progress well, I would be discharged soon. Just then, Mamita entered the room with a plate of fruits and insisted that I eat them. After eating an apple, I thanked them for their care and told them that I was feeling sleepy. I requested they come back later when they were free, and they all left the room. I closed my eyes and drifted into a peaceful sleep, grateful for the care and support of my loved ones.

The next morning, the doctor arrived and examined me thoroughly before signing my discharge form. However, he reminded me to take care of myself and get enough rest in my room. He also advised me to visit the hospital each day for dressing and changing the bandage to ensure proper healing. The nurse, on the other hand, handed me my prescribed medicines and advised me not to get my hair wet while taking a shower.

Returning to my room, I couldn't shake off the feeling that things wouldn't be the same with Shreya as they used to be before. During my stay at the MI room, she had taken care of me and spoiled me with her kindness and attention. As I entered my room, my roommates were excited to see me back at the hostel. I expressed my gratitude for their visits to the MI room multiple times. Sachin then suggested that I change out of the dress I wore in the MI room and join them for lunch in the dining hall. After changing my dress, I joined my roommates and walked with them to the dining hall. As soon as my friends saw me, their faces lit up with happiness. I went to our usual table and sat down with them. Shreya seemed to be glowing with joy. I met Ranjit after two days as he was busy with special classes. He told me that our physics teacher was asking about me and wanted to know when I would join the class. I assured him that I would be joining after two days, and before that, I needed to meet the principal. However,

I kept my true thoughts to myself. After lunch, my friends left for the academic block, and I made my way to the principal's office. Before leaving, I asked Mamita and Shreya to meet me at the MBA canteen at 4:30 PM, as I had something important to discuss with them.

When I arrived at ma'am's office, I was informed that Principal Ma'am was not there. Instead, her secretary asked me to wait and assured me that she would be back any moment as she had gone home to have lunch. Principal Ma'am soon arrived and saw me sitting on the sofa. She greeted me with a warm smile and asked how I was doing and when I had been discharged from the MI room. I replied that I was fine and wanted to discuss something important with her. Without hesitation, she invited me to her chamber. As we walked together, I couldn't help but notice how graceful and poised she was. I must confess, she was the finest and most graceful lady I had ever seen.

I was feeling lost and desperate, so I followed her to her chamber. She turned to me and asked, "Tell me, what do you want to discuss?" Taking a deep breath, I mustered up the courage to voice my concerns. "I need help and guidance, but I'm scared to say," I admitted. With a reassuring smile, she replied, "Tell me; I am here to help you." Hesitantly, I admitted that I was struggling with preparing for my upcoming board exams. "I don't have enough time now, and even the special classes won't be enough since it's already too late," I confessed with regret. I thought about leaving school and taking admission in a small school in the humanities stream. "I have four months left, and I'm sure I will pass in humanities," I added. To my surprise, she confirmed that I would indeed pass in humanities. However, I pointed out that if I appeared for the science stream, I would fail in physics and possibly even chemistry. When she asked how my parents would react to my decision, I replied that I would talk to them about it.

She then suggested that we think about it, and we will meet again during prep time. She promised to call all the humanities teachers, and together we could come up with a solution. I felt a weight lift off my shoulders knowing that I had someone willing to help me through this challenging time.

I went back to my room and anxiously waited for 4:30, the designated time to meet with Mamita and Shreya. I needed to discuss what was going on in my mind and seek their guidance. However, before I could head out, Ranjit came into the room and questioned my continuous avoidance of classes. I replied that I would make a decision today on when I would rejoin them. As soon as it was 4:15, I left my hostel and made my way to the MBA canteen where we had planned to meet. But upon reaching, I realized they were not there. As I sat there alone, my mind was filled with thoughts about my future and the important decision I needed to make. I ordered a cup of tea for myself and eagerly waited for Mamita and Shreya to join me. Finally, they arrived and apologized for being late, explaining that Shreya had taken a shower before coming. Shreya apologized with a smile and held her ears in a gesture of apology. I then ordered tea for them, and we went to the garden as there were no chairs available. I asked Mamita, who was studying humanities, how her preparations for the exam were going, and she shared that she had not started studying for her board exams seriously. Curious, I asked her about the difficulty level of the subjects. She replied that it was not difficult if one could memorize the content. I then asked her if it was possible to cover all the subjects in just four months. Suddenly, Mamita's facial expression changed, and she asked if I was considering shifting to humanities. I shared with them that I was indeed thinking about it seriously. Shreya was surprised and asked if I was serious about it. I confirmed, and she questioned what about my parents' plans for me to study medicine in Russia. I assured them that I would talk to my parents about my decision. I said after completing my 12th grade, I will join the prestigious Delhi University, and after graduation, I will pursue my higher studies in law or an MBA. She reassured me that with dedication and hard work, I could score well in the exams. I also told her that I have a good memory, to which she encouraged me to go for it. Mamita even offered to help me with her notes. I also mentioned to her that I need to meet the principal and teachers of the humanities department during prep time. If they are convinced, the principal may allow me to shift from science to humanities, and the teachers will also assist me. Both Shreya and Mamita advised me to stick to humanities as it aligns with my interests and strengths. Mamita suggested that if I study for 5 hours a day, I can cover the syllabus by February and still have a few weeks for revision before the exams.

After finishing our tea, I suggested that we go for a walk, and we ended up at the horse-riding area. As I wanted to show Shreya my horse, we walked towards the stable. However, she got scared upon entering, and I was also a bit hesitant in touching and patting my horse. Shreya then suggested that once my wound is healed and stitches are removed, I should show her how to ride. This excited Mamita too, and she said she would also join us on that day. Horse riding has brought Mamita and me closer together, and she even mentioned that we became friends because of this activity.

As we were making our way back, we passed by the North Block hostel. While crossing the basketball court, I spotted Ranjit and Debashish sitting there. However, no girls were allowed to enter as it was a boys' hostel. I asked them to wait for me, and I went there to bring them with me. Ranjit then jokingly commented on how I was not attending the special classes but instead roaming around. I told him that I had some news to share, which I would tell them later that night. Together, we all headed to the dining hall to have dinner and catch up on each other's lives. It was a delightful evening spent with my friends.

After finishing my dinner, I went to my room feeling a mix of excitement and nervousness. The preparation for my desired switch to the humanities field had officially begun as I made my way to the principal's office. As I entered, I saw ma'am and other teachers waiting for me. I was asked to take a seat, and ma'am wasted no time in getting straight to the point. She asked if I had made up my mind about switching to humanities, to which I confidently replied with a 'yes, ma'am.'. Ma'am then turned to the teachers and asked for their opinions on how they could help me in this transition. They mentioned that I would have to put in a lot of hard work and memorization to pass, but they assured me that with dedication, I could achieve a first division. Ma'am then gave me a paper and asked me to write an application requesting to switch to humanities. She also mentioned that she would be sending a copy to my parents. She called in the administrative staff to make the necessary changes to my details. Upon hearing ma'am's words, I was both anxious and excited to start attending humanities classes from tomorrow onwards. The teacher provided me with a list of subjects that I would be studying, including English, history, political science, psychology, sociology, and physical education. I was relieved to find out that English and physical education were already familiar subjects to me. The teachers assured me that they would provide notes and books for the subjects. I felt a sense of relief when she said I didn't have to buy all the books. She also advised me to rest and prepare well for the upcoming board exams. As I stepped out of her office, I felt like a weight had been lifted off my shoulders. Despite feeling light and relieved, I was determined to study hard and not repeat the mistake of neglecting humanities again.

During evening prep, I eagerly waited in my room for it to get over so I could finally head to the canteen and inform my friends about the new development. As soon as prep ended, my roommate walked in and greeted me with a concern for my well-being, asking how I was feeling and how my pain was. I assured them that I was fine and then went on to share the exciting news of shifting to humanities. I explained to them that I had been struggling with physics and saw no point in continuing with it. But they warned me that shifting to a new stream meant starting from the beginning and that I should study hard to catch up.

After having a conversation with my friends, I headed to the school canteen and was pleasantly surprised to find Mamita and Shreya already there. As soon as I sat down, they eagerly asked me about what happened with the principal. With a smile on my face, I told them that I had received the permission and the necessary changes were made in the school register. Not only that, but they also promised to send a copy of my application to my parents. I explained that once my parents received the letter, they would definitely call, and then I could convince them about my plan. Shreya was so happy for me that she offered to pay for our tea at the canteen today. Meanwhile, Mamita suggested that we chat while she went to get her books and notes. Shreya insisted that I eat something, but I was already full and declined her offer. She then went to make three cups of tea, and we started talking. That's when Mamita came with all the textbooks and told us to check the syllabus. She said she would give us notes tomorrow. I opened the NCERT books just to get an idea of the content and found it not too difficult. It seemed like all I needed to do was memorize it. Curious,

I asked Mamita if these were the only books for each subject. She replied that there was one more book, but studying just this one would be enough to pass. I assured them that I would put in my best effort and also spend free time with them, as these were our last few days in school before passing in a few months.

I returned to my room and immediately reached for my book on political science. Just as I was getting immersed in it, my friends Ranjit and Debashish entered my room. Immediately, their eyes fell on the book in my hand, and they asked me what I was reading. I closed the book and suggested that we go to Tau's canteen, as I had something important to share with them. They agreed, and we made our way to our favourite spot outside the campus. As we sat down with our tea, they couldn't contain their curiosity any longer and asked me what it was that I wanted to disclose.

When I informed them that I had switched my stream from Science to Humanities, they were taken aback and could not believe what I was saying. They bombarded me with questions, asking who gave me permission to do so. I explained to them that there was a meeting with the principal and teachers from the humanities department, where I expressed my interest in changing streams. Ranjit raised a valid concern and asked if I would be able to cover the syllabus in such a short time. I assured him that I would do my best and at least manage to pass. I also explained that if I were to continue with science, I was at risk of failing in physics and possibly chemistry as well. I knew that I would have to study hard and memorize a lot, and I am determined to succeed. Moreover, I shared that all the humanities teachers were cooperative and willing to help me catch up with the rest of the students. With their support and my dedication, I was confident that I could excel in my new stream.

I was excited to share my plans with my friends, as I had decided to study for 5 hours every day and spend the rest of my time with them. I also mentioned that after passing, I would apply to Delhi University. My friends were surprised that I had met the principal and made such big plans without telling them. I explained to them that it was a sudden decision and I didn't have time to inform them. Ranjit, with a sad face, asked if I wouldn't be joining the physics class anymore. I reassured them that my details were changed everywhere, and from tomorrow onwards, I would attend humanities classes. I told them that this decision made me feel so much lighter. Ranjit, feeling a bit tense about not having me in the special class, asked the staff from the canteen to bring him a cigarette. Debashish chimed in, saying that if I could excel in humanities and had a career plan, then I had made the right decision. I then asked Ranjit how his special classes were going and if there was any improvement. He replied, saying he wasn't sure, but he wasn't seeing much of a difference either.

While walking back from the canteen, Ranjit turned to me and asked, "What's the procedure for changing the stream?" I replied, "Well, you'll have to talk to Principal Ma'am and convince her that even with the special classes, you won't be able to pass in your current stream." When I came back to my room, I couldn't resist taking out my favourite book and diving into its pages. As I read, I couldn't help but feel determined to give my best, as I knew that if I put in my all, I wouldn't have any regrets later on. With this thought in mind, I went to sleep, eagerly anticipating the new beginning that awaited me tomorrow.

Upon waking up, I started my day by taking a refreshing shower and headed to the dining hall. As I finished my breakfast, I saw my friends Mamita, Shalini, Rachika, and Shreya leaving after their meal.

Mamita, who knew it was my first day in a new class, reminded me not to be late and that she would be waiting for me in class. She even invited me to sit with her, which made me feel relieved and grateful to have someone I know in the new class. Shalini and Rachika were surprised by Mamita's invitation and asked why I would sit with her in her class. Shreya then explained that I had transferred to the humanities stream as I found science uninteresting and had different career aspirations. This decision may have surprised my friends, but I knew it was the right path for me to follow.

As I was running late, I quickly went to my room to grab my notebook before heading to the academic block. When I arrived, I saw Mamita standing outside the classroom. As soon as she saw me, she took me inside and introduced me to the class, which took me by surprise. There were about 25-30 students in the class, unlike my previous science class, where there were over 70 students. Although I knew a few of them casually, I was nervous about being the new student in the class. I explained to them that I had recently shifted to humanities, and now they were my classmates. Just then, our history teacher entered the room and started taking attendance. To my surprise, he called out my name too, officially making me a part of the class. He then introduced me to everyone and asked them to help me catch up with the coursework. I felt relieved and grateful for such a warm welcome from my new classmates and teacher.

As I sat in my room, he began revising a few chapters from the beginning for me. He was willing to put in the effort to help me revise, and I paid full attention, taking note of important points. During our break, I sat with Mamita in class when our friends Ranjit and Debashish came to check on me. They asked how it was going, and I replied that it was going fine. As we stepped out of the room to grab some water, Shreya spotted me and came over to say hello. She asked how I was finding the lecture, and I gave her the same response as before.

I attended all the lectures and went for lunch as usual. However, on my way back, I bumped into my physics teacher, who stopped me and said, "I have heard you have run away from science." His tone was very sarcastic, and he continued, "I will see how you will perform now." His lack of optimism and belief in my abilities stung, but it lit a fire within me, and I was determined not only to pass but also to score well in my new field of study. With his words echoing in my mind, I promised myself to work hard and eventually achieve success.

After a long day of classes, I finally returned to the comfort of my room, ready to relax and unwind. But before I could do so, I knew there was an important task that needed to be done—creating a study schedule. With exams approaching, I needed to make sure that I was utilizing my time efficiently and effectively. After careful consideration, I decided to divide my study time into three sessions: two hours after school, one hour and thirty minutes during prep, and two hours at night. This way, I would have a total of five and a half hours dedicated solely to studying every day. I made sure to include breaks in between each session to avoid burnout and keep myself motivated. I sat at my desk, determined to finish the first chapter of my political science book. I made a promise to myself that I would study one chapter every day. However, I soon realized that studying in my room was not a feasible option as students kept coming in and out, causing constant distractions. It was clear that if I wanted to concentrate and make the most of my study time, I would have to find a quieter place. From tomorrow onwards, I decided to study in the library where I could have a peaceful environment. After studying for almost two hours, I went to the bookshop to buy some notebooks, as I have a habit of writing down important points that I have memorized. Later, during dinner at the dining hall, I informed my friends Shreya and Mamita that I would meet them for half an hour after our prep time. With a plan in place and all necessary materials at hand, I was confident that I would make the most of my study time and excel in my political science class.

As I made my way to the prep room and entered the humanities class, I couldn't help but feel a bit nervous. I didn't know anyone in the class, so I decided to take a seat at the back. I immediately pulled out my books and notes, determined to make the most out of this prep session. To my relief, I noticed that the sociology teacher was present to assist students in their studies. She approached me and encouraged me to focus on my studies, assuring me that the sociology syllabus can be completed in just two months if I put in the effort.

After the prep period had ended, I started making my way back to my room to keep my books and head to the canteen for some food. However, before I could reach my room, Warden Sir stopped me. He told me that I had changed streams and now needed to focus on studying. I explained to him that it was difficult for me to study in my room as it was a popular hangout spot for other students. Warden sir then suggested that I study in his office instead. He promised to provide me with a study table and chair the next day and even give me a spare key so that I could access the office at any time. I agreed and told him that I would study in the library after class and in his office during the night. After our conversation, I went back to my room to keep my books and then made my way to the canteen where my friends Mamita and Shreya were waiting for me.

As I entered the canteen, I saw Mamita sitting at a table with a pile of books on history and psychology in front of her. Seeing me, she gave me a warm smile and handed me the books, saying that they contain the entire syllabus for both subjects. I was pleasantly surprised and thanked her for her generosity. She then asked me to return the notes to her tomorrow after getting them photocopied. As she was feeling hungry, she went to order tea and snacks for both of us. As I was going through my notes, I heard Shreya's voice and looked up to see her standing there. She asked me how she was looking, wearing the same pink nightdress that she had on the first time I saw her and fell in love. Without hesitation, I told her that she didn't need to wear a nice dress to look good because she was already so beautiful. I complimented her on her beautiful eyes and told her that I often found myself getting lost in them. She blushed and sat down next to me. Our conversation then shifted to her upcoming unit tests and how she had a lot of studying to do. I encouraged her to work hard and not procrastinate like me, as it becomes difficult later on. Mamita called Shreya to help her carry Maggie and tea to our table. Both of them were big lovers of Maggie and would eat it almost every day. Shreya kindly offered to pass me my share of Maggie but declined, saying I wasn't particularly fond of it. She then stood up and walked towards the counter, leaving me wondering where she was going. When I asked her, she replied that she was going to get my favourite noodles, Yum Yum. I thanked her and told her that I would just have tea. Mamita asked if I had started studying, and I replied that I had started with political science, which I found very interesting. She shared that she liked psychology and sociology. Shreya then suggested that we plan a group outing for a movie before everyone got too busy with exam preparations. This made me extremely happy, as it was the first time she addressed me by my name, Asif. I couldn't help but express my love for her and told her that I would do anything for her. Shreya playfully asked why I was saying this now when she had just asked me something else. Mamita smiled and urged Shreya to reply with, "I love you too." But Shreya just smiled and said she wouldn't say it now. I then mentioned that I would ask Ranjit and Debashish about the outing but wasn't sure if they would be able to go as Ranjit was attending special classes. Nevertheless, I would still talk to them. I also suggested that we ask Shalini and Rachika to join us as well.

Over the next few days, I diligently followed my routine and found myself becoming more confident in my preparations. I attended lectures, took tests, and did reasonably well in all subjects despite the added pressure of being new to these subjects. My daily routine remained unchanged—attending lectures, going to the library after school, and studying in the warden's office after prep. However, due to my busy schedule, I was unable to hang out with friends and could only catch up with them during meals in the dining hall. But amidst all this, I found solace in meeting my love, Shreya, every day after prep before heading to the warden's office to study. I was proud of Shreya as her tests were over, and she had done exceptionally well, reaffirming her status as a dedicated and capable student. Our mutual support and encouragement kept us both motivated and focused on our academic goals.

One day after school, my friend Ranjit came to my room looking extremely dejected. He told me that he was finding it impossible to pass his science subjects and was considering changing his stream from science to humanities, just like I did 15-20 days back. Knowing that it was not too late for him to switch, I suggested he meet the principal today itself. I assured him that I was aware of the syllabus and he could start studying immediately if he gets the permission to change streams. In order to de-stress, I suggested we go for a group outing to watch a movie at Priya Cinema. Ranjit agreed and said that he also needed a break from all the stress and would join us on Sunday for the outing, but only if he is granted the permission to change his stream. Ranjit requested that I accompany him to the principal's office. I was hesitant at first, as I did not want to get involved in any trouble. However, I also wanted to support my friend and be there for him. When we arrived at the office, the principal greeted me and asked me how I was doing. She seemed to be aware of my academic performance as she mentioned being in constant touch with my teachers. As I was about to explain the reason for our visit, Ranjit and Kamal also expressed their desire to change streams. The principal was slightly annoyed but reminded them that they only had three months left, and it would be difficult to catch up with the syllabus in such a short time. She then turned to Ranjit and Kamal, questioning why they didn't switch when Asif did. They both remained silent but pleaded for her permission. Ranjit explained that if he were to write the science paper, he would most likely fail, whereas there were better chances of passing in humanities.

After thinking about it for a while, ma'am gave them paper to write their applications. She instructed them to use her landline phone to call their parents after completing the application. Ranjit took the initiative and called his father, who initially seemed angry but was eventually convinced by his son's explanation. Ma'am also talked to Ranjit's father and signed the application. They came out of the office looking extremely happy. They expressed their gratitude towards me and then followed me to my room. I gave them my notes and asked them to make photocopies and return them by tonight. Before dinnertime, Ranjit and Debashish came to my room and returned my notes. They suggested that we go and meet the other friends in the MBA canteen for dinner instead of going to the dining hall. I happily agreed and joined them on their way to the canteen.

As we were making our way towards the dining hall, my friends and I were pleasantly surprised to see Shalini and Rachika playing basketball with a group of kids. They were so engrossed in the game that they didn't notice us at first. But when they saw us, they quickly came over to greet us. Ranjit then invited them to join us for dinner at the canteen. To our surprise, they both asked if it was someone's birthday today. Ranjit then explained that he had changed his stream of study. Shalini and Rachika were shocked and asked what had prompted this sudden change. We couldn't blame them for their curiosity, as just a few days ago I had also made a similar decision. I asked Shalini to call Mamita and Shreya from the girls' hostel. When they arrived, I introduced Mamita to Ranjit as our new classmate. She was surprised and asked when this happened. I explained smilingly that he joined our class just a few hours ago. Mamita then advised him to get serious and study hard, as there was no time to waste now. As we were having dinner, I suggested that we all go to Priya Cinema on Sunday to watch a movie. However, I made it clear that this would be our last outing until our board exams were over. Everyone, except for me, Ranjit, Mamita, and Shreya, seemed hesitant but eventually agreed as they also wanted a break from studying. We decided to watch Jim Carrey's movie "Ace Ventura" at Priya Cinema, and all of us were looking forward to this much-needed break from our studies.

On a Saturday night, our group of friends gathered at the dining hall to discuss our plans for an outing the next day. The girls had already taken leave to go out, but we boys had a different plan. Unofficially, we had decided to sneak out from the backside of the school and meet them at the main road. As we were discussing our route, Shreya asked me to wear the black shirt she had given me. I couldn't help but smile at her suggestion, knowing that she had put thought into my outfit for the day. We all laughed and joked as we finalized our plans, excited for the adventure that awaited us tomorrow.

After having dinner, Shreya and I decided to take a short walk. It was a chilly November evening, and the weather was perfect for a romantic walk. As we walked, I couldn't help but admire Shreya's beauty. Her hair was flowing in the cold breeze, and she kept adjusting it. Every time she tied her hair, she looked even more adorable. I couldn't resist telling her how beautiful she looked today. Shreya, being her humble self, replied that it was just the breeze making me feel that way. We both shared a smile and continued our walk. However, during our conversation, she mentioned that after a few months, she would miss these walks as I would be graduating and leaving the campus. She was almost in tears as she said this. I reassured her that I would come back to visit every week as I would be in Delhi. She then shared how much she would miss me and how I always took care of her. I held her hand and reminded her to cherish the remaining months we have together. Eventually, I dropped her off at the girls' hostel and went to the warden's office to study. It was bittersweet to think about our impending separation, but I knew that our bond would remain strong regardless of the distance between us.

The next morning, I woke up feeling excited and ready for the day ahead. We had planned to meet at 9:30 in order to make it to Priya Cinema a little early before the show started. Our goal was to get there early so we could ensure we got tickets for the movie we wanted to see. After having breakfast, my friends Ranjit, Debashish, and I headed towards Tau's canteen. We knew that from there, we could catch a lift from some of the villagers to the main road. Luckily, we were able to get a lift quickly and didn't have to wait long. When we reached the main road, we met up with the girls and took two taxis to

Priya Cinema. In the car, Shreya and I sat together, holding hands in anticipation of the fun day ahead.

Upon arriving at Priya Cinema, Ranjit went to buy a ticket and saw there was a long queue to buy tickets. He noticed that there was a separate line for females and asked Shalini and Rachika to buy the tickets. They were able to get the tickets within fifteen minutes, and the show was scheduled from 12 to 3 PM. During the movie, I sat next to Shreya, and we took a break to go to the food counter. Shreya bought popcorn for us and asked me which cold drink I wanted. I declined the cold drink and asked her to get me water instead. As we were both eating popcorn from the same packet, our hands accidentally touched, and we ended up holding hands while watching the movie. It was a wonderful feeling, sharing a moment like that with my friend. Shreya then offered me some of her cold drink, and we ended up drinking from the same glass. It was a small gesture, but it brought us closer and made the movie experience even more enjoyable.

After the movie was over, my friends and I decided to go to a Tibetan restaurant for lunch. It was my first time trying momos, and I instantly fell in love with them. It was such a beautiful feeling to spend time with my friends outside of our usual hostel surroundings. We shared laughs and stories while enjoying delicious food. After our meal, we booked taxis to head back to our hostel. However, we decided to get down at the main road so that we could enter from the backside by climbing the wall.

After a few days, our school notified us to fill out the CBSE form for our upcoming board exams. With a mixture of excitement and nervousness, we filled out the required details and submitted the form. The countdown for the start of boards had officially begun. As winter vacation was approaching, the school also asked us to fill out a railway form for a reservation in case we wanted to go home during the break. However, our school had also arranged extra classes for those who decided to stay back. My friends and I all decided to stay and continue our studies. However, Shreya, who was a year younger than us, was going home in a few days. I was busy catching up on my studies but still made sure to meet her every day. The day before she was leaving, we met after prep, and she expressed her sadness about going home. She didn't want to go, but her parents were coming to take her home. She asked me to meet her parents and see her off. Though I wasn't keen on meeting them, I promised to do so for her sake.

The next day, I finally got the chance to meet Shreya's parents. To my surprise, Mamita was already there, waiting for me. Seeing her made me feel instantly at ease. Her parents were kind and welcoming, expressing their gratitude for taking care of their daughter and keeping her happy in boarding school. It was evident that Shreya had spoken highly of us to them. After some small talk, her parents took us to the canteen for refreshments. Afterward, Shreya went to her hostel to gather her belongings while I helped her carry her luggage to the parking lot. As we were saying our goodbyes, I could see tears in Shreya's eyes as she hugged Mamita and said goodbye to me before getting into the car. As the taxi left through the main gate, tears started to roll down my cheeks as well. Mamita comforted me and assured me that Shreya would be back in just two weeks. As I walked back to my room, I couldn't help but feel a sense of emptiness. Our hostel had been reduced to only 25 percent of its original strength, and the school was closed, leaving us with extra classes. Unfortunately, I was unable to attend these extra classes and spent most of my time in the library. My friends Ranjit and Debashish were also busy, and we would only catch-up during meal times in the dining hall. I had managed to cover 80-90% of my syllabus, studying for 18-19 hours a day.

But as the winter break came to an end, students started coming back to the hostel. Every day, I would eagerly wait for Shreya's return, but as more and more students came back, she was still nowhere to be seen. I asked Mamita to inform me when she arrives, and she assured me that Shreya would herself come looking for me as soon as she enters the campus.

I was sitting in the library, engrossed in my studies, when I suddenly heard Shreya's familiar voice. I looked up and saw her standing there with her luggage, making her way towards me. As soon as she saw me, she came running and hugged me tightly. I was overjoyed to see her after so long that I was almost speechless. She immediately noticed the tired look on my face and asked me if I had been getting enough sleep. Concerned for my well-being, she suggested that I take a break and go to bed early to recharge my energy. She had also brought something for me, which she promised to give me after my prep. We decided to grab some coffee at the canteen and catch up on each other's lives. After our refreshing coffee break, she went back to her hostel to unpack and freshen up.

We all gathered at the dinner table, exhausted from the preparations we had been busy with. As I looked around, I could see the fatigue in each of us, but it was a different kind of tiredness. A few months ago, Ranjit and I were both stressed and unsure about passing our boards. But now, we were confident and ready to ace the exams.

I met Shreya after prep, and she handed a packet to me and asked me to open it. Inside were homemade snacks and sweets along with a beautiful t-shirt. I was touched and thanked her for the thoughtful gifts. I asked her why she gave me a t-shirt, and she simply replied that she enjoyed giving me gifts. However, I could tell that she was exhausted from her journey from her hometown. So, before she left for her room to rest, she asked me to hide the snacks and sweets in my room as she had helped her mother prepare them especially for me. It was a heartwarming moment that reminded us of how much she cares for each of us.

With only one and a half months left before the start of my board exams, I could feel the pressure building up. The exams were starting from 1st March with English as the first exam, followed by psychology on 3rd March, history on 11th March, political science on 17th March, sociology on 19th March, and the last exam of physical education on 29th March. I had managed to complete the syllabus, and now I was focusing on revising every day so that I wouldn't forget anything. I had strategically kept history revision for last, as it involved a lot of dates to remember, and I wanted to keep them fresh in my mind. Shreya's exams were ending in the first week of March, and her new class lectures would start from 15th March. In order to stay focused and not get distracted, I had stopped meeting Shreya and only saw her occasionally at the dining hall.

Just two days before my English exam, Shreya gave me a pack of pens for which I was grateful. On the day of the exam, 1st March, we were given curd for good luck before leaving for Gyan Bharti School in Saket, where the exam was being held. Upon arrival, I checked my bag to make sure I had my admit card and the pens Shreya had given me. As soon as the exam started at 9 AM, I was relieved to see that the question paper was quite easy. I finished it well before time and was satisfied with my performance. After the exam, we all returned to school, and I headed straight to the dining hall to eat and then went to my room to catch up on some sleep as I had stayed up all night studying.

The psychology paper went as well as expected, and I was relieved. However, my next paper on 11th March was on history, and this was also my birthday. I had always struggled with remembering dates in history, so I was a little concerned about how the exam would go. But to my surprise, the history exam went extremely well, surpassing my expectations. After returning from the exam, I met Shreya at the dining hall. She wished me a happy birthday and told me she had an exam the next day, so she couldn't celebrate with me today. However, she promised to meet me tomorrow, and before leaving, she reminded me not to forget to treat her for my birthday tomorrow. We both laughed and made plans to go to the MBA canteen for dinner. With my next exam on 17th March and it being my favourite subject, Political Science, I finally felt a sense of relief and was able to enjoy my birthday celebrations with Shreya.

The next day, I was excited to meet Shreya at dinner time. We went to the MBA canteen for dinner, and I made sure to order all the food that she likes. She looked stunning in her beautiful dress. While waiting for our food, I shared the news that the school had booked a ticket for me to Bhagalpur on 2nd April with other students, including Shalini. Shreya's face went from sparkling to sad as she realized that we would be separated for some time. She asked me to promise her that I would visit her every week. I assured her that I felt the pain of separation more than you and promised to come and meet her regularly. After finishing our dinner, we went back to our respective hostels. As I had brought my Milton jug with me, I asked the canteen guy before leaving to fill it halfway so that I could drink it while studying at night and also share it with my roommates.

My political science paper was a mix of ease and length, but I thoroughly enjoyed writing it. Despite the challenge of its length, I found the topic interesting and engaging. As I left Gyan Bharti School, Mamita mentioned that she struggled with time management and was unable to complete the exam. However, she was still content with her performance.

Even Ranjit did well in the paper, and we were both relieved to have completed our sociology paper as well, marking the end of our board exams. The next and final paper on 29th March was on physical education, which was a relief considering it was the easiest subject for many of us. There was a big gap between exams, and we used that time to chat all night and play cards.

Now that all our major exams were over, we were finally free to do anything we wanted. I used to spend a lot of time with Shreya, as her exams were also over. Debashish was in the science stream and had his biology paper coming up, so we made sure not to disturb him and let him study in peace. After breakfast, Ranjit and I would often go to Tau's canteen, while in the afternoons, I would spend time with Mamita and wait for Shreya to join us after her school hours. We would often go horse riding or just roam around aimlessly. It was during these times that Shreya also discovered her love for horse riding. After our prep time in the evenings, Shreya and I would sit in the canteen for hours, chatting and enjoying our newfound freedom. The last exam on 29th March was relatively easy as there wasn't much to study for it. I was confident that the school would be generous in giving me marks in practical's since I was a part of the school's badminton team. After writing our last paper, we were officially free from all our exams, and it was a great feeling.

I just had 4 days to leave school permanently, and it was an emotional rollercoaster. I have made so many wonderful memories, created strong bonds with friends, and formed a special connection with Shreya. We spent maximum time together, and I cherished every moment with her. However, Shreya was always sad and would often cry. On 1st April, I gave her a letter and asked her to read it when I was gone. Her sadness became even more evident when she stopped eating properly. Worried about her well-being, I requested that Mamita talk to her and convince her to take care of herself. I even made a promise to Shreya that if she doesn't take care of herself, I will not come to visit her. On 2nd April, as we were saying our final goodbyes, Shreya also gave me a letter to read when I reached my hometown of Bhagalpur. It was heart-wrenching to leave Shreya behind, but I promised to call her every Saturday between 6 and 7, provided I was able to get a connection, as it was always busy. Despite the bittersweet ending, I am grateful for the wonderful memories and friendships that I have made during my time at school.

It was 5:30 PM, and I was getting ready to leave the boys' hostel. Suddenly, I saw Shreya waiting for me outside. I had my luggage with me, and she immediately took one bag from me to help. We walked towards the bus parking area where the school bus would take me and thirty other students to the railway station. As we reached the bus, I kept my luggage inside and stood with Shreya for a little while. The bus conductor asked me to take a seat, and that's when Shreya hugged me tightly and started crying. Seeing her tears, I couldn't hold back my own, and she handed me her handkerchief to wipe them away. She told me to keep it with me as a reminder of our love. As I sat on the bus, I couldn't stop looking at Shreya until the bus finally left the main gate. I was feeling sad, knowing that it would be 40-45 days before I could come back and see Shreya again. But I also had hope in my heart, knowing that I would be back to collect my board exam results. With a heavy heart, I left Delhi for my hometown, hoping to return soon and reunite with Shreya.

CHAPTER 9

EXCITEMENT OF AWAITING RESULT AND TAKING ADMISSION IN COLLEGE

I had finally reached Bhagalpur and was overjoyed to be reunited with my family. Despite having a cook at home, my mother insisted on cooking all my favourite dishes, knowing that I would soon be heading back to Delhi for further studies. I spent most of my time catching up with my cousins, laughing, and reminiscing about old memories. However, in the midst of all the excitement, I had forgotten to read a letter that Shreya had given me. After a few days, I finally took the time to read it in solitude on the terrace. As I unfolded the letter, the first words that caught my eye were "I love you, Asif." I was taken aback and couldn't believe that Shreya had such strong feelings for me. It was an emotional letter that she had never expressed when we were together. Reading it made me realize how much I meant to her. I desperately wanted to talk to her but had to wait until Saturday when she would be at the warden's office to take my call. Never before had I been so eager to speak to her. As I made my way down from the terrace, I joined my cousins for a game of cricket, but my mind was still reeling from the letter and the newfound realization of Shreya's love for me.

One day while having dinner with my family, my dad asked me what my plan was for further studies. I confidently told him that I wanted to take admission in Delhi University for my undergraduate degree, and after that, I wanted to either pursue law or prepare for the Common Admission Test (CAT) to get into a reputed MBA college. After dinner, my dad called his friend, who happened to be a prominent lawyer in the Supreme Court of India. He told him about my interest in the field of law, and my dad asked me to talk to him. I had spent two years in a boarding school in Delhi, and my dad's friend was disappointed that I never contacted him during those years. He jokingly said that he would have come to meet me with home-cooked food if I had just given him a call. He then proceeded to suggest that I should appear for the entrance test of the National Law School (NLS) in Bangalore. It was a five-year integrated course that would award me with an LLB degree upon completion. He mentioned that after graduating from NLS, I could either join a senior lawyer or opt for a master's degree in law. Excitedly, he informed me that the NLS entrance forms were out and asked me to fill them out as soon as possible. He also promised to send the study material for the entrance exam via courier, which would reach within 3-4 days.

I thanked him for his help and made my way to my room. As much as I appreciated his gesture, I couldn't shake off the feeling that I didn't want to go to Bangalore. My heart was set on studying at Delhi University, and I was determined to make it happen. After much contemplation and discussion with my family, I finally made the decision to appear for the entrance exam. The next day, I went to a bookshop that sold all the entrance forms for various universities. As I stood there, uncertain and anxious, I couldn't help but worry if the form for NLS would be available in Bhagalpur. If not, then my father would have to send someone all the way to Patna to get it for me.

But thankfully, luck was on my side that day, and the form was indeed available in the shop.

After purchasing the form for the National Law School, I met up with my friend Shalini at a nearby restaurant. I told her all about my decision to apply for NLS, and she was thrilled for me. However, she mentioned that she would also be joining a college in Bangalore, and we could possibly meet up on weekends. Shalini reminded me to prepare well for the entrance test. She also asked about our other friends, particularly Shreya, and mentioned that she was still in touch with our friend Rachika. Before leaving, she gave me her number and asked me to call her anytime for assistance in Delhi. Once I reached home, I filled out the form with the help of my father and sent it out with a demand draft in favour of NLS through speed post. The following few days were filled with excitement as I received the study material from my uncle and began my preparation for the entrance exam.

As I was reading the newspaper, I came across an article stating that CBSE will be declaring the results in mid-May. For a few seconds, my heart started beating faster, not because I was worried about passing, but because I wanted to score well to secure admission to Delhi University. I immediately called my friend Ranjit and informed him about the tentative result date. He advised me to book a ticket for Delhi as the admission process for DU would start by the end of May or the first week of June. My NLS entrance test was scheduled for 22nd May, so I had to be in Delhi before that. I told my dad to book a ticket for me, but he asked me to wait for a few days as he might also come with me. He asked me where I would stay if he couldn't come, and I hadn't given it much thought. Since I would be staying for almost a month, he booked a room for me at the Oasis Hotel in Paharganj, which is owned by his friend. He assured me that I would get a good discount and his friend would be there if I needed anything. He also mentioned that he would join me by the end of May during the time of admission at DU.

On a Saturday afternoon, I decided to call my friend Shreya. After multiple attempts, the call finally connected. I had chosen to call her from a PCO instead of my home so that I could talk freely without any fear. I shared with her that I would be coming to Delhi in 10 days. She was overjoyed to hear this news and immediately asked me where I would be staying and when we could meet. I informed her that I would be staying in a hotel in Paharganj and would visit her after my entrance test for NLS. This surprised her as she wondered why I was taking the test for a Bangalore college. I explained that I wanted to gain experience and that NLS was the best law school in India where students spend years preparing for the test. However, I had only studied for a month and did not have high hopes of clearing it. I also shared with her that my main reason for coming to Delhi was to apply to Delhi University. She eagerly asked when my results were expected, and I told her it would be in mid-May. She expressed how excited she was to meet me, and I replied that the feeling was mutual. We spoke for about 10-15 minutes before ending the call with the promise of keeping in touch and me calling her again once my reservation is confirmed. I also promised to share the phone number of my hotel with her so she could call me.

After waiting for 3-4 days, I finally received my admit card for the NLS entrance exam via speed post. My test centre was located in the Andhra Education Society in R K Puram, and the exam was scheduled on 22nd May from 12-3 p.m. I immediately asked my dad to book a ticket for Delhi on the 18th of May, as I needed to reach there a few days before my exam. However, my dad's work program got cancelled, and he couldn't accompany me, so I had to travel alone. This would be the first time I would be travelling without any family members and staying alone in Delhi. My mother and sisters were a little worried, but my dad reassured them that I am no longer a kid and I am capable of taking care of myself. He reminded them that I am now going to take admission in college, and it's time for me to be independent and handle my own responsibilities. He assured them that he has already made arrangements for my stay at Oasis Hotel and Nayeem Uddin, the manager, will pick me up from the station. Despite the initial apprehensions, I felt a sense of independence and responsibility as I embarked on this new journey towards college life.

As I prepared to leave for Delhi, a mix of emotions flooded through me. I was scared and worried about venturing out on my own, but deep down, I felt a sense of happiness at the freedom I would have. No longer would I have someone constantly watching over me like at home or boarding school. I could finally do what I wanted without any restrictions. My mother, in anticipation of my departure, started making my favourite snacks. My sisters, who always seemed to be fighting with me, stopped and instead showered me with love and attention. However, as the days passed and my departure date drew closer, everyone in my family became increasingly sad. This made me realize that I too was feeling homesick, and the thought of leaving them behind made me sad. I found it difficult to sleep at night as my mind was filled with bittersweet memories of home.

On 15th May, my mother woke me up earlier than usual and told me that Ranjit had called. I asked her to tell him that I will call him back after I wake up properly. However, she came back and said that it was urgent and Ranjit wanted to talk to me. I reluctantly went to the drawing room and grabbed the telephone. I was still half asleep when I answered the call and asked Ranjit what was so important that he had to call me at 7:30 AM. He then broke the news that CBSE had declared the results for 12th grade. My drowsiness vanished in an instant as I asked him who had told him about it. He informed me that he received a call from his friend regarding the result. I immediately asked him how I could check my result, to which he replied that I would have to call the school, but the line was constantly busy. He suggested waiting until evening when the line would be free or calling the principal at her residence. However, I was too scared to call her and decided to wait until evening to find out my result. As I sat on the sofa, holding the phone in my hand, I couldn't help but feel overwhelmed with emotions and thoughts. Many questions were running through my mind: Will I pass? Will I score well? Will my scores be good enough to get into Delhi University? My dad walked into the drawing room and noticed my anxious state. He asked me how I was awake so early and if everything was alright. I told him about the call I received from Ranjit, who informed me that the results were out. I could see the worry on my dad's face, but he remained calm and reassured me that if I had studied well, I would do well in the exams. However, I couldn't even enjoy breakfast properly as the pressure of the result was constantly weighing on my mind. Even my mother seemed stressed about it. All I could do now was wait for the evening when I could call my school and inquire about my results.

After breakfast, I went to the terrace with my cousins to take my mind off the stress of waiting for my exam results. As we chatted and laughed, I could feel myself relax and forget about my worries for a while. However, when I came back down, my mother informed me that there was a call for me from my school. The caller, Shreya, had tried to reach me twice already. My mother told me to sit in the drawing room as Shreya would call again. I sat there anxiously, waiting for Shreya's call. My mother came and sat with me, but I requested that she leave as I wanted to talk to Shreya alone. I was nervous about what she would tell me regarding my results. The thought of not meeting my expectations made my heart race with fear.

As soon as the phone rang, I jumped to receive the call. It was Shreya, and she sounded excited. She asked me where I had been because she had called me twice already. Without waiting for an answer, she exclaimed that I had scored 83% in my board exams. I couldn't believe what I was hearing and asked her to check again. Shreya reassured me that she had checked three times and even mentioned that my score was the third highest in the humanities stream. I was overjoyed and couldn't contain my happiness. I quickly asked about our other friends, Ranjit and Mamita, and Shreya informed me that Mamita had topped with 89% while Ranjit scored 72%. She praised me for achieving such a high score in such a short time. She also said something important that she had forgotten to mention—that she loved me a lot and hoped I wouldn't forget her once I joined college. In a hushed tone, I replied with equal affection, promising her that she would always hold a special place in my heart.

After disconnecting the call with Shreya, I quickly made my way to my mother's room to share the exciting news with her. I found her sitting there, engrossed in some work. With a big smile on my face, I told her that I had passed the exam. She immediately asked me how much I scored, and without hesitation, I proudly replied that I had scored 83%. My mother's face lit up with joy, and she lovingly kissed my head and blessed me. She then asked me to go and share the good news with my father in his office, which was just a short 300-meter walk from our home. As I entered his office, my father saw me and eagerly asked if I had checked my result. With a wide grin, I told him about my impressive score of 83%. He was overjoyed and handed me 5000 rupees to buy new clothes to celebrate my success. I told him that I would rather buy clothes in Delhi, as I would be going there in two days. He then instructed his staff to buy sweets and bring them home to celebrate together as a family.

After anxiously waiting for my sisters to return from school, I finally got the chance to tell them about my results. As I waited, I decided to call my friend Ranjit to share the news with him. He was overjoyed with his result. I also shared with him that I would be reaching Delhi on 19th May and staying at Oasis Hotel, giving him the contact number for any further communication. Finally, when my sisters arrived, I couldn't contain my excitement and immediately told them about my results. They were ecstatic and innocently asked if my score was good enough to get me into Delhi University. With a smile, I reassured them that yes, I had secured enough marks to get admission to Delhi University. The joy and happiness that filled the room were indescribable, and I couldn't wait to start this new chapter of my academic journey at one of the most prestigious universities in the country.

As I began packing my bag, I realized that it was growing bigger with each item I added. I carefully selected and packed all my clothes, making sure to include everything I would need. On the 17th night, the day before my departure, my mother gave me some snacks to take with me. Despite the bag being almost full, I managed to make room for the snacks. My father then asked me how much money I would need. I honestly had no idea, but he reassured me that I didn't have to worry about paying for the hotel as he would take care of it when he joined me at the end of May. He advised me to only carry money for food, travelling in Delhi, and buying application forms for Delhi University.

He handed me 20,000 rupees and reminded me to keep it safe. My mother also called me into her room and gave me an additional 5,000 for any emergencies. I wanted to decline, but she insisted, so I kept it with me. In total, I was carrying 30,000 with me. We all stayed up late talking and reminiscing about old memories before finally going to bed. However, the excitement and nervousness kept me from getting a good night's sleep as I woke up multiple times throughout the night, worried about my upcoming journey.

The next morning, while enjoying a cup of tea, I was greeted by an influx of relatives who had come to see me off on my journey. As I sipped on my tea, they all bombarded me with the same instructions: do not accept food from strangers on the train, do not get off at any station, keep my luggage safe, and wait for the hotel manager at New Delhi station. My train was scheduled to depart at 12:10 PM, so I had to leave by 11 AM. After changing into my travel clothes, I made sure I had all my belongings and was ready to leave by 11 AM. My entire family accompanied me to the station to bid me farewell. Before setting off, I double-checked my room to make sure I hadn't forgotten anything important. We left for the station in our car, and I was excited for my journey to Delhi. As we arrived at the railway station, we were greeted by my dad's staff, who were already waiting with a platform ticket for my family and themselves. They quickly took charge of my luggage and led us to the AC 3-tier bogie where my seat was located. While they adjusted my luggage in the compartment, I stayed outside talking to my family. As the clock struck 12 PM, my dad asked me to go inside and settle in my seat. Before getting on the train, I hugged everyone tightly, knowing that I would miss them during my stay in Delhi. My dad accompanied me and requested my co-passengers to look after me as I was travelling alone. From the window, I could see my family standing on the platform until the train started moving.

It was a bittersweet moment, but I was also looking forward to the new chapter of my life that awaited me in Delhi. My co-passengers turned out to be kind and caring, making sure that I was comfortable throughout the journey.

When my co-passengers woke me up in the morning, I was disoriented and groggy from my long train journey. They informed me that we had reached Tilak Bridge and that in 5 minutes, we would be arriving at New Delhi station. As the train slowed down, I collected all my luggage and waited for Nayeem Uddin, the hotel manager, to come to my seat. Since we were strangers to each other, he had my seat details to identify me. After everyone had left, a man in his late 30s approached me and asked if I was Asif sir. I nodded my head, and he kindly helped me carry my luggage outside the bogie. Worried about the weight of my four heavy bags, I asked if we should hire a coolie. But he assured me that it wouldn't be necessary as we only had to walk up one staircase and then take a short 200-meter walk to reach the cycle rickshaw that would take us to the hotel. This eased my mind as he seemed very cooperative and helpful. After getting down from the staircase, we took a rickshaw to our hotel, which was only a 5-minute ride. As we arrived, the hotel staff kindly took my luggage and kept it in my room on the ground floor, which happened to be just opposite the office of the hotel owner. Nayeem Uddin politely suggested that I freshen up after my journey. I was pleasantly surprised by the spacious room with a comfortable double bed. I unpacked my things and grabbed a towel and some clothes before heading out to smoke outside the hotel. Upon my return, Nayeem Uddin offered to call me by my first name, Asif, but added Ji, as he believed I was much younger than him. He even went the extra mile and offered me some tea to enjoy while I relaxed on the lobby's sofa. After taking a shower, I asked the room service staff if there were any good restaurants nearby, as I was very hungry. To my surprise, he offered to get food for me and recommended a delicious South Indian restaurant that served amazing Masala Dosa. I handed him a hundred rupees, and he came back with my food and returned thirty as change. After devouring my meal, I decided to take a well-deserved nap since I was exhausted from the journey. Later in the evening, I woke up and started studying for an upcoming entrance test.

It was a late evening when I received a call from my friend Shreya. As soon as I answered, her excited voice filled the phone line. She said she could feel from the air that I was in Delhi. We spoke for a few minutes, catching up on each other's lives. However, our conversation was cut short as Shreya had to return to her hostel due to an inspection going on in the girls' hostel. Before ending the call, she asked me when I would be coming to meet her and collect my exam results. I told her I would be coming on 23rd May, but she insisted that I do not postpone it any further as she would be leaving for her summer vacation on 28th May. After our conversation, I stepped outside to grab some food, still feeling excited about meeting Shreya and collecting my results.

When I returned to the hotel, the manager informed me that there was a call for me. My first thought was that my parents had called, so I quickly went to the PCO to call them back. However, they said they hadn't called, which left me confused. The only other person who had the hotel number was Ranjit, so I realized it must be him who called. I had already spoken to Shreya an hour ago, so I knew it wasn't her. Without knowing where Ranjit was, I decided to call his home in Ranchi. His father told me that he had left for Delhi two days ago and was staying in Mukherjee Nagar. Feeling disappointed that I couldn't reach Ranjit, I went back to my room and studied for some time before eventually falling asleep while watching a movie on television.

The next morning, I woke up and went to the lobby to grab a cup of tea. As I was sipping my tea, I saw Ranjit getting down from an auto-rickshaw. He spotted me sitting by the glass door and came over to hug me. I immediately ordered a cup of tea for him, and we started chatting. Ranjit informed me that the admission process for Delhi University would begin on 29th May and asked when my NLS entrance test was scheduled. I told him that it was the next day, and he offered to accompany me to R K Puram and wait for me to finish writing my exam. I thanked him gratefully, as I had no idea about the locality. I told him that my test was at 12 PM, so I would leave by 10 AM to reach there on time. He then asked me about my plans for collecting my results from school, and I told him that I would be going two days later. Ranjit suggested that we go together, so tomorrow he will stay at my hotel and bring his clothes along. After saying our goodbyes, I went back to my room and took out the analytical reasoning section of my study material, as it was the most challenging portion for me. Later, I went back to the lobby and asked the manager to wake me up at 8 AM the next day.

The following day, I was sitting in my room after having breakfast when I heard a knock on the door. To my surprise, it was Ranjit, along with his friend, who had also come to Delhi to take admission in DU. After offering them tea, I asked the manager how we could go to sector 2, R K Puram. He advised us to go to the railway station gate no. 2 and take a bus to R K Puram sector 1. Once we reached there, we could take an auto-rickshaw to our destination. I quickly grabbed my admit card, pen, and pencil, and we walked towards the railway station, which was only a kilometre away and would take us about 5-7 minutes to reach. We managed to get seats on the bus as it was starting from there and reached sector 1, R K Puram, by 11 AM. As we got off the bus, someone told us that our destination was within walking distance, so we started walking towards sector 2. As I entered the school, I quickly scanned the notice board to find my roll number. Once I found it, I made my way to the designated room for the test. As I sat down and looked at the question paper, my heart sank. It was much more difficult than I had anticipated, and I could only manage to solve 50% of the questions. At first, I felt disheartened and disappointed in myself. But then, it dawned on me that I had not put in enough effort into preparing for the test. While most students had been studying throughout the year, I had only one month to prepare. Ranjit asked me about my paper, and when I told him about my struggles, he reassured me and said that I should focus on getting admission to Delhi University. On our way back, we got off at Connaught Place, where we did some shopping and enjoyed a delicious sandwich. His friend took a bus to Mukherjee Nagar while we came back to Paharganj. We spent the whole night chatting and catching up. Despite the difficulty of the test, I couldn't help but feel happy and excited as I was going to meet my friend Shreya the next day.

The next day, we took a bus to Qutub Minar and planned to take a taxi from there to our boarding school. As the bus crossed Hauz Khas, a flood of old memories came rushing back to me. I could feel my excitement building up as we were getting closer to the school after almost 45 days away. We got off the bus and stopped for some tea before taking a taxi to the school. As we turned left from the main road towards the school, my heart was overflowing with anticipation to see Shreya. We reached the main gate within five minutes and headed straight to the administrative block. We showed them our identity cards and admit cards. The person in charge took our details and asked us to wait while he completed the necessary formalities before handing us our results and other provisional documents needed for admission at Delhi University. We were reminded that we needed to collect all of our original documents from 10th grade, which we had submitted two years ago when we first joined the school.

It was around 12 in the afternoon when I realized that Shreya would be in the academic block attending her lectures. To spend our time, we decided to meet the principal. When we reached the principal's office, she was delighted to see us and congratulated us on our results. She even invited us to her house for lunch, but I politely declined and said I had promised some juniors that I would have lunch with them. As we were leaving the principal's office, Ranjit suggested that I stay back and spend some time with Shreya while he goes to the railway station to receive his father. After collecting our results and other important documents, Ranjit left for the main gate to find a ride while I headed towards the dining hall, knowing that Shreya would most likely be there during lunchtime.

As I made my way towards the dining hall, I was surprised to see Shreya running towards me. She was breathing heavily and crying, unable to say anything. It had been a long time since we had seen each other, and her sudden appearance caught me off guard. She told me that her classmate had spotted me and informed her about my presence on campus. I tried to calm her down and asked her to stop crying as everyone was staring at us. I suggested we go to the MBA canteen to talk in peace. As we entered, the in-charge of the canteen greeted me with a warm smile, clearly happy to see me. Without even taking our order, his staff brought two cups of coffee for us. I asked Shreya what she would like to eat, and she replied that she would have my favourite Yum Yum noodles. It was heartwarming to see how much she remembered about me and our preferences even after so many days of not seeing each other.

As we were eating noodles, she mentioned that she wanted to bunk her afternoon classes and spend time with me in the canteen. I reminded her that I had to stay in the school till 6 PM, and it wouldn't be appropriate for me, a former student, to be seen roaming around with a girl on campus. She then asked about the DU admission process, and I informed her that it was starting from the 29th of May. I also mentioned that Ranjit would buy the application forms for me and come to my hotel so we could fill them out together.

I remember the bright smile on Shreya's face when I asked her to call me whenever she wants. I explained to her that it was not possible for me to call her as the school phones were always busy. The happiness radiating from both of us was palpable. She then requested me to meet her on the 28th at 4 PM at the railway station and gave me seat and bogie details. Curious, I asked her if she was going alone, to which she replied that her parents were coming to take her home. I was relieved to hear that, but still worried about how I would meet her in the presence of her family. However, Shreya assured me not to worry, as her parents knew me well, and I just had to say that I had come to drop someone off.

As I ordered tea again, I couldn't help but feel a sense of sadness wash over me. It was our last tea together today, as it was already 6 PM. The inevitable time for our separation had come. She started crying again, and I reached for her hand to comfort her. She was worried about me, living alone in a hotel. I reassured her that Ranjit often visits me, and the owner of the hotel is acquainted with my father. She insisted on me coming to the railway station on the 28th. I promised her that I would definitely come, knowing that it would mean a lot to her and to me. As we sipped on our tea, I couldn't help but reflect on the memories we had shared and how much she meant to me. I knew that despite the distance, our love would continue to thrive.

As we walked towards the main gate, our eyes were fixed on finding someone who was going out of the campus so that I could take help to go with him to the main road. After some time, I saw someone on a motorcycle going out. I approached him and asked for help, and he agreed to help me. I turned to my friend Shreya and assured her not to cry, as we would be meeting again in just four days. She hugged me tightly and said her goodbyes, telling me to take care. Although I was also feeling emotional, I tried my best to control my emotions. As I sat on the motorcycle and left the campus, the man who gave me a lift offered to drop me off at AIIMS, and from there I could take a bus. The thought of meeting Shreya again and the possibility of getting admission in DU filled me with happiness and hope.

For the next four days, I stayed at the hotel, and I didn't venture out to explore the city as I was busy watching movies on the television. However, I did have the opportunity to meet and interact with a few foreigners who were also staying at the hotel. It was fascinating to learn about their experiences of travelling and their different cultures. On the 28th of May, after having lunch, I changed into a fresh dress and headed to the railway station at 2:30 PM. I purchased a platform ticket and went to the inquiry counter to find out the platform number of the train on which Shreya was going to travel. As luck would have it, I spotted Shreya standing with her parents at around 3 PM. As I walked towards them, Shreya's father recognized me and gave me a warm smile. After greeting them, her father asked me what I was doing at the railway station. I replied that I had come to drop someone off. Shreya's eyes were flowing with love and gratitude as she wanted to thank me for coming. Her father then asked me about my board exam results, and I proudly told him that I had scored 83%. He then inquired about my future plans, and I shared that I was applying to

Delhi University and eventually wanted to pursue law or an MBA. Her father wished me all the best for my future endeavours.

I asked her and her father if they would like to have some tea. Her father replied yes but mentioned that the nearest tea kiosk was at a distance and they had luggage to carry. I offered to go and get the tea for them, and her father tried to give me some money in return. However, I refused and told him that I needed 100-rupee change. As I was about to leave, Shreya insisted on coming with me, as I wouldn't be able to carry four cups of tea alone. She thanked me for keeping my promise, and I replied by saying that I was also eager to meet her and that I should be thanking her for asking me to come. We returned with four cups of tea and talked to Shreya's family.

When the train entered the platform, I immediately offered to carry their luggage to their seats. After helping them settle in, I began to feel a bit uncomfortable for spending too much time with them. I knew I had to leave, so I bid them farewell. As I was about to exit the train, Shreya's mother blessed me, and Shreya walked me to the gate of the bogie. As the train started moving, I looked back and saw Shreya had tears in her eyes. In that moment, I couldn't hold back my feelings any longer, and I ran back to the train, shouting out that I loved her and promised to meet her when she returned from her vacation. Returning to my hotel, I couldn't help but think that now I needed to focus on getting admission to Delhi University.

In the evening, I received a call from Ranjit informing me that starting from tomorrow, we would have to apply to various colleges of Delhi University. He mentioned that he would bring the application forms to my hotel, and we would begin filling and submitting them to the different colleges. After our conversation, I stepped out of the hotel to grab dinner. On my way back, I called home, and my dad informed me that he would be taking a train on 1st June and would reach Delhi on 2nd June. Excited about my dad's visit, I went to sleep while watching a movie.

The next day, Ranjit came to my room at 8:30 AM and informed me that he had brought fifty forms for each of us. The cost of each form was only two rupees, so it did not affect our budget. I gave him 100 rupees for my form and started filling it out. The form was simple, requiring basic information such as name, the board's name, the marks obtained in four subjects, and the course we were applying for. As I was filling out my details, Ranjit asked me which course I was interested in. I told him that I just wanted to get into Delhi University. After a long discussion, we decided to apply for three courses in each college. We were excited about the possibilities and finally settled on History Honours, Political Science Honours, and Psychology Honours. Out of the fifty forms we had, we filled out fifteen for each course, totalling forty-five forms. We kept five forms unfilled, just in case we needed them later. Our first college experience was at Zakir Hussain College, which was conveniently located near Paharganj. We eagerly went to the college and visited three different departments to submit our forms. However, it was already late in the day, and we couldn't make it to any other colleges. Ranjit suggested meeting the next day at 8:30 AM outside SGTB Khalsa College in the north campus. He had to return to Mukherjee Nagar while I headed back to my hotel.

I arrived at SGTB Khalsa College at 8 AM, eager to submit my application for admission. As I waited for Ranjit outside the college, I couldn't help but admire the energetic atmosphere of the north campus. Students were arriving in groups, all hoping to secure a spot in their preferred colleges. As I observed them, I could see the exhaustion and tension on their faces from the long process of applying to multiple colleges. Finally, at 8:30 AM, Ranjit arrived, and we made our way inside the college. The campus was bustling with activity, and it took us around 20-25 minutes to submit our forms in three different departments.

In our college search journey, the next stop was Daulat Ram College. We went inside and submitted our admission forms. But as we were leaving, the guard at the gate stopped us and asked why we had entered. We explained that we were there to apply for admission. He then asked who we were applying for. In a rush to leave, we replied for ourselves, feeling quite irritated by the question. The guard then smiled and told us that this was a girls' college. Some girls standing at the gate overheard our conversation and burst into laughter. Embarrassed, we hurriedly left and headed to Ramjas College. As soon as we reached there, Ranjit started laughing, and I joined him. We could not control our laughter as we walked inside to submit the forms. Ranjit joked that if we were able to secure admission to Daulat Ram, we would be the luckiest ones. After Ramjas, we also submitted forms at St. Stephen's College, Hindu College, Kirori Mal College, and Hansraj College by evening. It was a tiring day, but we were glad that we could apply to all the colleges of North Campus in one day.

The next few days, I had a busy schedule as I submitted forms to various colleges in Delhi, including South Campus. In total, I applied to over 40 colleges, and now I am eagerly waiting for the cut-off results of different colleges. In just 10 days, the first cut-off list will be announced. On 2nd June, my father arrived in Delhi, and I went to the railway station to receive him. He informed me that he would be shifting to Delhi, and my mother and sister would join us once we found a flat. This news made me extremely happy as it meant that I would be able to attend college from the comfort of my own home instead of staying in a hostel or as a paying guest. My father got busy with work, and I spent most of my time at the hotel.

After few days, my dad asked me to accompany him in his search for a new flat. We visited several property dealers and saw multiple flats available for rent. However, my dad mentioned that he wanted to wait until we were properly settled before making a decision to purchase a flat. Finally, after much deliberation, we settled on a flat in the East End apartment located in Mayur Vihar. We quickly finalized the agreement and paid the necessary advance and brokerage fees to the broker before heading back to our hotel. We were informed that we would be able to move into our new flat on the 15th of June, as renovations and painting were still underway.

On 8th June, I got the news that DU colleges had declared their first cut-off list. My excitement knew no bounds as I had always dreamt of studying in one of the renowned colleges on the north campus. However, my hopes were shattered when I found out that I did not qualify for most of the colleges in the north campus. But to my surprise, I was qualified in a few south campus colleges. This left me in a dilemma—whether to take admission in the south campus or wait for the second cut-off list of the north campus colleges. I was relieved to know that I had been selected for History Honours at SGTB Khalsa College. To my delight, even my friend Ranjit had qualified for admission to Khalsa College. But when I reached the college, I was informed that all seats had been filled on a first-come-first-serve basis, and Ranjit had already secured his admission. This news left me feeling shocked and disheartened, as despite scoring good marks, I was still unable to secure a seat in the college of my choice. When Ranjit told me not to worry about getting into a top college in Delhi University, my disappointment began to fade. He assured me that there was a total of sixty-eight colleges in the university and many of them would come up with a third cut-off list. However, I couldn't help but feel sad about having to compromise on my dream of studying in a top college. It was all because of my laid-back attitude and procrastination. If only I had come early to Khalsa College, I might have had a chance to secure a seat there. I regretted not taking my college applications seriously earlier, but Ranjit's words gave me hope that I could still get into a good college and make the most out of my university experience.

After shifting from the hotel to Mayur Vihar, my dad and I were busy purchasing basic things for our new home. We even got the telephone fixed by MTNL, and I made sure to give my number to Ranjit and Shreya. However, as each day passed, I was growing increasingly frustrated as the third cut-off list for colleges was not being released. I had started looking for alternative options when my dad brought a glimmer of hope by informing me about the news he read in the newspaper—some colleges were coming out with their third cut-off list tomorrow. This news brought new life back to me, and my dad promised to accompany me to North Campus. To prepare for admission, I checked my bag to ensure that I had all the necessary documents required. The thought of finally getting into a college gave me a sense of excitement and anticipation.

The next day, my father and I arrived at the north campus at 8 AM. I was eager to secure a seat at Delhi University, and at 9 AM, while we were at the university main office, someone informed us that there were a few seats available at Ramjas College. We hurriedly took an auto to reach there, hoping to secure a seat. When we arrived, we found out that there was only one seat left in Political Science Hons. The college office instructed me to go to the Political Science department for a personal interview. Luckily, there were only 5-6 students in the department, and I quickly submitted my documents and waited for my turn for the interview. As I entered the room for my interview, I saw a woman in her late 50s who would be conducting my interview. She noticed my marks and questioned why I hadn't taken admission in any other college with such good marks. I explained that I had missed out on other colleges as I was late in reaching the college and also because I had always wanted to study in the prestigious north campus. She asked me why I preferred the north campus over the south campus, to which I replied that the competitive atmosphere and guidance from professors would help me excel in both my graduation and post-graduation studies.

During the conversation, ma'am asked me where I would be living since, I am originally from Bihar. I informed her that my family had recently moved to Delhi, and we had rented a flat in Mayur Vihar. She mentioned that there was a special bus from DTC that runs through Noida and stops at Mayur Vihar. Curious about my father's whereabouts, she asked me where he was. I replied that he was with me and sitting outside. She then requested to speak to him, and after a brief conversation, she handed me a paper with an 'admitted' stamp on it. She instructed me to go to the office, submit all my documents, and pay the necessary fees. Without wasting any time, I rushed towards the office and completed the necessary procedures.

After meticulously checking all the required documents, the college official handed me a slip and instructed me to pay the fees at the accounts department in the adjacent room. As I made my way there, I was informed that the fee for the first year of graduation was 5500 rupees. This came as a surprise to me, as my father had paid a whopping 120,000 rupees per annum for my boarding school education. However, I soon realized that being a government college, the fees were considerably reasonable. Filled with joy and gratitude, I rushed to the park where my father was sitting and hugged him tightly. He reciprocated my embrace and congratulated me on getting admission to such a prestigious institution. We then decided to celebrate over a cup of tea at the canteen and took a detour of the campus before leaving. On our way back home, we stopped at a PCO to call my mother in Bhagalpur and share the news of my admission with her. She was overjoyed and informed me that they would be moving to Delhi permanently in just 10 days. I couldn't contain my excitement upon hearing this. After talking to her, we took a taxi and headed back home. My college was starting after 15 days, so I was happy to spend time with my family before getting busy with the college routine.

CHAPTER 10

RAGGING AND MAKING FRIENDS FOR A LIFETIME

As I started preparing for my college, my excitement was mixed with fear of going to a new institution where I didn't know anyone. I went shopping and bought new dresses, shoes, and a bag, which made me very happy. However, the thought of ragging on campus made me even more nervous. My dad had to leave for Bhagalpur and would be back after 4-5 days with my mother and sister, leaving me alone in our flat. I spent most of my time watching movies, as I didn't know anyone in the housing society and hadn't made any friends yet. The only people I knew were the owners of the nearby grocery store, where I had gone a couple of times to buy some things. My dad called me and asked me to come to the train station the day after tomorrow in a taxi. He explained that they were carrying a lot of luggage and it would be convenient to have two taxis. I immediately called the local taxi stand and booked two taxis for the designated day. The train was scheduled to arrive around 11 AM, so I asked the taxis to come by at 9:30 AM. I made sure to keep an extra half an hour in case we encountered any traffic on the way.

The day of my parents' arrival had finally arrived, and I was both excited and anxious. I had made sure to lock my house properly before leaving for the railway station, not wanting to take any chances with safety. As the Magadh Express arrived at the platform, I quickly made my way to the bogie where my parents were sitting. However, I was shocked to see just how much luggage they were carrying. My dad asked me to get two coolies to help with the load. The coolies were initially hesitant, asking for a higher price than I had expected. After some negotiation, we finally came to a mutually agreed figure, and they took the luggage as we headed towards the car parking area where our taxi was waiting for us. After a long and tiring journey of almost 24 hours, my family finally reached Delhi. We quickly unloaded all the luggage in one taxi, and I sat in it while my family took the other taxi. Once we reached home, I immediately got to work and made tea for everyone. They were all exhausted from the journey, so I decided to order lunch from a local restaurant. After everyone had eaten, we all went to sleep to rest and recharge for the evening. As we were all gathered in the living room, we made a list of things we needed for the kitchen. My mother and I then went to the Sector 18 market for some shopping. On our way back, we got some food packed for dinner. It was a relief to be almost free from my responsibilities after taking care of everything for the past few days. However, it was short-lived as my college was starting in just 5 days. Despite that, I was looking forward to starting this new chapter in my life with excitement and anticipation.

On the first day of college, I woke up early, eager and excited to start this new chapter in my life. After taking a quick shower, I got dressed and was ready to head out by 7 AM. My mother, who had been up since before dawn, insisted that I eat breakfast before leaving. However, I was so nervous and anxious that I couldn't bring myself to eat anything. I promised her that I would eat something in college and quickly made my way to the nearest cycle rickshaw stand to catch a ride to the sector 1 bus stand (also known as Gole Chakkar). From there, I hopped onto a bus headed towards Kashmiri Gate bus adda, where I then switched to another bus that would take me directly to Ramjas College. As the bus approached the gate of the college, my heart started beating faster with anticipation and nerves. I took a deep breath and stepped out of the bus, ready to embark on this new journey at Ramjas College.

After getting off the bus, I found myself standing near the gate of the college. As I looked around, I noticed that there were many students standing outside, most of whom seemed confident and were probably seniors. Feeling intimidated, I avoided making direct eye contact with them and quickly made my way into the college premises. However, once inside, I realized that I had no idea where to go. I was too scared to ask anyone for help, so in a state of nervousness and uncertainty, I started walking towards the Political Science department where I had given an interview at the time of admission. Along the way, I saw groups of seniors chatting and laughing, making me feel even more out of place. Although I did notice a few students who seemed like freshmen, I couldn't muster up the courage to approach them and strike up a conversation.

When I was about to enter the political department, I was stopped by a few seniors. They asked me my name and my department, but before they could ask anything else, they abruptly left as a professor was approaching us. As they left, they mentioned that we would meet again and that they would come to my classroom to talk more. As I stood there, I noticed a boy who seemed nervous. I approached him and asked him where the class for first-year students was located.

He informed me that he was also searching for it. Together, we found a notice board and checked for our classroom. We were both relieved to find out that our classroom, P1, was on the same floor. We then went to the classroom together, starting off our first day in the political department.

As I entered the classroom, I couldn't help but notice how small it was. There were only a few students sitting there, and I went and took a seat next to a skinny, tan boy. His face looked familiar to me, and I soon realized that I had seen him before. Before I could ask him, the professor entered and introduced himself to the class. He gave us a brief overview of the subject of political science and then asked each of us to introduce ourselves. After taking attendance, he explained the syllabus for the course and informed us that classes would officially start the next day. With only twenty-three students in the class, it was clear that this would be an intimate learning experience. He also gave us details about the books we needed to buy and mentioned that we could also borrow them from the library. The subject that he would be teaching us was "Principles of Political Science.". As the class came to an end, the professor bid us farewell and said he would see us all tomorrow for our first official class.

During a conversation, Utkarsh asked me if I had studied at St. Joseph School in Bhagalpur. I replied that I had, but only for a brief period before changing schools. To my surprise, Utkarsh said he also attended the same school and even gave me some names of students we both knew. We realized we had some common friends and started talking more about our time at St. Joseph. Curious about where he currently lived, I asked him, and he mentioned that he was from the hostel. I then inquired about the issue of ragging in the school, and he replied that we would discuss it later. It was then that the boy sitting next to Utkarsh introduced himself as Karanveer Singh. From his accent and appearance, it was evident that he was from Delhi.

After the professor left the classroom, Utkarsh and I were engaged in a conversation when ma'am entered the room. It was the same ma'am who had interviewed me during my admission process. She introduced herself as the head of the department and informed us that she would be teaching us the Constitution of India. Ma'am then took attendance and asked each one of us to introduce ourselves. With a warm smile, she welcomed all of us and gave us a brief history of Ramjas College. She then explained the course syllabus and gave us details about the textbook we would be using. Ma'am also mentioned that our timetable would be posted on the notice board later that day and asked us to note it down and attend classes regularly. Before leaving, she wished us all the best for our academic journey.

As soon as the teacher left the classroom, a few seniors sneaked in and locked the door from the inside. My heart raced with fear as I knew that this was the beginning of our ragging. They asked each of us to introduce ourselves, and I couldn't help but notice how calm and relaxed Utkarsh was. I wondered how he could be so bold in such a terrifying situation. It turned out that the seniors already knew Utkarsh, as they were also from the same hostel. When it was my turn, they asked me to sing but quickly stopped me and insulted my singing voice, making me feel embarrassed and small. They then turned to Utkarsh and asked if he had made any friends yet, to which he looked at me and Karanveer before telling them about us. Despite the fear and tension in the air, I experienced a feeling of solace upon realizing that I had formed a friendship on my first day of college.

They asked the boy sitting at the first bench to give them an introduction. His name was Abhinav, and he was partially blind.

They kindly told him that if he needed anything, he could let Utkarsh know, and he would inform them. As Abhinav turned to face Utkarsh, I could see that he struggled with his vision. The group then asked me and my friend Karanveer to meet them at the hostel later. I immediately regretted talking to Utkarsh and making him my new friend, as I realized Utkarsh was from the hostel and close to seniors. Being with Utkarsh will always keep us on the radar of seniors.

After the seniors left, my classmates and I waited for the professor to arrive for our next class. However, after a long wait, it was evident that no professor was coming. Utkarsh suggested that we go check on the professor ourselves. I knew he would be safe from getting caught by the seniors, but I was hesitant to go with him as I feared getting caught myself. Utkarsh then asked Karanveer to come along, but even he refused to go. Utkarsh went alone and came back with the news that there was no class and the next one was at 2 PM. Karanveer suggested that we stick together to avoid any run-ins with the seniors. Utkarsh urged us to come with him, but we were adamant and told him that if we stayed with him, the seniors would definitely rag us. He replied saying that whether we stayed with him or not, eventually the seniors would catch us all. He left alone while Karanveer and I decided to leave the college premises to escape from being caught by the seniors. We didn't want to take any chances and risk getting into trouble with them.

As I walked outside with Karanveer, I saw my senior from boarding school standing there. He immediately recognized me and asked about the course I had joined. I gave him all the details, and he mentioned that he was studying English Hons. He then kindly offered to help me if I needed any assistance. I thanked him and shared my concern about ragging. He assured me not to worry and to actually enjoy the ragging process. He also added that those living in the hostel may have to face more intense ragging. However, he assured me that it would only last for the next 7 to 10 days, and things would eventually settle down. A group of seniors who had come to our class and asked us to meet them at the hostel also joined us. When Karanveer and I saw each other, we knew that we were in trouble. The seniors then approached Atul Bhai, who was my senior from boarding school, and inquired about how he knew me. Atul bhai revealed that I was his junior from school and considered me as his brother. The hostel seniors said that they also see us as brothers and that's why they called us to get to know us better. Atul bhai then asked where we were heading next, to which I replied that we were going to grab something to eat. However, he advised us to avoid going to the canteen during the ragging period. As we stepped out of the college, Karanveer expressed his concern about the upcoming ragging period, which would last for another 10 days at least. I assured him not to worry and suggested that we should stay low and avoid going anywhere alone. We also decided to leave the college premises as soon as our classes were over during the ragging period.

When we returned after lunch, Utkarsh surprised us with a timetable that he had copied from the notice board. We were grateful for this as it would help us plan our schedules better. However, after our last class for the day got over, we made plans to head home. But Utkarsh seemed insistent on us going to the hostel with him as some seniors had asked him to bring us. We tried to decline, saying we would go tomorrow, but Utkarsh was adamant and said that we didn't have an option. He also assured us that these seniors were not as bad as they seemed and it would be beneficial for us to get close to them. He even mentioned that they could help us deal with ragging in college.

The hostel was located near the football ground, just behind the college buildings. As we walked towards the hostel, we saw many senior students sitting at a tea shop outside the hostel. Upon seeing us, they shouted at us to come. Utkarsh said that we were going to meet Rahul sir, our super senior and the hostel president. The seniors told us to meet them when we were returning. As we entered the gate, we were greeted by a beautiful garden at the centre with rooms on three sides and two floors. Some seniors were sitting in the park under the shade of a tree on a bench; they were badly dressed in shorts, banyans (vests), and slippers. They shouted at us and called us "FUCCHAS" (Freshers). Utkarsh told them that we were going to meet Rahul sir. We found him standing in the lobby outside his room, and he asked us to wait in the park as he was coming there to meet us.

As we waited for Rahul sir in the garden, my nerves were on edge as I saw the faces of all the seniors staring at us with anger. I could feel the intensity of the ragging that was about to happen, and I tried to mentally prepare myself for it. When Rahul sir finally arrived, accompanied by a group of his friends, he asked us to relax and assured us that they would only ask us questions and play games, without causing any harm. However, as we stood there with only three of us, facing almost twenty people sitting and glaring at us, I couldn't help but feel intimidated. My friend Karanveer and I nervously introduced ourselves, but my attention was drawn to some of the seniors who were casually smoking as if it was not even against college rules. This only added to my anxiety about what was to come. One of the seniors, who appeared to be quite weak and was wearing thick glasses, approached us and asked us to undress and stand in our undergarments. We were taken aback by this unexpected request and pleaded with them to ask for something else. However, Utkarsh obediently started removing his clothes and stood in his underwear. The senior praised him for his obedience, and then Karanveer and I were also forced to undress. They then asked us to play kabaddi with a twist—instead of saying kabaddi-kabaddi, we had to say Fuchha-Fuchha. As we started playing, one of the seniors shouted at us to speak louder. They were all laughing and hurling abuses at us. Although I felt like crying, I managed to control my emotions. The seniors then asked us to play a game called Stappo, and I noticed tears in Karanveer's eyes, but he was also trying to hold them back. Looking at Utkarsh, I could see that he was actually enjoying the whole situation. Rahul sir noticed that we were all visibly upset and immediately intervened. He sternly told the seniors to stop ragging us and announced that it was enough for the day. He then invited us to sit with him on a bench and reassured us that ragging is a part of tradition and we should not take it personally. He also reminded us that all the seniors now know us and would come to our aid if any day scholars tried to rag or threaten us. Furthermore, he offered to guide us in our studies. As I looked over at my friend Utkarsh, I noticed he was still in his underwear, as we had quickly changed back into our clothes before sitting on the bench. Rahul sir then took us to a tea shop and offered us tea. As we sipped our tea, the stress and humiliation from earlier seemed to dissipate. After finishing his tea, Rahul sir left, and I asked Utkarsh how he could remain so nonchalant despite being in such a vulnerable position. He explained that he was used to it as he had been ragged by hostel seniors for the past two days since joining the hostel. In fact, this was not the first time he had been in underwear in front of everyone. With that, Karanveer reminded us that it was getting late and we should make our way towards the main gate to catch the bus back home at 5:30. And so, we bid farewell to Utkarsh and made our way out to the main gate.

As a new student at the university, I was well aware of the potential for ragging from seniors. So, when I saw the special bus to Mayur

Vihar, I intentionally avoided boarding it in order to avoid any unwanted confrontations with my college seniors. Instead, I took the white line bus from the bus adda, all the while feeling anxious about how I would survive the remaining ten days without falling victim to ragging. My mind was filled with thoughts of how I could escape this situation, and I desperately wanted to talk to my friend Shreya for some comfort. She was in her hometown for summer vacations, and I couldn't reach her for the past few days. When I finally reached home late at 7:30 PM, my parents were understandably worried. But I didn't mention anything about bragging to them and simply told them that there were some formalities to fulfill on my first day. The thought of facing ragging had left me stressed and anxious, and I couldn't wait for these ten days to be over.

The next day after waking up, I immediately checked my timetable to see my schedule for the day. I noticed that my first class was starting at 8:30 AM, so I quickly got ready and left for college at 7 AM. Since I lived in Mayur Vihar, which was quite far from my college, I had to take two buses to reach there. As soon as I reached college, I attended my first lecture on the Constitution of India and took notes of everything that our professor taught. My friends and I had not bought the syllabus books yet, so we decided to go to Kamla Nagar market during our break to purchase them. We went to a bookshop and bought all the books that our professor had recommended. On our way back, Karanveer asked us to call him Karan, as his family and friends call him by this name instead of Karanveer.

During lunch break, Utkarsh decided to go to the hostel to have lunch at the hostel mess. Meanwhile, my friend Karan and I went towards the main gate. However, our plan was interrupted by a few seniors who seemed like day scholars. They asked us to go and propose to a girl who was sitting near the gate in the garden. The girl was surrounded by other seniors who were also sitting in groups. The seniors instructed us to go together and propose to the same girl and then fight with each other to see who loves her more. We were hesitant and explained to the seniors that we could get into trouble for this kind of behaviour, and the girl could file a complaint or even slap us. But the seniors were firm in their demand. Reluctantly, we went to the group, and both of us proposed to the same girl, starting a fake fight over who loves her more. The girl immediately understood that we were being ragged and told us not to fight as she loves both of us. She was very understanding and kind towards us, diffusing the situation with her cooperation and friendly attitude. The seniors who had sent us to propose to girls called us back and inquired about our next class schedule. We informed them that our next class was starting at 2 PM. However, upon checking their watch, they realized that it was already 2:10 PM and urged us to run to our class. We were filled with fear as we didn't want to enter the class late and interrupt the lecture. But we mustered up the courage to ask for our professor's permission to enter. She scolded us for being late on the first day of class, but we explained that we were stopped by the seniors. Understanding our situation, she allowed us to enter and take our seats.

After our class, as we were making our way to the main gate to catch the bus, we were approached by some seniors from the hostel. At first, we were apprehensive, thinking they might rag us again. However, to our surprise, they spoke to us politely and asked us to bring two freshers to the hostel every day for ragging from tomorrow and avoid being ragged by them. They promised they would not rag us. As we boarded the bus, Karan expressed his concern about convincing our batchmates to come with us. I shared his worry, and we both agreed to figure it out the next day.

The next day I was on my way to my department when I noticed Abhinav standing near the main gate. I approached him and asked if he was also going to class. He replied affirmatively and then curiously asked who I was. I introduced myself as Asif, his classmate. As we began walking towards our class, I couldn't help but notice that Abhinav was not completely blind. He had some vision, but it seemed to be in a blue hue. He was wearing thick glasses and mentioned that he could only see things close to his eyes. I asked him where he lived. He responded by saying that he was currently staying with a relative, but today he would be allotted a room in the hostel on a handicap quota. He said this very casually, as if it was normal to be blind. He also mentioned that he was from Roorkee and his father held a senior position in a PSU. I found him to be a very decent person and asked him to spend time with us. He replied that he had no friends and happily agreed to spend time with me. Together, we went to class and sat together.

When Karan joined us, I didn't waste any time informing him that Abhinav had become our friend and we were going to stick together. After the first lecture, Karan and I were anxious because our other friend Utkarsh hadn't shown up. We were aware of the hostile atmosphere in the hostel and didn't have the courage to go and check on him. That's when Abhinav stepped in and said he would do it, mentioning that being visually impaired worked in his favour as no one would disturb a disabled student. It was then that I realized how smart and resourceful Abhinav was, using his disability to his advantage.

Three of us, Karan, Abhinav, and I, were walking towards the hostel. As we approached the entrance, Karan and I stopped outside, and Abhinav, who has a vision impairment, volunteered to go alone. While we were standing outside the hostel, waiting for Abhinav to return, a group of seniors suddenly appeared. They were not from our hostel, as we had never seen them around before. Hostelers always had a different air about them, as if they ruled the entire campus. The seniors curiously asked us what we were doing near the hostel, to which we replied that we were waiting for our friends. Without hesitation, they invited us to follow them to the football field. Once there, they gave each of us a one-rupee coin and asked us to measure the field using only the coins. It seemed like a fun and childish demand, and we eagerly accepted the challenge. However, after a few minutes of measuring and crawling on the ground, my leg started hurting. When I turned to see the seniors, they were nowhere in sight. It was then that I realized how foolish we must have looked, measuring a football field with coins in the scorching heat of Delhi. Karan also stood up and asked me what would be the size of the field if we measured it with coins. Realizing that this was just a waste of our energy, I made a wild guess and said it would be around two lakhs coin. When we returned to the designated meeting spot, we saw Abhinav already standing there. He informed us that Utkarsh was not in the hostel as he had gone to visit his sister's house. It turns out that Utkarsh's parents were coming to visit him from Bhagalpur today.

After our college day came to an end, my friends Karan, Abhinav, and I headed towards the main gate. As we walked, my stomach began to grumble, and I couldn't resist the idea of going to the canteen. However, when we saw some seniors standing near the canteen, we decided to avoid it and explore outside the college premises instead. Abhinav, who was a big fan of Delhi's local chaat (snacks), suggested that we go to Kamla Nagar, which was within walking distance from our college. However, due to Abhinav's aversion to walking, we decided to take a cycle rickshaw. He then shared that he had been to Kamla Nagar with a childhood friend from Roorkee who had recently joined Miranda House. We arrived at a famous chaat shop and ordered their famous Dahi Bhalle. Having tried Dahi Bhalle in many places before, I must say that this shop had the best one yet. To make our meal complete, we also ordered lassi.

As I walked back to the bus stand with my friend Karan, Abhinav informed us about the upcoming freshers' party at college. With just 10 days left before the summer break, it was going to be the last celebration before the college reopens in August. While Abhinav was excited for the party, Karan and I were relieved that the ragging would finally be over. As we waited for the bus, Abhinav decided to take an auto-rickshaw instead. Upon reaching home, my mother informed me about a call from my junior, Shreya. She had mentioned that it was something important and would call again later that night. As I changed into comfortable clothes, I couldn't help but wonder what could be so important that Shreya wanted to talk to me about.

As I was strolling through the housing society in the evening, I stumbled upon a badminton court where a group of girls and boys my age were engrossed in a game. Being an avid badminton player myself, I couldn't resist the urge to join in. I politely requested they let me play one game, and they happily obliged. After the game, we got to talking, and they invited me to join them regularly for games. Later that night, as I was watching television, my phone rang, and it was Shreya on the other end. She sounded both happy and annoyed, mentioning that it had been 10 days since we last spoke. She reminded me of my promise to not forget her after joining college. I finally confided in Shreya and requested her to listen to my explanation. I told her how I didn't have a home telephone number and how difficult it was to juggle college and travelling for three hours every day. I also explained in detail about the ragging incidents in my hostel where my friends and I were undressed and forced to play games like kabaddi and Stappo. Surprisingly, she apologized for being harsh and even gave me her home telephone number, assuring me that she would pick up the phone most of the time. I assured her that she was always on my mind and promised to make more time for our relationship.

The atmosphere in college had drastically changed as the students were busy preparing for the fresher's party. The seniors were actively involved and would come to our classes, encouraging us to participate in the celebrations. Many students from our class had taken part in various events and activities. As a result, classes were often postponed due to low attendance as most students were occupied with preparations. However, my friends and I did not participate as we had no interest in the event. Surprisingly, even the tradition of ragging, which was once a common practice among seniors, had almost ceased. We would usually spend our time roaming around the college, except in the canteen and hostel areas where freshers were still being ragged. This was a perfect opportunity for us to bond and strengthen our friendship without any distractions.

Abhinav had recently moved to a hostel, and he would often invite me and our friend Karan to come and visit him, but we kept putting it off, saying we would go after our summer vacations. We not only explored our own college but also hung out at different places like the law faculty canteen and the canteen at D School (Delhi School of Economics). However, our regular hangout spot was Kamla Nagar. As I spent more time with my friends, I realised that I hadn't spoken to any other classmates except for Karan, Utkarsh, and Abhinav. It seemed like we were forming our own world and had no interest in anyone else's business. We were content with our close-knit group and didn't feel the need to socialize with others. Our friendship was strong, and we were happy in our own little bubble. The preparations for the party were in full swing, with almost half of the football field decorated and lights fixed for the event starting at 5 PM. We were particularly looking forward to the performance by one of the bands. However, just one day before the party, we made plans to meet at 4 PM and spend some time together at the party before heading to Connaught Place to catch a movie.

The next day was a lazy morning for me as I woke up late, knowing that I had to go to college in the afternoon after lunch. As I sat down for breakfast, I remembered that I had to call Shreya and catch up with her. Luckily, she answered the phone, and we started talking. She told me that she always waits for my call every day and understands that I am still adjusting to college life. After updating her about my classes, I mentioned the freshers party that was happening later that day. Shreya was excited to hear about it and asked me what I was planning to wear. I told her that I had not decided yet but was thinking of wearing a white shirt with light faded jeans and sneakers. However, Shreya suggested that I wear something more eye-catching for the party. I explained to her that I don't really enjoy parties, but I was going just for the sake of formality and to spend time with my friends. Shreya had warned me about the presence of many girls at the party and advised me not to mingle or approach them. I assured her that I would be careful and that my friends and I had plans of going to Connaught Place after spending some time at the party. I asked her when her school would be reopening after summer vacations, and she informed me that it would be on 25 July. I promised her that I would come and meet her after that, as my college would start from 1 August, and I would have some free time. I expressed my genuine desire to meet her, and she was delighted to hear that. As I was getting late, I had to disconnect the call and quickly finish my shower and lunch and get ready by 2:30 PM. Before leaving, my mother gave me 2000 rupees, even though

I had enough money. Despite having enough money, I accepted it and left for the party.

When I reached college, the atmosphere was unlike anything I had ever experienced before. It was vibrant and electric, filled with excitement and energy. All the students were dressed in their best clothes, especially the freshers. As I waited for my friend Karan, I heard a honking sound. I turned around and saw Karan pulling up in his car. He asked me to hop in, and we set off to explore the north campus. We visited almost all the colleges and took in the sights and sounds of this bustling student hub. As we passed by Miranda House, Karan stopped his car and suggested we grab a quick tea from the kiosk across the main gate. He looked around and exclaimed, "You know, Asif, all the beautiful and intelligent girls' study here." He mentioned that one of his friends also studies at Miranda House, and we should visit her one day to make some new friends.

After tea, Karan and I drove to our college and parked our car in the designated parking area. As we were getting out of the car, we were greeted by Rahul sir, who was the hostel president and also from our department. He asked us where we had been and why we hadn't met again. I explained to him that we were scared to go back to the hostel after the ragging incident. He reassured us that everything was back to normal and there was no more ragging. He even invited us to visit him in the hostel if we needed any help. Then, he asked us where we were headed next, to which we replied that we were waiting for our friends Utkarsh and Abhinav. He suggested that we go with him to the hostel and meet them there, but we insisted on waiting for them outside. However, he insisted that we join him as he promised that no one would rag us anymore and we would be safe with him. Eventually, we agreed to go with him to the hostel, feeling grateful for his kind gesture and assurance of safety.

We were hesitant to return to the hostel after our previous unpleasant experience, but we decided to give it another chance. To our surprise, the atmosphere was completely different this time. As soon as we entered, we were greeted with warm smiles and friendly faces. One guy in particular, who wore thick glasses and was quite thin, approached us. He was the same guy who was very active while raging at us and invited us to have tea with him. We were taken aback but intrigued, so we followed him outside the hostel gate to a nearby tea shop. He introduced himself as Chandan from the MA history department. His friends, who were also drinking tea, called him Chua or 'Mouse.'. They explained that even junior students in the hostel address him as 'Chua sir.'. It was impressive to learn that Chandan had cleared the UPSC prelims exam. We and our friend Karan were in awe of him. Chandan sir then looked at us and said we could call him by any name we felt comfortable with. This unexpected encounter with Chandan and his friends left us feeling welcomed and accepted in the hostel. We returned to the hostel, and Chandan sir showed us Utkarsh's room. As we knocked on the door of room no. 8, a fat guy opened it and introduced himself as Dhawan from the B.com department. He informed us that Utkarsh went for a shower and would be back soon. We were chatting when suddenly, Abhinav appeared at the door. He couldn't see us properly and came close to us, surprised to find us in the hostel. When Utkarsh arrived, he was equally surprised to see us there. He jokingly called us "Fattu" and asked how come we are here. We continued talking when a senior entered and asked for a cigarette from Utkarsh, who took one from his almirah and gave it to him. My friend Karan then mentioned that he also smokes, and I admitted that I do too. Abhinav, who doesn't smoke, joked that by staying with us, he would become a passive smoker. Utkarsh lit up a cigarette and said we could share it. After smoking, we all left for the fresher's party, creating memories that we would cherish for years to come.

The atmosphere at the football field was electric, filled with energy and excitement. More than two to three thousand students from various colleges had gathered to enjoy the festivities. The stage was set for a catwalk by the freshers, followed by a band performance at 8 PM. The seniors and juniors put up an array of cultural shows that added to the fun-filled atmosphere. As the clock struck 6:15, we bid farewell to the party and headed towards Connaught Place. After parking our car at Palika Bazaar parking, we hurried towards the cinema hall, as the movie was scheduled to start at 7:30 PM. Thankfully, we managed to get our tickets and entered the hall. We made sure to take care of Abhinav, who had a problem with his eyes.

After watching a movie, my friends Karan, Abhinav, Utkarsh, and I decided to head to Khan Market for some delicious chicken rolls. As it was getting late, Karan offered to drop me off at my housing society in Mayur Vihar. I was relieved and grateful as I didn't have to worry about taking a bus late at night. Once we reached my society, Karan said goodbye and continued to drop off Abhinav and Utkarsh at their hostel. As I walked towards my building, I couldn't help but feel happy that I have made such good friends in college. I knew that the next three years of my college life would be easier and more memorable with them by my side. I was grateful for their company and excited for all the adventures we would have together.

CHAPTER 11

BREWING BONDS AND CONFLICTS IN COLLEGE

After a fun-filled summer vacation, I was excited to join my college. As the classes began, we attended all the lectures regularly. During breaks, my friends and I would either go to the canteen or to the hostel. The hostel quickly became our favourite spot on campus, as it was a place where we could relax and be free from all the regulations of college. With each passing day, our friendship grew stronger as we spent more time together. I also started taking the U special bus to college, but on days when it was overcrowded, I would prefer to avoid it. Overall, joining college after summer vacations was a new and exciting experience for me, and I couldn't wait to see what else it had in store for us.

One day after a long and tiring day in class, we went to the hostel to unwind and catch up with each other. Utkarsh, however, had other plans as he changed his outfit and mentioned that he was going to Miranda House to meet his friend, Sikha Gupta. We were all surprised and asked how he knew her. Utkarsh revealed that she was from his previous school, where he completed his 12th grade. He then invited us to join him, but Karan and I declined while Abhinav agreed to go along. Abhinav mentioned that he would also meet his childhood friend Priyanka, who was studying English Honours at Miranda House. Since Karan and I had no other plans, we also went with them. Although Miranda House was about one kilometre away from Ramjas, Utkarsh assured us that the back gate, which was just half a kilometre away, would make the walk shorter. He added that most of the girls used the back gate as it was closer to their hostel.

As we reached MH, Utkarsh immediately asked a girl passing by to call Sikha Gupta from the hostel. However, the girl had no idea who Sikha was. Utkarsh explained that she was a first-year student in Economics Honours. Abhinav also requested that she call Priyanka, a first-year student in English Honours. While we waited for their arrival, we decided to go to a nearby tea shop across the road and ordered some tea for ourselves. As we were sipping on our tea and having a good time, we suddenly heard someone calling out for Utkarsh. He waved back as the girl was standing on the other side of the road. We urged him to go alone as we were enjoying our tea at the moment.

Utkarsh had disappeared for a while and returned with her. He introduced us to her, and we couldn't help but notice her beauty, intelligence, and confidence. As we got to talking, Sikha complained that Utkarsh had not invited her to the fresher's party. I couldn't help but smile sardonically and asked why he hadn't invited her. I said if I were in his place, I would have definitely invited my friend. However, Utkarsh quickly shut me down and explained that we had only attended the party for half an hour before heading to Connaught Place to watch a movie. Sikha playfully retorted that she also enjoys watching movies and requested that next time, we inform her of any plans we make.

She had a warm smile on her face, looked at me, and said that Asif would now be responsible for informing her as we were now friends. I chimed in, assuring her that of course she would be invited from now on.

While we were talking at the tea shop, I noticed a girl walking towards us. Curious, I asked Abhinav, "Is she your friend Priyanka?" He replied, "You know I can't see things at a distance; let her come closer." As the girl reached us, she hugged Abhinav, and he introduced us to her. It turns out Sikha and Priyanka were both from the same college but had never met before. They shook hands and started chatting. Sikha asked Priyanka if Abhinav had invited her to the fresher's party. Priyanka replied that she was meeting Abhinav for the first time after joining college. Sikha then shared that these boys were living the typical college life by going to movies and hanging out at various places. Karan chimed in, saying that we also go to the law faculty or D School canteen almost every day after college. He invited the girls to join them there sometime. Sikha expressed that she needed to leave, but before doing so, she made sure to take down the hostel room number of Priyanka so that they could meet up later. Priyanka was extremely welcoming, and we ended up spending a significant amount of time together. As we were sitting, I noticed a particular bus labelled 'U Special' approaching, and there was an available seat. I quickly signalled the bus driver to stop and informed my friends that I would be taking this bus as it would directly take me to Mayur Vihar. The best part was that as a student, I didn't have to purchase a ticket as it was free of cost.

Over the course of time, Sikha and Priyanka had become very close friends. They would often visit us in Ramjas after class, and we would all go to the law faculty canteen together. It was a convenient meeting spot, located midway between Miranda House and Ramjas College. One day, as we were sitting in the canteen, Sikha excitedly announced that it was her birthday tomorrow and invited us to celebrate with her at McDonald's in Kamla Nagar. She mentioned that she had also invited a few other friends from her college. After an hour, Sikha asked Priyanka to leave with her to go back to their college. However, Priyanka made an excuse and said she would come later as she had some work to finish with Abhinav. When Sikha left, Priyanka suggested that we all pool our money to buy her a special gift. With five of us as friends, we decided to contribute 500 rupees each, making it a total of 2500 rupees. Priyanka mentioned that she would come to our college the next day during lunch to collect the money. She also added that if any of us were free, we could accompany her to Kamla Nagar to buy the gift together, or else she would go alone. The next day after attending our lecture, my friends and I headed towards the main gate, where we saw Priyanka standing with her friend. We were excited to catch up with her, and each of us gave her 500 rupees. However, Karan requested that she go alone as we had an assignment to complete. Abhinav, on the other hand, insisted on going with them. As they left, I asked Karan why he lied about having an assignment when we didn't actually have one. He explained that Priyanka, being a girl, would want to visit the entire Kamla Nagar market to buy the perfect gift, unlike us, who would settle for anything. We then decided to go to the canteen and grab something to eat while waiting for them.

As we stepped into the canteen, we saw our professor, who teaches the Constitution of India. We noticed her sipping on a cup of tea, and I could tell she was deep in thought. We mustered up the courage to ask her if we could join her, and she happily obliged. As we sat down, she asked us about our future plans after graduation. Utkarsh expressed his desire to prepare for the UPSC exams and join JNU, while Karan shared his dream of studying photography abroad. I mentioned my interest in pursuing law or appearing for CAT to get into a good MBA college. With a stern but caring tone, our professor advised us not to waste our time and start preparing for our futures. She emphasized the importance of taking advantage of the time we have now, as it will never come back once it's gone. To Karan, she admitted that she had no knowledge about photography. As she finished her tea, she bid us goodbye and left us with valuable advice for our future. Utkarsh was filled with determination and motivation as he declared that he would start preparing for the UPSC exams from the next day. I reminded him that to appear for the exams, he would need a graduation degree. He shared with me that he had heard from Chua sir that the course for UPSC was quite lengthy and challenging, which is why he had also started preparing during his graduation. Karan then asked me about my plans for the CAT exams, to which I replied that I would begin preparing after my second year. I jokingly added that my memory was not strong enough to remember everything after three years of studying. We then ordered some tea and patties from the canteen. As we sipped on our tea and enjoyed the delicious patties, I couldn't help but express my love for the canteen's patties. After finishing our snacks, we headed to our department to attend the last lecture of the day.

Unfortunately, Abhinav was unable to attend the lecture with us, so we left for the hostel after the class ended. We needed to change our t-shirts before heading to Sikha's birthday party. To our surprise, we saw Abhinav already at the hostel, all dressed up and standing in Utkarsh's room. We were curious and asked him why he didn't come to the lecture. He explained that after shopping for Sikha's gift, they got delayed as the gift wrapping took longer than expected. When asked about the gift, Abhinav revealed that they had bought a dress for Sikha. However, we were not really interested in knowing what kind of dress it was, as our main focus was on attending the birthday party and having a good time.

After changing our t-shirts, we headed to Kamla Nagar. As we arrived, we noticed a group of 10-12 girls standing with Sikha and Priyanka. We were the only boys who were invited, and Sikha kindly introduced us to her friends. Curious, Utkarsh asked why they were all standing outside. To our surprise, Sikha informed us that she had requested the McDonald's staff to arrange four tables for our group. We started chatting and catching up when the McDonald's staff came to us and asked us to come inside as the tables had been arranged. We followed them inside and found our tables ready for us.

While my friends and I were enjoying our meal at McDonald's, Karan suddenly leaned in close to my ear and asked me if I liked anyone. I replied that I had no interest in anyone as I already had a girlfriend. He seemed surprised and mentioned that I had never told them about her. I explained that she was studying at a boarding school and that I was planning to meet her the coming Sunday. Excitedly, Karan said that he would also come with me. I politely told him that we would talk about it later. However, before I could say anything else, Priyanka noticed us talking and asked what we were discussing. Karan quickly blurted out that he was going with me to meet my girlfriend at the boarding school on Sunday. To my surprise, Sikha overheard and said she would join us as well. Before we knew it, our other friends Utkarsh, Abhinav, and Priyanka also expressed their interest in coming along. We decided to discuss the details later at the law faculty canteen the next day. As we were leaving McDonald's, one of Sikha's friends asked if she could also join us at the canteen tomorrow. To be honest, we didn't want any more friends to join us as we already had a close-knit group. After walking to our college instead of taking a cycle rickshaw, we gathered at Ramjas Gate for a few more minutes before the girls headed back to their hostel. My friends and I then went to our hostel to grab our bags before catching a bus to Mayur Vihar.

The next day, I woke up excited to go to college and meet my friends. However, as I reached the classroom, I realized that none of my friends were there for the first lecture. I was disappointed and thought of bunking class to go to the hostel and visit my friend Utkarsh's room. But then, I remembered the trouble I had faced in my 12th grade for bunking classes and decided to attend the lecture. After the first class, my friend Karan came and joined me for the second lecture. I asked him where he was, and he replied that he had woken up late. During the lunch break, we went to the canteen to grab something to eat. To my surprise, Utkarsh and Abhinav also joined us, and we all ordered a veg thali. After finishing our delicious thali, we all headed to our public administration class. I have always been interested in this subject and never missed a single class. However, Utkarsh and Kamal seemed less enthusiastic about it and told me they wanted to skip the class and go to the law faculty instead. My friend Abhinav and I insisted on attending the class and promised them that we would join them in an hour.

After our class ended for the day, we decided to head to the law faculty. As we approached the canteen, we noticed our friends sitting outside the canteen under the shade of a tree. It was a pleasant day, and the canteen had kept chairs outside for the students to relax. Sikha and Priyanka were also there with their friend from Miranda House. We went over to them and joined in on their conversation. Utkarsh jokingly referred to them as our class toppers. I remembered that the new girl had introduced herself to me yesterday, but I had forgotten her name and felt embarrassed about asking her again. However,

Abhinav was more direct and asked her name directly. She introduced herself as Chaaya. Sikha then asked me when I was planning to go to the boarding school on Sunday to meet my girlfriend. She also asked for my girlfriend's name, which is Shreya. Sikha expressed her desire to join us as she was tired of her hostel life and wanted a change of scenery. I told them that I would be leaving around 9 AM from Mayur Vihar. They asked where my school was located, and I informed them that it was in Mehrauli, about 2 km from the main road in between farmhouses. Karan offered to pick me up in his car from Mayur Vihar, while Sikha said she would take her cousin's car from South Ex as she was familiar with driving in Delhi. She requested Karan drop her off at South Ex part 1 before going to pick me up. I advised Karan not to come to Mayur Vihar, as I would directly reach South Ex around 8:30 AM. Now it was Karan's responsibility to pick everyone up from North Campus and meet me at South Ex. I also mentioned that I won't be coming tomorrow as I was tired of the 3-hour commute every day. Sikha gave me her cousin's address and asked me to come there on Sunday. After finalizing the plan, I said goodbye and took the U special bus to Mayur Vihar.

On Sunday morning, I woke up early and excitedly told my parents that I was planning to spend the day with my friends. I promised to return home by 7 PM and, after a quick shower, got ready in a comfortable pair of jeans and a black shirt that Shreya had given me. I hopped on a direct bus to South Ex, luckily finding one that was also heading towards Dhaula Kuan. As soon as I reached South Ex part 1, I made my way to Shikha's cousin's house. However, upon reaching there, I was unsure whether to go inside or wait for them outside. Spotting a tea shop nearby, I decided to grab a cup of tea and patiently wait for them to arrive. Karan's car was nowhere to be seen, which meant that they had not reached yet. I checked my watch, and it was already 8:45, even though we were supposed to meet at 8:30. I decided to wait for them until 9, and if they still didn't show up, I would take the bus to Qutub Minar. Just when I was about to give up hope, I saw Karan's car approaching. They must have spotted me standing at the tea shop, as Karan stopped there. Everyone got out, and Sikha suggested we go to her cousin's house. Chaaya decided to go with her while the rest of us stayed behind. Within a few minutes, I saw Sikha driving a luxurious car towards us with Chaaya already inside. Utkarsh quickly hopped into the car, followed by Abhinav, Priyanka, and myself sitting with Karan. I suggested that they follow us, and if they got lost, we would all meet at Qutub Minar. We were finally on our way, and I couldn't wait for the adventures that awaited us at our destination.

I had informed Shreya that I would be coming to meet her today with my friends. I knew she had been waiting for us and was looking forward to our visit. As we made our way to Qutub Minar, both cars met, and I asked my friend Sikha to follow us. I also requested my friend Karan, who was driving our car, to slow down so that Sikha could keep up. From the main road near the school, we took a left turn towards the school. I couldn't contain my happiness as I would finally be meeting Shreya after a long time. As we reached the main gate, the guard recognized me and opened the gate for us. I quickly informed him that the other car was with me, and we parked our cars and made our way towards the girls' hostel. My friends were impressed with the vast infrastructure and size of the school.

As I was walking towards the girls' hostel, I met Warden Sir on the way. He had a big smile on his face and seemed very happy to see me. My friends who were with me also greeted him, and he exchanged pleasantries with them. Warden sir then suggested that we go and meet Principal Ma'am, as she would also be delighted to see us. However,

I thought it would be better to first finish the formality of meeting her before going to see her. So, we all went to Principal Ma'am's office, but she was not there. The staff informed us that since it was Sunday, she comes in late, around 12 PM. The staff offered to call her and inform her about our visit, but I declined, not wanting to disturb her on a weekend. Instead, I suggested that we come back at 12 PM to meet her. And so, we left with the plan to return later and meet Principal Ma'am.

My friends and I decided to visit Shreya at her hostel. We approached the guard and asked him to inform Shreya that she had a visitor. After a few minutes, Shreya came out wearing a beautiful salwar suit, looking absolutely gorgeous. My friend Priyanka couldn't help but compliment her on her beauty, and Shreya smiled in response. I then introduced Shreya to my friends, and we all decided to go to the canteen to catch up. The canteen staff brought us coffee, and Shreya kindly asked my friends what they would like to eat. It took them a while to decide, but they finally made their choices. As for me, Shreya knew my favourite noodles and ordered them for me without me even having to say anything. After we finished eating, my friend Karan suggested that they explore the school while Shreya and I catch up. I informed them that if they couldn't find us in the canteen, they could come to the principal's office.

When my friends left, Shreya surprised me by thanking me. I was confused and asked her for what. She replied that she was grateful because I had come to meet her and even introduced my friends to her. She also mentioned that she was worried about her upcoming board exams, and I advised her to start preparing from now on. Shreya then excitedly shared that she would be participating in a badminton tournament. I was happy to hear that she was still pursuing her love for badminton. I asked her if she had tried horse riding as well, and she revealed that she had gone a few times, but without me and Mamita, she didn't enjoy it as much. I was surprised to learn that Mamita was now studying at IP College, as we had lost touch after school. I asked Shreya if she had Mamita's contact number, and she informed me that Mamita was currently staying with her cousins and gave me her telephone number. During a conversation with Shreya, she asked me how far IP College was from my college. I replied that it was not too far, as I pass by it every day on my way to college. She then mentioned that our mutual friends Shalini and Rachika were studying in Bangalore and had visited once to collect some documents. I suggested we go together to the principal's office, but she insisted that I should go with my friends. I knew she wanted to avoid meeting me in front of the principal. Shreya then commented on how smart my friends are, referring to the girls. I proudly agreed, mentioning that they were from Miranda House, one of the most prestigious women's colleges in India. Shreya seemed impressed by this and asked how I met them. I explained that Priyanka was a childhood friend of Abhinav, and Sikha went to school with Utkarsh.

As I walked towards the dining hall with Shreya, I couldn't help but feel a sense of familiarity and comfort. I wanted to have lunch there, but as I was with my friends, I didn't want to leave them and eat alone. However, as I passed by the basketball court, I saw my friends heading in my direction. I joined them and suggested that we go and meet my principal. As we entered her office, her staff informed us that ma'am was waiting for me. I couldn't help but feel a sense of nervousness and excitement as I was ushered into her office. Ma'am greeted me with a warm smile and expressed her delight at seeing me. It dawned on me then that I was here to meet Shreya. I realized that next year, when she would be completely done with school, I wouldn't be coming back here as often. Ma'am asked me about the college I had taken admission in, and I proudly replied that I was a student of Ramjas College, Delhi University. I then informed her that I had come with my friends from the university to show them around my school. She was curious to know where my friends were, and when I told her they were waiting for me outside her chamber, she asked me to call them in. Soon, I was back with my friends, and I introduced them to Ma'am. She was delighted to meet them and even more surprised to know that the girls are from Miranda House, another reputed college of the university. Ma'am was so impressed by their presence that she called her staff and asked them to bring some tea for us. She even invited my friends to come again and meet students and discuss Delhi University and career options. Ma'am then inquired if I had met any juniors yet, to which I replied that I was planning to meet them soon. To my surprise, she even came out of her office to bid us goodbye before we left.

As we came out of the principal's office, I saw Shreya standing near the telephone booth, and we went to her and decided to go for a walk towards the nearby ground. As we strolled along the football field, Shreya suddenly asked me if I would like to meet the horse-riding instructor and my horse. My friends were taken aback as they had no idea that I knew how to ride a horse. Curious and intrigued, we made our way to the stable, only to find out that our instructor was not there. However, my friends were delighted to see so many beautiful horses in the stable and insisted that I show them my horse-riding skills. I had to politely refuse as our instructor was not present, but I did take them to my horse and showed them some basic commands and tricks.

As the evening wore on and the sun started to set, Sikha remarked that it was getting late. I could sense the sadness in Shreya's face as it was time for me to leave. We made our way towards the parking area, surrounded by the chatter and laughter of our group of friends. As we reached our cars, all the girls gathered around Shreya and gave her big hugs, saying how much they would miss her and how she should come back to visit whenever she had free time. As they all sat in the car, I stood with Shreya for a while before bidding her goodbye. She told me how much she missed me and my care for her. I used to stand by her side all the time, and she longed for my presence. She asked me when I would come back again, to which I promised her that I would come very soon. I reminded her to focus on her studies and promised to keep in touch. We shook hands, and I went to sit in the car with my friends. As we drove away, we all waved to Shreya, who stood there with tears in her eyes. We shouted "Bye" to her and left the school premises with a promise to come back soon. Chaaya mentioned that Shreya was a nice girl and asked me to always keep her happy and not to break her heart. With a heavy heart, I left the school compound, determined to keep my promise and make Shreya happy.

I asked Karan to drop me off at South Ex, as there was a direct bus from there. However, Karan was adamant about dropping me off at my home instead. I tried to reason with him, explaining that it was already getting late and by the time he would come back to pick up others, it would be dark. But he insisted on dropping me all the way home. Eventually, both of our cars stopped at the bus stand in South Ex, and everyone came out to say their goodbyes to me. I hopped on the bus to Mayur Vihar and reached after sunset.

Unfortunately, for the next three days, I was unable to attend college due to a terrible fever. However, as soon as I recovered, I eagerly made my way to campus. To my surprise, when I arrived and stepped off the bus, the atmosphere was different. There were only a handful of students around, and the usual hustle and bustle of campus life was missing. Confused, I made my way to my class only to find out that all classes for the day had been cancelled. I assumed that perhaps the college was closed for some special occasion and headed to the hostel. As I entered the hostel corridor, I was met by a group of angry seniors who immediately questioned why I had come to college. Fearful, I asked them why they were so upset. They then proceeded to ask if anyone had seen me coming. Worried, I asked them what had happened. One of the seniors replied with a stern tone, "After how many days have you finally decided to come to college? Go and ask Utkarsh and don't even think about going home without informing someone from the hostel." With a heavy heart and growing anxiety, I made my way to find Utkarsh, unsure of what was going on and why it was such a big deal that I had come after three days.

When I entered Utkarsh's room, I was surprised to see it was packed with seniors. Utkarsh and Abhinav were also there, and it seemed like they were in some kind of trouble. Chua sir asked me why I had come today, and Utkarsh quickly interjected, explaining that he had been absent for three days and was not present yesterday. One of the seniors then asked why they were asking about him, to which Utkarsh replied that they knew he was friends with me and we were always together. After this, the seniors left, but not before advising me to stay in the hostel until evening and to inform them if I needed to leave. This whole situation left me feeling curious and a bit anxious, wondering what could have possibly happened in those three days that caused so much concern among the seniors. I couldn't help but wonder what kind of trouble Utkarsh had gotten himself into.

As soon as the seniors left, I couldn't help but ask in a panicked tone about what had happened yesterday. Utkarsh, looking visibly disturbed, revealed that there was a huge fight in the canteen that involved the entire hostel. Curiosity got the best of me, and I asked for more details about how it all started. However, Abhinav remained silent and just listened to Utkarsh's account of the incident. According to him, after class yesterday, they had gone to the canteen and were waiting in line for their tea. But when the staff started serving, Abhinav accidentally took someone else's coffee instead of his tea. This led to the guy getting angry, and he not only verbally abused Abhinav but also slapped him and pushed him to the ground. In the heat of the moment, Utkarsh retaliated by slapping the guy back, only to find out that he was a senior and a local student whose house was close to the college. Utkarsh explained that this particular student had a large group of friends and cousins who often hung out at the college, and they all joined in to attack them, around 8-9 guys in total.

Fortunately, there were a few guys from the hostel who proved to be true heroes in a time of need. They bravely jumped into the fight to rescue their hostel junior, who was being attacked by some locals. Someone ran towards the hostel to inform everyone. The entire hostel was in chaos as all the hostelers armed themselves with sticks and joined in to defend their junior. In no time, the canteen was turned into a battlefield with loud cries and sounds of sticks clashing. The college administration, including the principal, intervened and managed to rescue the local students from the hostelers' wrath. I asked them about their well-being and inquired about Karan and Utkarsh. He said he is fine. Abhinav replied, "Those idiots had hit me knowing that I am blind." I comforted him by saying that everything was over now.

Utkarsh declared that it was just the beginning as that group returned after an hour with a large number of people in cars and jeeps. They were shouting and using abusive language, claiming that they would not spare any hostelers. They barged into the college and even came close to the hostel area. The situation became so intense that the principal had to call the police to control it. However, even after the police intervention, they continued to shout and threaten to take revenge. He said they showed up outside the college today as well, looking for us. I asked Utkarsh how I could possibly be involved in this chaos. He explained that they had mentioned the involvement of a day scholar who was a friend of theirs and believed that I had called everyone from the hostel to join in. Utkarsh further stated that they did not know my name, but they could recognize me by my face and knew that I was a student of the political science department. The situation seemed to be escalating, and I couldn't help but wonder how things would unfold in the days to come.

As I heard Utkarsh's words, I couldn't help but feel a wave of panic wash over me. Memories of a similar situation in boarding school came rushing back, making me feel tense and worried. I had been stuck inside the hostel, too afraid to go back home. The warden's office was locked, and I couldn't contact my family because the warden was with the principal. It was 2 PM when the warden finally came to the hostel and asked Abhinav, Utkarsh, Rahul sir, and a few other students to come with him to the principal's office for a compromise. My heart raced as Rahul sir requested the warden take me with them. He explained that he had only come back to college after three days, and his name was being dragged into this issue. He was afraid of me being beaten up if I was found alone.

The principal asked Abhinav to explain what happened yesterday, and he began by explaining that he was handicapped with partial blindness. Due to his condition, he can only see things from a close distance. Abhinav then narrated that by mistake, he took another student's coffee, thinking it was tea. Without noticing his vision issue, the student started abusing and punching him, ultimately pushing him to the ground. In the midst of this chaos, Utkarsh and Kran came to his rescue, but they also ended up getting involved in the fight. As there were 8-9 people on the other side, including some non-college students, we were overpowered. Some seniors from the hostel who were present in the canteen also joined in to help, which only added more fuel to the already burning fire. When the principal asked me if I was also from the hostel, I clarified that I was not and had just returned to college after being unwell for three days. Despite this, my name was being unnecessarily dragged into the situation.

One of the persons sitting in front of the principal during the disciplinary meeting was the local MLA, who happened to be familiar with the family of the boy involved in the fight. The MLA understood that it was not entirely our fault and acknowledged that mistakes can happen in youth. He urged everyone present to put an end to the matter and promised that no group would repeat such actions. The principal sternly reminded everyone that any further trouble would result in expulsion from college. The inspector also intervened, stating that he would send a constable to monitor the situation daily. With a warning in mind, we all shook hands and left the principal's office, hoping for a peaceful resolution.

When we came out of the principal's office, I saw Ma'am walking towards the parking area. I quickly mustered up the courage to ask her for a favour. I told her I didn't want to take the bus from there due to safety concerns and requested that she drop me off at Ring Road instead. She responded by saying that I had not attended her lecture, yet I had time to fight. I explained to her that I was not well and had only come to college today. However, my name was being dragged unnecessarily as some of my friends were involved in a fight. She then asked me where I lived, and I told her that I lived in Mayur Vihar. Ma'am then said that she was going to Patparganj and could drop me there, from where I could take a bus to Mayur Vihar, which is around 6-7 kilometres away. I thanked her and requested that she wait for a minute while I quickly ran back to the hostel to get my bag. With a grateful heart, I hopped into her car, and we drove towards Patparganj, and from there I took the bus to my home.

The next few months in college were filled with cold tension after the fight that had broken out with local students. The local student who had started the fight was in his final year and would be graduating in a few months. We were always careful when going out, as the situation was still tense. For some time, we even stopped going to Kamla Nagar market, as that local student lived there. Instead, we would go to the law faculty and meet our friends from Miranda House. With the final examinations approaching, everyone became serious about their studies. I remember not going to college for a whole month before my final exams, as I wanted to fully focus on my preparations. I only went once to take my admit card. Luckily, the final exams went very well, and the results were declared. With the exception of Hindi, I achieved excellent grades. However, my performance in Hindi was abysmal, and I failed. Now I have to clear it next year. To our surprise, Utkarsh had topped the class while Abhinav, Karan, and I were also in the top 10. I had scored thirty-two marks less than Utkarsh and was eagerly waiting to join college as a senior. It was a bittersweet moment as we said goodbye to our seniors who were graduating.

CHAPTER 12

YEARS OF COLLEGE WITH CAREER ASPIRATION AND POLITICAL PASSION

Now that I had completed my first year of college, I was eagerly anticipating the start of my second year. Tomorrow was the day I would finally return to campus after a long break of fifteen days. As I was preparing for my first day, I received a call from my friend Karan. He wanted to know what time I would be arriving at college tomorrow. I told him that since it was the first day of college after entering our second year, I would come late at 10 AM because I needed to get my new identity card, library card, and complete the registration process. The next morning, I took the bus and made my way to college. As I stepped off the bus, it was a wonderful feeling to be a senior now. I could see many new faces, fresh and excited to start their college journey just like I was a year ago.

I have befriended many people, but my core friend circle always remained limited to Karan, Utkarsh, and Abhinav. As I entered the hostel premises, I saw a familiar face—it was Saurabh, our batchmate from English Honours and also a hostel mate. He was known as "Neta Ji" in the hostel circle due to his leadership skills. As we greeted each other, he asked about my result, and I happily shared that I had performed well. He then asked if I was going to meet our friends. With a smile, he informed me that they had stayed up all night dealing with the ragging of junior students in the hostel.

As I entered Utkarsh's room, I found him sleeping soundly. As a prank, I decided to wake him up by throwing a bucket of water on him. Little did I know that this would trigger a water war between all the hostelers. Utkarsh got irritated and started to throw pillows at me, and soon enough, other students joined in. It was chaos as everyone grabbed buckets and started tossing water at each other. I saw Utkarsh heading towards the toilet with a bucket, and I quickly ran to the safety of the garden, knowing he would try to drench me. But to my surprise, there were already 15-20 students in the garden with buckets of water. I pleaded with Utkarsh not to throw water on me as I had to go home later, and my dress would get wet. But he assured me that I could wear his clothes instead. Even Abhinav, who initially tried to stop us, joined in the fun. Upon entering the hostel, Karan was surprised to see us playing with water. Saurabh (Neta Ji) caught him and brought him to the garden, where he was visibly angry but had no choice but to join in on the fun. This lasted for almost an hour, with Utkarsh lending me and Karan clothes to wear. After this, we decided to go to the tea shop outside the hostel. Karan suggested that we finish the registration process after having tea, but Utkarsh and Abhinav said they would do it later. So, Karan and I went to our departments and completed the registration process.

After registration, Karan and I decided to grab a quick bite at the canteen as Karan was feeling hungry since he had missed his breakfast. As we walked towards the canteen, we couldn't help but notice a group of freshers being ragged by their seniors. Karan immediately expressed his disapproval of the concept of ragging, stating that it creates a sense of fear and insecurity among the new students. I agreed with him, but I also mentioned that if done in a positive manner, ragging can help develop a bond between seniors and juniors. However, many seniors often take it too far and exploit their power over the vulnerable new students. This not only ruins the relationship between the two batches but also leaves a negative impact on the juniors. As seniors, it is our responsibility to guide and mentor our juniors rather than subjecting them to unnecessary humiliation and bullying.

Karan and I went to our department to check the notice board for the updated timetable. To our surprise, our first lecture was starting at 9:30 instead of the usual 8:30 that we were used to attending in our first year. As we were leaving the Political Science department, we spotted Abhinav and Utkarsh walking towards the main gate. Utkarsh was wearing shorts, a clear sign that he was not headed to the department for registration. We called out to them, asking where they were headed. They stopped upon hearing our voices, and we went over to them to ask. They informed us that they were on their way to the law faculty canteen to meet our friend, Sikha. She wanted to discuss some important issue with them. Excited to catch up with them after two months of not seeing each other due to exams, Karan and I decided to tag along and joined them.

Priyanka, Sikha, and Chaaya were eagerly waiting to see us after more than 45 days. As soon as we saw each other, our faces lit up with happiness. Sikha smiled at me and congratulated me on my good marks, but then asked me why I had failed in Hindi. She was surprised because Hindi teachers are known for giving extra marks. I felt a little embarrassed and asked her how much she had scored in Hindi. She replied that she had gotten sixty-two marks. I smiled and confidently said that I would surely score more than sixty-two marks in my second attempt. We were all catching up when Utkarsh asked what we wanted to talk about. Sikha then revealed that she was thinking of contesting for the hostel president position this year and wanted to fight for the college president position next year. We were all taken aback as we had never seen this side of her before. She then asked for our opinions on her decision. I personally had no idea about all this, but I encouraged her to go for it if she was confident. Chaaya added that Sikha was quite popular in the hostel and everyone loved her, so she would have a good chance of winning. Sikha said that she needed our help, to which Karan questioned how we could help her when we were not even allowed to enter her college, let alone the hostel. Sikha explained that all we needed to do was make posters and help with campaigning content. We all happily agreed to support our friend in her endeavour.

The next few days were a whirlwind of lectures and assignments, and I was determined to make the most of it. After a disastrous 12th-grade mistake, I was determined not to make the same mistakes and was very particular about attending all my classes. It was crucial for us to have at least 80% attendance in order to be eligible to write the final exams. In our free time after college, my friends and I worked on making posters for Sikha's campaign in the hostel elections. Despite our best efforts, we struggled to come up with creative ideas and often received input from others in the hostel. We would then go to Miranda House, where Sikha, Priyanka, and Chaaya were busy campaigning, to hand over the posters.

One day on my way to the hostel, I overheard a group of freshers playfully teasing and abusing each other. I was taken aback and upset by their behaviour, especially since they saw me and were still in a playful mood during what seemed like ragging time. I couldn't believe they were behaving this way on the college campus. I asked them to follow me to the hostel, but they pleaded with me not to take them there and do whatever I wanted to do right then and there. However, my anger blinded me, and I didn't listen to them. As soon as we entered the hostel, I shouted for all the students to come out of their rooms because we had "Fuccha" (freshers) among us. To my surprise, almost all the hostel students came out as if they were waiting for this moment.

Karan had reached college early and was staying in the hostel in Utkarsh's room. Utkarsh, Abhinav, and Karan were joined by a group of other students. However, Karan was not pleased with the addition of these students and asked why they were brought there. He believed that they would only cause trouble and make others cry. I explained to him that they were caught abusing in the college, and Utkarsh had asked them to sing as punishment. At first, everything seemed fine, and everyone was having a good time. But as time passed, the intensity of ragging increased, and after half an hour, the juniors were standing in their underwear. One of the seniors, Saurabh (Neta Ji), asked if they had girlfriends, and when they said no, he made them propose to each other while talking in a girl's voice. It was hilarious to watch them in their underwear, making proposals. Everyone was laughing, even Karan, who was initially against ragging. To add some spice to the situation, I asked another student to act like a news reporter and give live coverage of the proposal. However, things took a turn when the juniors started crying. I immediately put a stop to the ragging and asked everyone to let them go. I reminded them all that ragging should never cross the line and they should never abuse anyone on campus, as it tarnishes the image of our college. The incident ended on a funny note, but it also served as a lesson for all of us about the consequences of ragging.

Karan had arrived at college earlier than usual and was in Utkarsh's room. Karan was surprised to see freshers and asked me why I brought them here. He warned that the hostelers will bully and make them cry. However, I explained that they were abusing each other on campus, and I guess they are not afraid of ragging. As we were chatting, Utkarsh asked them to sing. Everything seemed fine until the ragging started to escalate. After half an hour, the juniors were standing in their underwear, and one of the seniors, Saurabh (Neta Ji), asked if they had girlfriends. When they replied no, Saurabh came up with a hilarious idea of having one of the juniors propose to another in a girl's voice while instructing the other not to accept it. Everyone was laughing uncontrollably, even Karan, who was initially against ragging. To add more spice to the situation, one of their friends acted as a news reporter and gave live coverage of the proposal. However, things took a turn when the juniors started crying. Realizing that things were getting out of hand, Karan intervened and asked everyone to stop and let the juniors go. He also reminded them not to abuse anyone on campus, even after the ragging period, as it can harm the college's reputation.

The day before the hostel election in Miranda House, my friends and I decided to go and meet Sikha to wish her all the best. We were excited to see her campaign for the hostel president position, but when we met her, she looked exhausted. She told us that she had been going to every room in the hostel to convince the students to vote for her. Some rooms even required a second visit as they were not convinced during the first one. We asked her about her chances of winning, and she said that as of now, everything seemed positive, but one could never predict what could happen overnight. She also mentioned that she had to cut our meeting short as she had to meet a few more students before the election day. We wished her luck and left, hoping that all her hard work and efforts would pay off in the end.

The next day was filled with excitement and anticipation as the much-awaited election took place in the Miranda House hostel. By 4 PM, the results were out, and Sikha emerged as the winner with a remarkable margin. We were overjoyed and decided to pay her a visit at Miranda House to congratulate her. Despite being busy with formalities, Sikha took the time to come out to meet us and was overwhelmed with gratitude for our support. She hugged us tightly and thanked us for being there for her. We couldn't be prouder of her victory and asked her to treat us to celebrate. With a smile on her face, she promised to take us to Connaught Place for lunch once she is free in the coming days. It was a day filled with joy, pride, and celebration as we witnessed our friend's success in the hostel election.

It was a regular day at the law faculty canteen when I spotted Sikha walking in with a shopping bag. As she joined our table, Abhinav asked about the rest of our group. Sikha explained that she had gone to Kamla Nagar for shopping. As we enjoyed our aloo paratha and tea, Priyanka and Chaaya arrived and joined us, claiming to be starving and helping themselves to our plates. Priyanka asked Sikha about her shopping, and she revealed that she had a surprise for all of us. She had bought gifts as a 'thank you' gesture and asked us to finish our food before showing us. Utkarsh, being curious, urged us to eat faster. We all washed our hands, and Sikha pulled out t-shirts from her bag—grey ones with Ramjas College, University of Delhi written on them for the boys and navy-blue ones with Miranda House, University of Delhi written on them for the girls. I was ecstatic as I had been wanting a t-shirt with my college name printed on it for months. As we checked the sizes and fittings, Sikha announced that we would be wearing them the next day for our lunch plans at Connaught Place. My first thought was that I would have to skip classes, but we had already made plans to leave campus at 12 PM. The excitement in the air was palpable as we eagerly looked forward to our lunch outing in our new college t-shirts.

The next day I went to attend my first lecture. After the lecture, I went to the hostel where my friends Karan, Abhinav, and Utkarsh were waiting for me. They were all wearing new t-shirts with "Ramjas College, University of Delhi" written on them, which were given to them by Sikha. They asked me why I wasn't wearing the new t-shirt, and I told them that I had kept it in my bag. I quickly took it out and wore it, feeling a sense of pride with the college name printed on it. The t-shirt was not just a piece of clothing but a symbol of my identity as a student of Delhi University. I couldn't help but show off a little, wanting everyone to know that I was a part of this prestigious institution.

My friends and I went to Miranda House to meet our friends and proceed to Connaught Place. As soon as we reached, we saw our friends wearing navy blue t-shirts with "Miranda House" written on them. They looked beautiful and confident in their college t-shirts. After talking for a few minutes, we decided to head to Connaught Place for lunch. As we entered the restaurant, we could feel the curious glances of people around us, probably because we were all wearing our college t-shirts. After a delicious lunch, we went for some window shopping, and that's when I noticed Sikha buying cigarettes. It was surprising for me as I had never seen her smoke before. To my surprise, she even offered us a cigarette, and we all lit it and walked towards the bus stand. While my friends took the bus to the bus adda, I took a bus to Mayur Vihar. It was a fun day filled with new experiences and getting to know my friends better.

As October arrived, the university campus was buzzing with excitement over the upcoming university election. Initially, I had no interest in getting involved until I ran into Ved Bhai, a senior from my boarding school who was contesting for president in the DUSU (Delhi University Student Union) election. He was studying at Bhagat Singh College in the south campus and came to our college with over 100 supporters for campaigning. I was pleasantly surprised to see him, and we caught up on old times. However, things changed when he asked me to campaign for him in Ramjas College and all colleges in the north campus. I was hesitant at first, but Ved Bhai convinced me and even provided me with pamphlets to distribute.

After he left, I was left feeling lost and unsure of what to do. I couldn't turn to my friends for advice as they were all in support of a different party. Feeling alone in my decision-making, I decided to talk to Karan, who was also a day scholar like me. As soon as I opened up to him about my dilemma, he immediately offered his support and said, "Don't worry, I will come with you to visit all the colleges."

At the beginning of the campaign, I took the initiative to involve my own department in supporting Ved Bhai for the position of president. My classmates were surprised, as I had never interacted with them before, despite being in the same class. However, I approached them politely and explained my reasons for supporting Ved Bhai. I also distributed pamphlets containing information about other candidates from his party running for vice president, secretary, and joint secretary positions. My main focus was on promoting Ved Bhai's candidacy. Although my classmates did not make any promises, they said they would consider voting for him. Along with my friend Karan, I visited all departments in our college and urged them to support Ved Bhai's campaign.

Karan expressed his disappointment with our college for supporting a different party and suggested that we visit other colleges instead. With the help of our friends from St. Stephen's, we started our campaign by standing at the entry gates of colleges throughout the north campus. Our main aim was to distribute pamphlets and convince students to vote for Ved Bhai. We visited popular colleges like Hindu College, Hansraj College, Kirori Mal College, Daulat Ram College, SRCC, Khalsa College, Delhi School of Economics, the law faculty, and Miranda House. At each college, we stood in front and tried to reach out to as many students as possible. Fortunately, at Miranda House, I received support from Shikha and others. However, our efforts were met with mixed responses from the students. One day while returning from Hindu College, we were stopped by students from the opposite party who asked us to stop campaigning for Ved Bhai. They believed that there was no chance for him or his party to get votes in the north campus. Despite this setback, we remained determined and continued our campaign, hoping to make a difference in the upcoming elections.

During the campaign for the election, Karan and I bunked classes for almost two weeks. The fever of the election had taken over our minds, and we were fully immersed in it. We were constantly discussing and debating the candidates and their policies, and we even joined in on the rallies and marches. The atmosphere during those two weeks was intense, with heated arguments and fights breaking out between two groups supporting different candidates. We realized that we had neglected our studies for too long and decided to resume our classes after the election.

On the scheduled day of the election, I made my way to college early in the morning. As I walked through the gates, I couldn't help but notice the hustle and bustle of preparation for the voting process. Ved Bhai, who was running for the position of president, had sent his trusted associates to each college to ensure a smooth and fair election. My classmate Karn and I went to meet the person in charge of overseeing the voting in our college on behalf of Ved Bhai. He praised us for our hard work and promised to put in a good word for us with Ved if he won. However, I was taken aback by his statement and told him that I didn't need any favors. I was campaigning for Ved Bhai because he was my senior from boarding school, and we shared a strong bond. After casting our votes, Karn and I left for the hostel to meet our friends. To our surprise, we were met with anger and disapproval from hostelers. They accused us of going against the hostel by supporting Ved and his party. I immediately clarified that I had no interest in politics and was simply supporting Ved, as he was my senior from boarding school, and we had a good relationship. I assured them that I did not ask anyone to vote for others from his party. Thankfully, they understood, and everything went back to normal. As we sat in Utkarsh's room, Saurabh entered and announced that he would be contesting for college president next year. He asked for our support, and Utkarsh assured him that we would always support anyone from the hostel.

After a few days of anticipation, the results for the Delhi University Students' Union (DUSU) were finally declared. Ved Bhai and his party have won two positions out of five, with Ved Bhai himself being elected as president and one position of joint secretary. He wasted no time in expressing his gratitude to the students and colleges who supported him and personally visited each college to thank them. When he came to our college, he asked his friend to look for me. I was in the canteen at that time when I received a message that Ved bhai wanted to meet me. Feeling both excited and nervous, I immediately went to meet him. He shared with me that he didn't receive as many votes from the colleges in North Campus as he had hoped, but he acknowledged my hard work and dedication towards his campaign. He also assured me that if I ever faced any problems, I could count on him.

The election result was finally declared, and we resumed our lectures. However, the professors seemed to be in a bad mood, especially ma'am. She scolded us for our poor attendance and warned us that even if we attended every day, it would still not be enough. With the month of December approaching, everyone began to take their studies more seriously. One day, while we were sitting in Utkarsh's room, he announced that he would be going to Bhagalpur and returning just before the exams. He planned to prepare for the exam there and assured us that he would get a medical certificate from Mukherjee Nagar. Abhinav had been regular in attending lectures, but Karan and I were already short of attendance to appear for the exam. Karan suggested that we also get medical certificates in order to take the exam. I asked Utkarsh when he would be getting the certificate, to which he replied that he would get it in February after his return from Bhagalpur. He even invited us to come with him at that time to get our own medical certificates.

The day before Utkarsh was set to leave for Bhagalpur, he invited us to join him on a quick trip to the bookshop in Kamla Nagar. He needed a few books, and upon arriving at the bookstore, Utkarsh headed straight for the section containing ten years' question papers for all subjects. He explained that these question papers would be sufficient for us to prepare and score well in our exams. Inspired by his confidence, we also purchased the question papers and left the store feeling excited and prepared for our upcoming exams.

After Utkarsh left, my friend Karan and I became very irregular with our classes. We started bunking often, and I only went to school to meet my close friends Abhinav, Priyanka, Sikha, and Chaaya. I was seriously preparing for my final exams from home, as in political science what is mostly required is memorization, and I was fairly good at it. I also paid more attention to Hindi as I had failed in my first year. This time, I was confident that I would pass as I had studied hard. During this time, I also made an effort to meet Shreya every Sunday and bridge the gap between us since I hadn't been giving her proper time before. Thankfully, everything was back to normal, and we were both happy. She even started calling me every day from her hostel, showing that our relationship was still strong.

In February, I went to collect my admit card for the upcoming exams. To my surprise, I found out that my friend Utkarsh had also returned, and I could see a newfound confidence in him, which made me believe that he was well-prepared for the exam. Utkarsh took me and our friend Karan to Mukherjee Nagar to get the medical certificate. As we were on our way, I couldn't help but think about what I would say to the doctor in order to get the certificate. However, when we reached the reception and asked for the certificate, I was pleasantly surprised by how smoothly the process went. The staff at the counter took our details, and within a few minutes, they handed us our medical certificates, duly signed by a doctor and stamped, and charged 200 rupees from each of us, which we paid without hesitation. Overall, it was a smooth and efficient process that left me feeling relieved and ready for the upcoming exams. While returning, we decided to meet Sikha, Priyanka, and Chaaya at the law faculty. We went to pick up Abhinav and then headed to the law faculty to meet the girls. It was a fun and enjoyable experience as we spent hours chatting and reminiscing about old times. After a while, I had to leave as I had to catch a bus to Mayur Vihar.

I appeared in all my exams and was confident that I did well, even in Hindi. The results were yet to be declared, but I was not worried as I was certain that I would receive good marks. While waiting for the results at home, we had an unexpected visitor—a family friend who also happened to be the commissioner of police in Delhi. He asked me about my plans for the future, to which I replied that I was considering either pursuing law or getting into a good MBA college. However, he suggested that I should try for the UPSC exams. I expressed my doubts about the difficulty of the exam, to which he responded that it would be easy if I cleared it and tough if I didn't. He questioned how I could label it easy or tough without even attempting it. Not wanting to engage in a debate, I simply said that I would give it a try.

After dinner, I accompanied them to their car. To my surprise, there were two cars waiting for them—one for the police, equipped with guns, and the other for him and his family. As we approached the car, all the policemen came out and saluted him before opening the door for him and his family. This sight left a lasting impression on my mind and made me realize the importance of an IPS officer. The next day, I went to a bookstore and bought a few books as I had heard about someone preparing for the UPSC exam. I sought his guidance, and he advised me to start with NCERT books of all subjects from class 6 to 12. He emphasized building a strong foundation and recommended that I join a coaching institute after 6 months of self-study. With my determination renewed, I purchased all the books and began my journey towards achieving my dream of clearing the UPSC exam.

Resuming my college in the third year was a bittersweet feeling for me. It was my last year on campus, and I was determined to make the most of it. My goal was to study hard and also spend quality time with my friends. The first-year students had joined the college, but I didn't feel any excitement towards it. My life revolved around attending lectures and meeting my friends at the law faculty canteen after college. I was highly focused in class, and even my teachers noticed my dedication, thanks to my impressive marks in the second-year exam. This year, I decided to change things up and started going to the library regularly. Many times, I would spend hours in the library until 6 PM. Surprisingly, my friends were also taking their studies seriously. Utkarsh had even started preparing for the UPSC exam. I didn't reveal to them that I was also preparing for the same exam. For almost a month, I followed this routine of studying and spending time in the library diligently, determined to make the most of my last year in college.

One day, my friends and I were sitting in Utkarsh's room when Saurabh (Neta Ji) walked in. He informed us that there would be college elections in fifteen days and he was planning to run for the position of college president. Utkarsh mentioned that there would be a hostel meeting later that night where everyone would come together and decide who they wanted to support in the elections. When Saurabh left, I asked Utkarsh about his chances of winning the election. He replied confidently, stating that Saurabh was quite popular in college and the hostel residents would most likely support him if he ran for president. I questioned why there was still a need for a meeting if his chances were so bright. Utkarsh explained that the meeting was just a formality to make sure there were no other contestants from the hostel.

After attending the last lecture, my friends and I decided to go to the law faculty. As we entered, we saw Sikha and Chaaya sitting in a corner. Abhinav immediately asked Priyanka, to which Sikha replied that she was angry as she also wanted to contest in the college election. This created a dilemma for us as we were torn between supporting two friends. Sikha explained that the college election was bigger than her previous hostel election, and she would need a lot of help. We assured her that we would talk to Priyanka and try to find a solution. Karan suggested that we go to Miranda House to meet Priyanka. I urged Sikha to leave immediately so that Priyanka wouldn't think we were not supporting anyone. After they left, we discussed how to approach Priyanka and resolve the differences between her and Sikha. Abhinav came up with the idea of convincing Priyanka to contest for the role of vice president. After having a cup of tea, we headed towards Miranda House to talk to Priyanka and find a solution to the problem at hand.

We visited Miranda House and approached a girl near the gate, asking her to call Priyanka from the 3rd year. After a few minutes, Priyanka came with a group of unfamiliar girls. We invited her to join us for tea at the law faculty, but she declined, saying she was tired. We insisted on talking to her alone, so she asked her friends to leave and said she would join them later. Utkarsh asked her why she didn't come to the law faculty with Sikha and Chaaya, to which Priyanka replied that there was tension between her and Sikha. Abhinav, who was Priyanka's childhood friend, took the lead and asked her what happened between them. Priyanka revealed that Sikha wanted to contest for the position of president, causing a strain in their relationship. Abhinav revealed to her that Sikha had been diligently preparing for the upcoming election for the past two years. Priyanka confidently stated that she had a better chance of winning the election. However, Karan questioned, "Why aren't you supporting Sikha, especially since Sikha had put in two years of hard work?" Priyanka then shared her own desire to contest in the election. In order to resolve the conflict, I suggested to her to show a bigger heart and contest for the position of vice president. After understanding our point, Priyanka ultimately agreed to run for vice president. This decision would not only strengthen their chances of winning but also promote teamwork and cooperation within the group. It was a win-win situation for both. After Abhinav asked Priyanka to go inside and call Sikha, she immediately went inside and came out with Sikha. The two girls hugged each other, expressing their excitement, and promised to help each other in the upcoming election. Everyone present there was happy to see the two girls standing together and supporting each other. We then suggested that they should start campaigning and assured them that we would make posters to promote their candidacy. After discussing their campaign strategies, both of them went inside to prepare for the upcoming election. Utkarsh and Abhinav returned to their hostel while Karan and I took a bus to go back home.

In the next few days, our schedule was filled with attending lectures and creating posters to support our friends, Sikha and Priyanka. Meanwhile, Saurabh was selected as the hostel's candidate for the college president position at Ramjas. As Karan and I were close to many students, we were also given the task of campaigning for Saurabh. Our group consisted of five students, including Abhinav, Karan, Utkarsh, Vipin, and myself. Although Karan and I were not particularly close to Vipin, he was known as "Ara Cat" among the hostel students due to his typical Bihari accent and his belief that he was smart and modern. This nickname caught on quickly as it perfectly captured his personality, making him stand out among the other students. Despite our initial reservations about Vipin, we all worked together towards a common goal of supporting Saurabh for college president.

Our group of five made it a mission to visit every department of our college, campaigning for Saurabh. We would gather outside the college gate during lecture breaks and spread the word about Saurabh. Unlike previous DUSU elections, we made sure not to miss any lectures this time. However, our dedication to Saurabh's campaign did not falter. After college, around 4 PM, we would head to Miranda House to catch up on the updates for our friends Sikha and Priyanka's election preparations. This routine of campaigning and keeping up with our friends' elections was taking a toll on my UPSC preparation, but I knew I had to stand by my friends. With both the elections being held in just one week, I was determined to support them till the very end.

On election day at Ramjas College, my friend Karan and I stood at the main gate, trying to convince students to vote for Saurabh. As the voting time was coming to an end, we rushed to the polling station to cast our own votes. The results were set to be announced at 7 PM, so Karan and I decided to stay at the hostel for the night. In the evening, while we were at a nearby tea shop, we heard loud music coming from the hostel. Curious, we went to check it out and were pleasantly surprised to see a huge celebration going on. Saurabh had won the election and was now the new president of Ramjas College. Everyone was dancing and having a great time, and Saurabh even came and hugged us. Ara Cat, in his typical accent, exclaimed, "Sala, itna mehnat kiye hain, jitna tou tha hei." (He had to win; we have worked so hard.). It was a joyous and proud moment for all of us in the hostel.

Abhinav excitedly informed us that today was also the election day at Miranda House, and the results must have been declared by now. Without wasting any time, we rushed towards the college. The atmosphere was electrifying as we could hear girls screaming with joy inside the campus. We approached a girl who was coming out of the college and asked her about the results. She happily told us that Sikha had won the position of president and Priyanka had become the vice president. We requested her to inform Sikha or Priyanka that we were waiting outside. After a few minutes, both of them came running towards us with beaming smiles on their faces. Their happiness was palpable, and they said they would meet us tomorrow as they had to go and meet the principal. We then returned to our hostel and joined in the celebration with other students. The whole night was filled with excitement, and we stayed awake.

After the election, life returned to its normal routine, and I was able to focus on my studies once again. I made it a habit to come to college every day and put in my best effort to excel in my studies. Sundays were the only days I allowed myself to rest, as I did not have to go meet Shreya, who had moved to Bangalore to pursue her BBA. Despite the distance, we made sure to stay in touch and catch up on our lives through weekly phone calls on Sundays. These conversations were always a highlight of my week, as it felt like nothing had changed between us despite the physical distance. Our relationship remained strong and supportive, even though we were in different cities.

In just a few months, our final examinations will be upon us. I am relieved to say that this year, for the first time, I am well-prepared for the exams as our syllabus has been completed. It is a great feeling to know that I have already started studying months before the actual exams. Along with the exam preparation, there was also excitement in the air for the upcoming farewell party in January. We invited our friends from Miranda House to join us in the celebration. However, I have already informed my professors that after the farewell party, I will not be coming back to college, as I plan to study at home. I have requested that they mark my attendance. Thankfully, all my professors agreed and understood my situation and have promised to mark me present even if I am not physically present in class.

The day of my college farewell had finally arrived, and I was filled with mixed emotions. I had bought a new dress that I couldn't wait to wear. As I reached college in the afternoon, I made sure to carry my dress in my bag so that I could change into it later. The party was scheduled to start at 6 PM and last till midnight. Karan had offered to drop me home after the party in his car. At 6:30, we went to the main gate to meet our friends Priyanka, Chaaya, and Sikha, who would be joining us. They were all dressed beautifully, and we entered the college together. The party was being held on the ground where there was loud music playing, and students were dancing. We found a spot for ourselves, and soon Sikha and Chaaya dragged us onto the dance floor. Karan was a great dancer, and he joined in with them while Priyanka, Abhinav, Utkarsh, and I watched them dance. When the cultural program began, our excitement soon turned into boredom, and we decided to take a break and show our college to our friends. We proudly showed them around our campus, including the hostel where Abhinav and Utkarsh lived. As the clock struck 9 PM, dinner was served, and it was announced that it was only for third-year students. However, we insisted that our friends join us for dinner, assuring them that no one would say anything as most of the organizers were known to us. The dinner was a simple vegetarian meal, but everyone enjoyed it. As it started getting late, we realized that the girls had to return to their hostel by 10 PM. We offered to accompany them back as it was getting dark, and we didn't want them to feel unsafe. After dropping the girls off, Karan, Abhinav, and Utkarsh kindly offered to drop me off at my home as well.

Before the commencement of my exams, I made a trip to my college to collect my admit card. The atmosphere was filled with nervous excitement as we were all gearing up for the exams. As the days passed and the exams began, we were all completely consumed by our studies and the pressure of performing well. However, on the last day of our exams, we were hit with a wave of emotions as we realized that this would be our last day in college. From tomorrow onwards, we would all be embarking on different paths, and our college days would be nothing but memories. It was a sad moment to say goodbye to our friends and professors, knowing that we might never see each other again. As we walked out of the exam hall, we couldn't help but feel nostalgic about the time spent in college and the memories we had created.

After completing our final paper, we all gathered at Miranda House to meet our friends who would soon be going home. It was an emotional moment as we sat in the law faculty canteen and reminisced about the past three years we had spent together. There were tears in everyone's eyes as we realized that our time as college students had come to an end. Later, we went to Kamla Nagar, and around 8 PM, the most painful word of the day had to be said: "Goodbye." As we walked towards the Miranda House college gate, tears started rolling down our cheeks. We exchanged home telephone numbers and made a promise to keep in touch. It was a bittersweet moment as our college life came to an end, but at the same time, we were excited for the new beginnings that awaited us.

www.ingramcontent.com/pod-product-compliance
Lightning Source LLC
LaVergne TN
LVHW041151150826
845673LV00001B/135

* 9 7 9 8 8 9 6 1 0 6 6 6 1 *